COMA
AND NEAR-DEATH EXPERIENCE

"This wonderful, well-researched, groundbreaking book explores the mysterious inner world of patients in coma. It points the way to more humane and effective treatment for those patients who are the most vulnerable and unable to speak for themselves. In addition, the authors include a fascinating investigation of other dimensions of consciousness, such as those experienced in NDEs, OBEs, dream states, and induced visions. Significantly, they point out that these experiences may be the overlooked bridge uniting science and spirituality."

ROBERTA MOORE, M.A., M.B.A., FILMMAKER AND FORMER
PROFESSOR AT FLORIDA SOUTHWESTERN STATE COLLEGE

"So good! So needed!"

JEFFREY J. KRIPAL, ASSOCIATE DEAN OF FACULTY
AND GRADUATE STUDIES, RICE UNIVERSITY

"A must-read for anyone who is touched by critical illness, whether they are a patient, family member, or a clinician."

E. WESLEY ELY, M.D., PROFESSOR OF MEDICINE,
VANDERBILT UNIVERSITY MEDICAL CENTER

"I want all my students to read this book!"

JILL LARKIN STORER, BSN, RN, CCRN,
CLINICAL EDUCATOR IN CRITICAL CARE

COMA
AND NEAR-DEATH EXPERIENCE

The Beautiful, Disturbing,
and Dangerous World
of the Unconscious

A Sacred Planet Book

ALAN AND BEVERLEY PEARCE

Park Street Press
Rochester, Vermont

Park Street Press
One Park Street
Rochester, Vermont 05767
www.ParkStPress.com

Park Street Press is a division of Inner Traditions International

Sacred Planet Books are curated by Richard Grossinger, Inner Traditions editorial board member and cofounder and former publisher of North Atlantic Books. The Sacred Planet collection, published under the umbrella of the Inner Traditions family of imprints, includes works on the themes of consciousness, cosmology, alternative medicine, dreams, climate, permaculture, alchemy, shamanic studies, oracles, astrology, crystals, hyperobjects, locutions, and subtle bodies.

Cataloging-in-Publication Data for this title is available from the Library of Congress

ISBN 978-1-64411-921-1 (print)
ISBN 978-1-64411-922-8 (ebook)

Printed and bound in the United States by Lake Book Manufacturing, LLC.

10 9 8 7 6 5 4 3 2 1

Text design and layout by Kenleigh Manseau
This book was typeset in Garamond Premier Pro with Rival Sans and Laski Slab used as display typefaces

To send correspondence to the authors of this book, mail a first-class letter to the authors c/o Inner Traditions • Bear & Company, One Park Street, Rochester, VT 05767, and we will forward the communication, or contact the authors directly at **alanpearce.com**.

Scan the QR code and save 25% at InnerTraditions.com. Browse over 2,000 titles on spirituality, the occult, ancient mysteries, new science, holistic health, and natural medicine.

To our darling Rebeckah
1982–2021

and the best of friends,
J. Philip Wood
1956–2022

And to everyone who has entered a coma
To those who came back
And to those who did not

Contents

PART 1
· · · · · · · · ·
A World More Vivid
than Life Itself

A Wake-Up Call

E. Wesley Ely, MD

In the last half century, critical care medicine has made tremendous strides in reducing untimely deaths among the sickest patients in the hospital. Thanks to scientific progress in understanding the severely deranged physiology intrinsic to critical illness, we are increasingly adept at supporting patients through the ravages of diseases that have claimed too many lives in years past.

In an effort to reduce suffering, a culture of deep sedation and medically induced coma crept into our intensive care units (ICUs) and was rationalized as a more humane approach to clinical care. Decades of research on ICU survivors, however, has challenged this long-held belief. Many survivors develop long-term, debilitating side effects from their ICU stay, including muscle wasting, mental health problems, and cognitive impairment. These are collectively termed post-intensive care syndrome or PICS.

Patients have recounted harrowing stories of hallucinations and false memories while sedated, delirious, and comatose in the ICU. We increasingly understand that delirium and coma are not benign sequelae of critical illness but can instead lead to persistent cognitive and mental health impairments that prevent patients from returning to "normal."

To add insult to injury, patients' voices have been notably, and inappropriately, absent from the many discussions regarding delirium, coma, and altered consciousness during critical illness.

In this pioneering book, Alan and Beverley Pearce give a voice to survivors and their perceptions of altered reality while at the brink of death. These stories also highlight the profound long-term effects that these experiences have on survivors, from the inability to manage finances and the loss of employment to the end of their ability to serve as functional matriarchs and patriarchs of their families.

This is a must-read for anyone who is touched by critical illness, whether they are a patient, a family member, or a clinician.

E. WESLEY ELY, MD, is a subspecialist in pulmonary and critical care medicine as well as a practicing intensivist with a focus on geriatric ICU care. He is a professor of medicine at Vanderbilt University Medical Center whose research has focused on improving the care and outcomes of critically ill patients with ICU-acquired brain disease (manifested acutely as delirium and chronically as long-term cognitive impairment).

Coma and Consciousness: The Yawning Abyss

Jeffrey J. Kripal

In the spring of 2020, I did an interview on BBC Radio 3's *Arts and Ideas* show with the philosopher Shahidha Bari. The COVID-19 pandemic was just beginning. It was April of that fearful, terrible year.[1] Induced comas and intubation would quickly become ways of life, or ways of death. Everyone would come to know about them. And fear them. One of my best friends was the head filmmaker and videographer at a very large hospital here in Houston. He would see the worst up close. And he would give me reports. It was not good. We were all afraid.

Shahidha was interviewing me about my sort-of-new book, *The Flip,* which had appeared a few years before in the United States but had just been published again in the United Kingdom.[2] It was really bad timing. Or really good timing. The book is about the metaphysical openings that scientists, medical professionals, and engineers often experience that shake them to their spiritual core—sometimes when near death, sometimes while on psychedelics, sometimes in their dream life. Many of these individuals end up letting go of their earlier materialism or belief that everything is ultimately insentient matter, dead stuff doing mathematical things and only looking alive. That view comes to seem wildly implausible after their openings—a bit silly, really. They further realize, with something of a shock, that their science, medicine, and engineering did not need that particular interpretation anyway. It is just an interpretation. It is not the science. It is not the medicine. It is not the engineering. These professionals "flip" in the sense that they no longer live in a world in which matter is primary or the only existent. Now, mind, subjectivity, or consciousness is somehow fundamental. It is not that they think this. They know it. How, it is not really very clear. But they do. And that is just a bit unsettling.

Toward the end of the interview, Shahidha asked me a question that seemed obvious at the time but nevertheless surprised me, caught me off guard. It involved the early pandemic. "Is the coronavirus," she asked in perfect seriousness, "the kind of extreme experience that will bring about a flip?"

Wow, there's a question I hadn't heard before (and I had heard a lot of questions). I replied that I didn't think that was how we should be thinking of COVID-19 at that point (I suppose that was my hesitation). But I had to admit: "I am absolutely certain that all of this suffering, and all of this fear, and all of this dying is producing all kinds of extraordinary experiences, most of which we will never hear about because our culture does not allow these stories to be told." I suggested the same was true of the nuclear disaster caused by the Japanese tsunami a few years before the interview or the endless, stupid murders and the horrific sufferings of the war in Vietnam a few decades before that. Like these earlier human disasters, the current pandemic would result in countless altered states of consciousness and near-death experiences, this time on ventilators. Those who were fortunate enough to come back from those mind-spaces—which, alas, was not everyone—would report extraordinary experiences, but medical professionals would be unable to hear them. They would frame them as so much nonsense or ignore them entirely. I suggested that millions would be flipped but that the medical materialism that runs beneath or above our culture would not be, could not be. Modern medicine would save many but would in the end fail us spectacularly, both spiritually and intellectually.

Alas, I was correct. The vacuous phrases "COVID mania" and "COVID delirium," among others, were used by the medical establishment and then by the obedient media to describe—or, rather, not describe at all—what was being said by those emerging from induced comas and terrible traumas. There was a yawning abyss between what was being described by those who knew and what was being claimed by those who knew nothing at all. If anyone in the medical establishment really listened to what was being said, I certainly did not hear about them. There was one great nothing.

Until this book. I agreed, immediately, to write a contribution to it. That is always a mistake, I have learned, as I never have time. I agreed anyway. I remembered my conversation with Shahidha. I had time for this. I wanted to learn. I wanted to read. I wanted to see someone think through the issues I had tried to think through in *The Flip* but apply them to an urgent real-world situation: the artificial induction through sedation of coma and its consequences—some of them brain destroying, some of them cosmic in nature—during and after the pandemic. How do we think, together, about brain dysfunction, hallucination, parallel universes, other lives, reincarnation, the relationship between mind and brain, psychopathology, modern medicine, and early death? Where do we draw the line or make the cut? Can we? I wanted someone to answer Shahidha's question more fully than I could in April 2020.

They have.

Please read this book. It is not what you probably think it is. It is not a book only about coma and sedation and why we should think twice about this dubious and destructive medical practice. It is also a book about the nature of consciousness itself. It is a book about the profound moral ambiguity of shutting down the brain as filter for a time. It is about risk, danger, brain damage, and transcendence. It is also about the near-death experience, schizophrenia, psychedelics, savants, and out-of-body experiences. It is about us. Please read this book. And please do not fall back on easy answers, be they scientific and secular or religious and spiritual. There are no easy answers. That's the point.

JEFFREY J. KRIPAL is associate dean of the humanities and the J. Newton Rayzor Professor of Philosophy and Religious Thought at Rice University in Houston, Texas. He is also the associate director of the Center for Theory and Research at the Esalen Institute in Big Sur, California. Jeff is the author of ten books, including, most recently, *The Superhumanities: Historical Precedents, Moral Objections, New Realities* (2022), where he envisions the future centrality and urgency of the humanities in conversation with the history of science, the philosophy of mind, and our shared ethical, political, and ecological challenges. He is presently working on a three-volume study of paranormal currents in the sciences, modern esoteric literature, and the hidden history of science fiction for the University of Chicago Press collectively entitled *The Super Story: Science (Fiction) and Some Emergent Mythologies*. There, he intuits and writes about a new emerging spectrum of superhumanities (in both senses of that expression). The website jeffreyjkripal.com contains his full body of work.

A Whole Other Life

Nick MacDonald can be hilariously funny or surprisingly spiritual. He is a good-looking, well-built man in his midthirties who had been living life to the full. In the last few years, he has dropped the pace and settled down to small-town life in America's Midwest. He thinks he chose the place because he liked the peculiar pink color of the locally produced ice cream.

He runs a successful garden business and is widely acknowledged as being good with his hands. "My old man was a big-time motorcycle mechanic and he taught me a little bit," he says modestly. Nick achieved brief fame and a welcome into the community when he won the town's hotdog-eating competition. He is regarded as a mean baseball player with lots of good friends. He initially tried his hand at dairy farming but now teaches people how to "grow all kinds of shit."

His last relationship broke down soon after his partner gave birth to a baby girl. Since then he has been living alone. One day—totally out of the blue—Nick started to feel rather peculiar. The floor began to give way. "I was free falling, and I was free falling into complete nothingness." Then everything went curiously orange in color.

Nick instinctively knew that he was desperately ill. When he finally prizes his eyes open, he finds himself stretched out in a hospital bed, tubes and lines running out of his face and body. Monitors beep and flash. He is having serious problems with his memory.

He has no recollection of the young woman who comes to visit, claiming to be his fiancée. She tells him how ill he's been, how close to death. Pneumonia and sepsis. She shows him the diary she faithfully kept for every one of the fourteen days he spent in a coma.

Next up are a range of people all attempting to convince Nick he is not who he thinks he is. He is not the Nick who did a combat tour with the U.S. Army or who ate all the hotdogs, nor did he lose toes to frostbite several years back. He is the Nick who owns and operates his own pizza parlor. He has never been known for his manual dexterity and would sooner buy new than fix anything.

He shuts his eyes and tries to will himself back to the town with the pink ice cream. But it won't happen. He wonders now which is the dream—the world with the pizzas and the raven-haired fiancée or the one where he works outdoors with his hands and has frostbite scars?

"Let that blow your mind for a minute," says Nick.

Now he is stuck here and must play along. Struggling with the initial problems that put him into the coma—and with the harrowing aftereffects of the coma itself—Nick faces a lengthy uphill battle. "I had to learn to walk, talk, and eat all over again. It was very humbling," he says of his forty days in the hospital.

It feels like my consciousness, spirit, or soul packed and went to another world just like this one and picked up a life there. It still blows my mind to recall that place. I was in a world just like this but just slightly different. The atmosphere was slightly orange instead of ours, which is blue. There were still a lot of the same places but they were not the same or in the same location as they are here. It was like the United States but not like the United States on a map. It was just mixed up.

The two weeks I was in a coma felt to me like twenty years. I lived a whole other life while I was under. So much so that when I finally was brought back to this world, realm, dimension, or whatever you want to call it, I was actually sad I was awake and didn't get to see how my other life there played out. I literally missed it, the *people, the experiences, the things I learned. I feel these emotions very strongly to this day.*

I also don't know what I looked like there. I assume I looked the same as I do here but never once in the twenty years under did I ever see my reflection. I don't like to say this was a dream because these experiences were so real to me. The vividness was so clear. I just can't explain a dream like that.

Amid the confusion and never-ending flashbacks, Nick found himself torn with loss.

All of a sudden, I was ripped out of my alternate reality and that was it—it was over. No conclusion, no closure. As far as meaningful relationships go, yes, I had several. Sometimes I feel like I had more there than I do here. And they were pretty deep, too. Three years later, I still feel that emotion from love and loss. It's crazy.

My family didn't come out and say it, but I could tell they thought I was insane. They didn't want to engage much on the fact that I was somewhere else. They didn't understand. I get it. How could they?

Most coma survivors will say that nobody can ever hope to understand unless they have undergone the experience themselves. For a few, comas may be a merciful blank. Others report lying frozen, aware of everything around them, silently screaming, yet unable to even blink. For many, this is a terrifying world of never-ending nightmares, more vivid than life itself, which burn themselves deep into the memory.

Others undergo nothing but joy and an overwhelming sensation of pure love akin to the psychedelic experience, while many accounts resemble the near-death experience (NDE), featuring past-life reviews, meetings with deceased loved ones, and a total oneness with the universe—events that are not limited to clinical settings and can be induced in numerous ways or may even happen spontaneously.

Alternate lives such as Nick's—lived to the full, seemingly lasting decades while mere days pass in the ICU—appear without parallel in any experience other than coma, with the possible exception of apparent past lives experienced by Buddhist monks and others deep in meditation. Something is clearly going on that defies scientific or medical explanation.

Equally shocking—and equally unknown to the public at large and most medical professionals—the apparently benign procedure of deep sedation to coma levels in the ICU is killing patients needlessly and consigning the majority of survivors to ruined lives of lasting brain damage, deep psychological trauma, and chronic physical complications.

Prolonged deep sedation is proven to damage the brain so severely that tens of points can be wiped off IQs, rendering survivors mentally impaired, while the lack of mobility results in serious nerve, muscle, and skeletal damage, hastening early death. For a small but growing number in the medical world, comas are not just highly dangerous but irresponsible to the point where hospitals and medical staff could, in the future, face lawsuits for malpractice.

Although the World Health Organization maintains no figures for the number of people placed in medically induced comas each year, the numbers are likely to be in the millions, a figure substantially multiplied during the COVID-19 pandemic.

The word *coma* comes from the Greek *koma*, meaning "deep sleep," and refers to a prolonged state of deep and unresponsive unconsciousness brought about by illness or injury or medically induced by anesthetics similar to those used in surgery. In essence, coma is a profound shutdown of brain function.

The first medically induced comas were not attempted until the late 1950s or early 1960s, when the first mechanical ventilators came into use and relaxant drugs were then used to paralyze the patient. These early ventilators resembled clunky domestic washing machines in size and construction. No one can say who the first patient was to undergo the experience.

Austrian doctor Peter Safar (1924–2003) is credited with pioneering the concept of advanced life support when he started keeping patients sedated and ventilated in a special environment in Baltimore City Hospital in 1958. However, others believe that the first ICU was established at Kommunehospitalet in Copenhagen in December 1953 by the pioneering Danish anesthetist Bjørn Aage Ibsen (1915–2007). Yet others argue that the British nurse Florence Nightingale created intensive care when she moved those most desperately ill closest to the nurses' station during the Crimean War.

Sometime in the 1990s—when more sophisticated, microprocessor-controlled ventilators became available—doctors treating patients for the invariably fatal acute respiratory distress syndrome (ARDS) noticed that patients appeared far more comfortable when heavily sedated, and so they began using sedatives generally reserved for the operating room. In turn, the sedated patients needed help breathing, so were placed on the new ventilators, and it was noticed that they were oxygenating better. It seemed the way to go.

"They saw how much more comfortable they looked," Kali Dayton, DNP, AGACNP-BC, an intensive care unit (ICU) nurse practitioner and consultant in Washington State, told us.* "They saw how much easier it was that they didn't have to talk to them, didn't have to do anything with them. And so that practice of putting them in coma seeped into treating other kinds of patients."

But the surgical sedatives had previously only been employed for brief periods of time and usually on patients with functioning kidneys, which help remove the sedatives from the system. No one had ever thought to give continuous high doses over weeks and months. And yet this became standard practice for all manner of critical ill patients for a decade or more. And then, gradually, clinicians became aware of something deeply troubling.

Too many patients were dying in the hospital and soon after discharge. Those who survived developed long-term debilitating effects, the result of severe nerve damage and muscle wastage. Mental faculties went haywire, with survivors often unable to recognize even close loved ones. The new term *post-intensive care syndrome* (PICS) was coined. "Patients with PICS are robbed of their normal cognitive, emotional, and physical

*Unless otherwise specified, all quotes from Dayton are from interviews we had with her.

capacity and cannot resume their previous life," noted Dr. E. Wesley Ely of Vanderbilt University School of Medicine in his 2017 report highlighting the dangers of these poorly understood practices.[1] Additionally, one-third of those discharged develop post-traumatic stress disorder (PTSD), more commonly seen in combat veterans and victims of physical or sexual assault.

From the few coma survivors who could find anyone to listen, there were accounts from deep within coma of alternate realities and parallel universes, some staggeringly beautiful, others defying all imagination in the depth of their horror. Those who gave voice to these terrifying or life-changing experiences were told to put them out of their minds, as these were nothing more than false memories and hallucinations. The term *ICU delirium* became a universal diagnosis, a seemingly mild affliction that would soon fade away.

While these experiences appear easy to dismiss, the lasting physical and mental damage began to draw concern as the evidence against coma care mounted. As such, some ICUs decided to ease back dramatically on the sedatives and pay more attention to patient mobility and interaction. It was found that by allowing patients to remain awake, they could chat with nursing staff via text on their phones, connect with their families in the same way, and even run a business from their laptops, all while sitting upright and allowing the mechanical ventilator to breathe for them.

This way, patients became more invested in their own recovery while avoiding instances of delirium or muscle wastage, and they could work with staff to achieve an early exit from the ICU. And, if heavy sedation had to be employed, the patient would be awakened daily in what were termed "sedation vacations." This was a practice gaining increasing acceptance. But then the COVID-19 pandemic hit in 2020.

Suddenly, every ICU in the world found itself overwhelmed. ICU staff, instead of their usual two-to-one patient-nurse ratios, were ministering to multiple patients, and burnout was becoming a serious issue for staff. It made sense to place patients in a more manageable condition, and so the heavy use of sedatives returned. This put strain on the supply chain and different medications began to be employed, with far greater use of the more powerful benzodiazepines.

"They went right back to those protocols of the 1990s," says Dayton. "And now they're using some of the worst drugs for the longest periods of time." Staff had to be drafted into ICUs from elsewhere in the hospital who had no idea of earlier ICU procedures that focused on keeping the patient alert and mobile.

"And all these new people came rushing into the ICU who'd never been in an ICU before because we had so many COVID patients," Dr. Ely tells us. "People were drawn in from cardiology clinics and pediatric clinics, and they didn't even know how to run an ICU, they just thought, *Oh, this is how you do it*. So a bad new culture was built almost overnight."

Sedatives and coma, they were now told, were the best way to deal with COVID-19, giving the body a chance to rest and letting nature and medication do what they could. Heavy sedation became the norm again, and coma treatment became almost automatic.

Dr. Ely and his team studied more than two thousand COVID patients from fifteen countries and demonstrably proved that the two or more weeks, on average, spent in coma were devastating to patients. "It's a left turn. It's a bad idea. It's inappropriate. It's not good medicine," he stressed to us. "But it's easy because it knocks the patient out."

Today, despite a wealth of evidence to the contrary, most doctors believe that the patient, once comatose, is at total rest, allowing the body the chance to recuperate. The brain is offline. The event will be a blank in their lives. And while many a doctor will tell families that the comatose patient is resting and the sedatives aid a deeper sleep, multiple research papers and a growing number of studies have shown that the sedatives employed disrupt brain activity so severely that REM sleep is not possible. "It's not that brains are turned off during medically induced comas," insists Dayton. "It's that they're injured and broken."

Many clinicians also believe that a long stay in the ICU can be highly traumatic, and so they try to shield the patient from unnecessary harm with different levels of sedation. In some cases, deep sedation is used to control unruly or agitated patients, those who tug at the lines and feeding tubes running in and out of their body. In many instances, patients are also physically restrained to prevent them harming themselves. But no medical practitioner can be sure just how far they are pushing the patient, as the effects of different sedatives vary from person to person. Many will drift in and out of differing levels of consciousness. Others go so very deep that they enter realms rarely glimpsed before. Others who go too far—and manage to return—report standing on the threshold of this life and the next, glimpsing another level of existence.

Intensive care staff rarely get the opportunity to discuss the ICU stay with patients. Those coming out of deep sedation are generally too confused—or incapable of speech because of damage to vocal cords—that by the time they leave the unit no coherent accounts can be gathered. Few medical personnel ever feel the need to explore further because the nebulous term *ICU delirium* is seen as explanation enough. Yet, for the patients, such a diagnosis appears to explain nothing and even downplays the true severity to the point where many feel insulted.

There is an obvious contradiction between the patients' experience and the doctors' understanding. Delirium and hallucinations are conscious states of mind that cannot be experienced while sedated to the deepest levels of unconsciousness because the brain is effectively offline. Many doctors acknowledge it is impossible to have any recollections from within coma, and so any memories recalled by coma survivors can only have been hastily conjured up after regaining consciousness. This, they say, is the brain's way of making sense of the missing period in their lives. Yet this theory is deeply at odds with the actual experiences that people report from inside coma, which are invariably rich in detail and all too often described as more real than any waking reality.

Those who leave the hospital are rarely given any indication of the damage they have suffered, nor guidance on how to make sense of an experience that will stay with them for life. Many feel they have been cut adrift without any explanation, rendered amazed and puzzled by what they have just been through and reluctant to tell even close loved ones. Many are left to question every aspect of reality: not sure if they have died and come back or if they traveled to realms and dimensions that the modern world would consign to fantasy. Almost without exception, those who have visited these other realms from within their coma all describe themselves as insane, mad, bonkers, or crazy. They can see no other explanation.

Coma patients are clearly entering the strangest mental arenas, and they appear to be doing so because the heavy sedation switches off a key element within the brain that enables us to process our everyday, waking consciousness, and this allows a greater expansion of the mind, as experienced by those in the deepest states of meditation, by others undergoing psychedelic states, and even by those teetering between this life and the next.

There is also compelling evidence that certain chemicals are released in the human body at times of extreme stress and impending death that produce the mystical effects experienced in coma, either to ease our passing or open a doorway to what lies beyond.

So here we are in the twenty-first century, and we like to believe that science can explain just about anything. But explanations are in short supply when it comes to events that thousands upon thousands of people experience daily within their comas. Despite centuries of scientific and medical progress, consciousness—something every one of us experiences moment by moment—remains a mystery. No doctor or scientist can tell us how this comes about or where the seat of consciousness is. They cannot even point to the location of their own minds, because nobody can truly say where the mind resides.

And while today's scientists are at a loss to explain our everyday level of consciousness, there remain other equally mysterious levels of consciousness that can be achieved by a variety of means, be they medically induced, recreational, or part of a spiritual quest. But for too many, these are no-go areas with an active refusal to explore, fearing to take science into the realms of New Age mumbo-jumbo or spiritual fantasies. And yet there is an overwhelming body of evidence and countless first-hand accounts* that demonstrate the mind is capable of far more than we currently understand.

We take a journey into those realms—levels of consciousness and other regions of the mind that can no longer be dismissed as hallucinations, false memories, or the result of confusion or delirium—that prove equally as real as our current, waking level of consciousness. Until these experiences can be taken seriously and greater effort is made to understand the doors that comas appear to unlock, people will be consigned every day to the darkest recesses of the mind, waved off with the best of intensions to embark on solo voyages beyond the imagination.

And, of those who survive, the overwhelming majority are doomed to live half-lives, shadows of their former selves, with many regretting that they ever returned.

---

*If not specified otherwise, the accounts of coma patients, nurses, doctors, and scientists shared in this book are from interviews we conducted.

A World More Vivid
than Life Itself

1

You're Not Just Sleeping Your Time Away

From Confusion and Bliss to the Gates of Hell

Adison Pusateri, BSN, RN, is a highly experienced nurse who has spent the past seven years working nightshifts from 7:00 p.m. to 7:00 a.m. in the intensive care unit (ICU) of a Denver hospital, one typical of those across the United States and much of the developed world. As working environments go, it is hot, smelly, noisy, and a ceaseless hive of activity. As an environment for the sick to get well, it doesn't get much worse.

"In my experience, for whatever reason, when it's close to shift change is when things get a little crazy," says Pusateri. "I can't tell you how many times a status quo patient has had some sort of event—whether it be small or large and life threatening—close to the end of my shift or immediately when I am coming on shift."

In this Denver ICU there is never a quiet moment. The pandemic has stretched people and equipment to their limits. Each patient requires constant care. "Depending how sick the patient is will determine how sedated the doctor will want to keep them in order for their body to rest," she explains.

"Heavily sedated, the patient will have large central lines with multiple IV infusions constantly running. The central lines might be in their neck or groin. They will be fed through a tube if on a ventilator, and this will either go into their throat along with the breathing tube or into their nose.

"These people will almost always have a tube up into their bladder and sometimes a rectal tube to collect stool so they don't mess the bed. However, it will still leak frequently. These patients often smell horrible after a day or two because a sponge bath can only go so far."

Pusateri says her patients rarely lie still. Some need physical restraints to stop them tugging on the lines and tubes. "People in medically induced comas are nothing like what is portrayed in the media on television or in fiction. Something to know about someone in a medically induced coma is that the only reason they are in one is because they are near death. Even heavily sedated, they will still tear up and I have seen unconscious people cry," Pusateri tells us. "So almost never would I refer to someone in this situation as appearing 'peaceful.'"

When I was sedated the first time, I cried. I sobbed and begged the doctors and nurses not to let me die.

This is the recollection of Darren Buttrick, who, at forty-nine years of age and gym fit, caught COVID-19 in March 2020 and became so ill that doctors told him to say goodbye to his family.

There were lots of machines bleeping, lots of noise, and what felt like someone playing with my ears and neck. It felt like dangly earrings, but that was the central line in my neck that would bleep and deliver the drugs I needed.

Darren—in common with the vast majority of ICU patients—gets confused and quickly agitated. They tell him he needs to rest. *Time now for a nice sleep.* The nurse takes his hand and strokes gently. She counts slowly to ten. This is when panic sets in for Darren, who fears he may never wake up.

I again begged them to save me, with tears rolling down my face. I was heartbroken and so frightened. She got to three and I don't remember anything else.

What came next for Janine Sarah Withers from Tredegar in Wales was no blank but an entirely altered reality. She believes she had COVID-19, but in December 2019 few were thinking about the pandemic and no one in Wales was testing for it. Whatever she had quickly turned to pneumonia, causing lung failure.

It was horrific and life changing. Believe me, during this time you're not just sleeping the time away. You can feel and hear far too much of what's happening. It's the most terrifying nightmare you will ever have. I lay there totally paralyzed, screaming inside my head but not able to make a sound.

Janine was not yet in a coma. She was being sedated and closely monitored. She flitted in and out of consciousness. This is when things first start to become strange in the ICU.

"Many people experience animals in their room," explains Pusateri. "They see people who aren't there. Bugs and snakes. A lot of my delirious patients will think they're somewhere else other than the hospital. They think they're in a different point in time. Or think they're in a completely different situation. One patient was convinced that they were on a cruise ship, sunbathing on deck."

Chrissy Statham has a clear memory of just when things started to get unearthly in an ICU in Suffolk, UK, where she was being treated for type A influenza and pneumonia.

I remember my oldest son visiting and writing on a chalkboard, Behave with the nurses. I remember a lift, shelves, and a sink, with a door to my left, then it all went blank.

This is where it gets weird. For some reason, I was in bed and some football players came to visit me. I had a hand puppet on my arm and somehow I was expected to wave the puppet at the footballers, but it was just too heavy. The pressure on my chest was unbearable and I couldn't join in. I had no energy. I blacked out again.

During the forty-five days of coma that followed, Chrissy experienced a never-ending succession of painfully vivid and utterly distressing nightmarish scenes.

I was hanging on a meat hook over the ocean, surrounded by mountains. Then I was dumped in a coal mining bucket and transported through tunnels where women were having their hands cut off for sharks to eat.

I also remember being in London during the war, near the river, then being evacuated to the country, where I was running to save my life and seeing death all around me.

Worse still, she has a clear recollection of being raped and not being able to do anything about it.

A radio playing somewhere in the background gave color to the odd imaginings of Jo Nelson, who very likely had COVID-19 back in December 2019 and was rushed to Aintree University Hospital, not far from the famous British racecourse. She was being sedated in the ICU when she heard the announcer urging her to call in and win big time. Just answer one easy question.

They were running this every hour, on the hour, and I just kept phoning in and [each time] I kept winning [she laughs]. I remember looking at my online banking and seeing the money change every hour. I couldn't wait to tell my husband. One thousand pounds each time! I just remember feeling amazing, knowing we were sorted financially.

Eventually, Jo lost nine days of her life when she was placed into a coma. She experienced a never-ending cycle of death.

These "nightmares" were all about people I'm close to, and in the dreams they either died themselves or had little ones and they died. When I properly woke up, I genuinely thought all these people were dead, it was so real. I can remember every single minute of it; some of the "dreams" lasted whole days at a time, with me going to endless funerals. It was just heartbreaking.

A pet greyhound called Ted was a regular bedside visitor for composer Stephen Watkins as he recovered in an Essex ICU in the UK from an aneurysm operation that left him with a blood clot on the heart.

Ted would come through the door with my other dog, Toffee, just behind him. They'd be walking on their hind legs. They both would be wearing nurses' uniforms and have COVID masks on, and Ted would have a thermometer between his paws. Then he'd shove it in my mouth. And there'd be other nurses around, just ordinary nurses doing their jobs, and Ted would just wink at me and say, Don't tell 'em, Dad.

Events such as these are described as the classic symptoms of ICU delirium—"an acute and fluctuating disturbance of consciousness and cognition, a common manifestation of acute brain dysfunction in critically ill patients, occurring in up to 80 percent of the sickest intensive care unit populations."

Pusateri sees a lot of it. "We royally mess up their sleep schedule. Almost always a patient will be awoken by staff every one to two hours, all day and all night. This, in addition to all the noises in an ICU, the constant beeping and alarms, leads to severe sleep deprivation." From her experience, few ever manage more than three hours of disturbed sleep a day.

Within ICUs, there are two distinct types of delirium. Hyperactive delirium refers to patients who are not comatose. They are confused, have short attention spans, sudden mood swings, agitation, combativeness, and disorderly thinking. They often misinterpret events around them. Hypoactive delirium is when a patient is totally unresponsive and will not awaken of their own accord. Events believed to have been experienced within this state are classed as false memories or hallucinations.

Both are infinitely more serious than they sound and can be rightly classified as medical emergencies because they involve different levels of brain failure. Those with delirium are twice as likely to die in the hospital and three times as likely to die within six months of discharge. Those that survive are likely to spend far more time in the ICU and regularly require admission to care facilities later. They are at high risk of post-traumatic stress disorder (PTSD) and permanent cognitive impairments, termed post-ICU dementia and PICS.

Generally, the main causes of ICU delirium are sleep deprivation, isolation, and lack of mobility and human contact, together with the varying levels of sedation brought about by the remarkably varied cocktail of sedatives and analgesics employed, from opiates to ketamine. Additionally, low oxygen saturation, known as "sats," due to struggling lungs or blood clots, can lead to brain damage.

When Deborah Mayo was admitted to the UK's Leicester Royal Hospital with suspected swine flu in February 2015, she was immediately rushed to the ICU and swiftly given a combination of sedatives and paralyzing drugs in a bid to stabilize her. She was thirty-eight years old at the time. She recalls:

The docs asked if I kept pigeons as I had the lungs of a pigeon keeper. I had the lungs of a very old person and my status was "incompatible with life," a term that still sends shivers down my spine.

The doctor tells her husband, Adam, that she has also suffered a cardiac arrest and now has sepsis, which can quickly result in multiple organ failure. She will be lucky to survive the night. But she does. Drifting in and out of consciousness, Deborah fears for her husband and how he is going to cope.

We've only been married two years. I take care of everything. The finances are all on my PC and all password protected. How was he going to pay the mortgage? What was our mortgage account number? Who was our mortgage with? All these thoughts, silly as it sounds, crossed my mind.

The next four days would be a half-remembered world of worry and stress, of being turned face down or face up in her bed, while nurses fussed about, adjusting machines and administering insulin, antibiotics, and analgesics. Then, in the following fourteen days, Deborah would undergo hypoactive delirium or, as she terms it, "One mind fuck of a coma."

But first, in common with many others, the hospital around Deborah initially weaves itself into her altered state. This is hyperactive delirium. She remembers being in a portable ward, like a large ambulance, and she was in the only bed, alone.

She recalls the ambulance driving around until finally coming to a stop at Northampton's Royal & Derngate theater complex, where the doctors and nurses all hop out for a fun night of clubbing, abandoning Deborah in the large ambulance.

The ceiling was Perspex but opaque and there were bodies writhing in blood above me. I was screaming in fear as latex-covered beings surrounded me. I remember a nurse coming to visit me after she'd been clubbing, and I said I'd report her. She then thrust a tube down my throat, which I desperately tried to remove. She screamed at me and said it's for my own good. I was suffocating.

COVID-19 patient Darren was surprised when he suddenly became conscious again. He recalls:

I remember seeing lot of people in space suits. I felt in a different world, very frightened. There were people laying in front of me and to the side of me. They were on their backs and on ventilators and in comas, and just the ringing sound of machines, the bleeping keeping them alive.

I remember looking at the wall clock and watching every minute pass, and feeling so frightened and agitated and not well. I wanted to go home. My friend had a birthday party in two days, the house insurance needed paying. Where's my phone?

Panic again sets in. Darren is ripping the central line from his throat. He grabs hold of the feeding tube to his nose before, seconds later, he slips into oblivion once more.

It took seven staff to pin me down. The doctor decided to put me back to sleep and ventilate me again. They said I was calling out, Dad, come and save me. Please help me. I need you to get me out of here.

Pusateri explains what happens when a patient is sick enough to be medically paralyzed:

This is with a drug that inhibits the patient's muscles from moving at all. This includes the diaphragm that everyone uses to breathe, so they have to be on the ventilator. This is because their lungs are so still or fluid filled.

While sedated and unconscious, they will retain their brainstem reflexes and fight the ventilator, gag on the breathing tube, move around in bed, sometimes vomit around the breathing tube. They will almost always experience some level of edema, when the fluid shifts from the vascular space into the tissues and cause swelling that can be so bad that fluid will weep from their skin. Often times it can be enough to saturate their bed sheets.

One patient, who already had intimate knowledge of the ICU he found himself in, insists he was self-aware.

On the ventilator, in a medically induced coma, I was self-aware. I could hear and process everything that was going on. Conversations

were happening around me that I knew the answers to, but I was
trapped inside my body. My body would not allow me to respond.

This is Corey Agricola, a chaplain at the vast UAB Hospital in Birmingham, Alabama. He likes to wave his hands around when he talks in his musical Southern accent. His smile is vast and highly infectious. Corey is also an eight-year veteran of the US Marine Corps who one day was in peak physical condition "doing 'maxes' at the gym and bench-pressing three hundred pounds deadlift," and the next is flat on his back in the very hospital where he works. Suddenly, he's not expected to live. He has a massive and mysterious infection determined to resist all treatment.

On top of the infection that's likely to kill him, Corey is fretting for a whole different reason. In a few days, he's all set to propose to the woman he intends to marry. He plans to spring the surprise from the basket of a hot-air balloon that he's already paid for up front. "I could see the days on a little calendar on the wall in front of my bed, and I could see the days taken down. And I can see what they're doing to me. I gotta hurry up and get out of here because we're gonna miss the deadline."

Those around him have other pressing concerns. Options are running out.

They tried many different antibiotics, and they were down to their
last one. They told my fiancée that this is the last one we can try. We
think he's got about four days to live.

Corey has to listen to all this. He can see it all, too.

I was seeing things that were actually in the room but I wasn't in a
position to see them. I could see the monitor with my blood pressure
reading. And I could see it going up and down—it would drop all the
way to fifty over twenty and all the way up to one-ninety over one-
twenty. I mean, it was just crazy—but I could see it in my mind, you
know. In my mind! And it all corresponded, I learned later.

The decision to place patients like Darren and Corey into a coma is usually a team decision. "The intensive care doctor will have the final decision," explains Pusateri. "But it's the nurses and respiratory therapists who will communicate the need for it ninety-nine percent of the time."

When that happens, the patient is kept in the same ICU and under even closer observation. "Occasionally, a patient on a ventilator may not be sedated at all, depending on what's going on," Pusateri points out. "Sometimes they are completely awake. But, typically, if they are intubated they will start off on minimal sedation, and the sedation will be increased if they are fighting the ventilator too much or are too agitated."

The word *coma* is actually something of a misnomer. "A medically induced coma isn't really an all-or-nothing scenario," Pusateri tells us. "It's more of a spectrum of consciousness." It is also a bit of a hit-or-miss situation. Some drugs do not work well on some patients. Weight is a serious consideration, and anyone with a history of certain kinds of recreational drug use will be all the harder to knock out. Elderly people suffering dementia will need considerably fewer sedatives. She continues:

> We use something called the RASS score to rate how sedated someone is. It stands for Richmond Agitation-Sedation Scale. It goes from +4 (extremely agitated and violent) to −5 (completely unarousable). Most often the goal, which is ordered by the doctor, will be a RASS score of 0 to −2.
>
> If the patient needs to be paralyzed, the goal will always be RASS −5. This is because if they are undersedated but paralyzed, they may be awake and you won't know.

This, Pusateri is keen to stress, "is extremely cruel—to be awake but unable to move or even blink."

To see just how deeply unconscious the patient is, electrodes are placed on their face and fired with a small electrical stimulus. Pusateri will then look to see if the eyebrows twitch or not. By rights, there should now be minimal brain activity beyond basic life-support functions. The patient is in what is also known as "apparent death"—all signs of life or vitality are absent and the person appears to be dead because of very feeble or minimal functioning of body systems. Corey, the hospital chaplain, recalls:

> I felt like I was coming out of my body, like I was floating away. And then, as they tried to bring me back off the propofol, I came back into my body. And there I was, present in the room, but it was now a totally different experience. I was in scenes from my life in the past. I was in a different hospital, the one where I lived in Houston, Texas, for nine years and pastored a church out there.

As Corey drifts deeper into the realms of actual coma, he should not be experiencing anything at all. According to current medical understanding, he no longer has access to his memories, nor can he process new ones. The pictures playing out in his mind are not registering on his brain. Any brain scan would be flatlining. Yet, somehow, Corey Agricola is finally airborne.

> I felt like I was flying, and it was so real. I remember flying and being able to reach my hand down to pick up the snow from the mountain peaks. And it was, you know, cold to my hands.

Corey also finds himself flying back in time, visiting parts of his old life he had once captured on camera. He is reliving the actual Kodak moment, stepping into the framed photographs that decorate his home.

> Yeah, I was back to those moments. I went back probably twenty years or so to a time where I had my Jeep Wrangler and used to love going on rides or just around the countryside here in Alabama. I wanted to unwind or get away, you know. I would just drive around and see a different part of the state, and I was back on one of those rides.

The old photographs flick past in Corey's mind. Here's one from even further back.

It was just so real, being with my dad in Montana. It felt like I was there. I could smell it all. I had all my senses. Oh, yeah, I was talking to people. You know, talking to my dad. It's like I was back there one hundred percent.

Stephen Taylor, a retired medical statistician, was already unconscious when he arrived at the ICU in the Royal Liverpool University Hospital. His colon had suddenly burst while he was at home, and he was quickly developing sepsis. The doctors take one look at him and conclude that his chance of survival is about one in one hundred. Swiftly, he is heavily sedated and placed on a ventilator. It would be ten days before Stephen would open his eyes again. His experiences were so strange that he felt compelled to write them down, one of the few survivors able to do so. He recalls:

The entirety of my stay in critical care was a period of strange, vivid dreams and nightmares. In the beginning, I was aware of a yellow world where all is bathed and suffused with its radiant, glowing light, propagating feelings of healing and comfort, enveloping everything in its warmth.

And then the scene changes. Stephen is traveling with his family by car through the lush Belgian countryside in brilliant, white sunshine, speeding along a fast highway, when suddenly there's a crash and the yellow world evaporates.

The next thing he knows, he's being shown an exterior shot of a beautiful, modern building as he stands on a large, green lawn amid a vista of rolling countryside, fields and farmland, garden flowers, mature trees, and woodland. Distant, hazy hills shimmer on a blue horizon. In front of him stands an imposing structure, four stories high and sweeping away in a beautiful, graceful, curving arc that follows the contours of the hills. The walls are thick, pink granite with a shining metal and glass frontage. He marvels at the thick, opaque glass roof.

Now he enters the building, leaving behind the bright afternoon sun and walks into a lofty atrium with a polished gray granite staircase climbing to a balcony. In front of him is a tall, splashing fountain. He sees a reception desk, recognizes he is in a hospital, and sees himself as a patient within. Stephen is about to check in to a rather creepy Belgian hospital run by black-habited nuns and overseen with haughty authority by a wheelchair-bound Mother Superior. He will be here for the next week and more.

Zara Slattery is a graphic artist living on England's South Coast who contracted a flesh-eating bacteria in 2013 while visiting her mother in the hospital. Zara spent two weeks in a coma while doctors fought to save her life. Her coma experience would be one of inexplicable guilt and utter fear from the very beginning. She would eventually turn her hospital stay into the nightmarish graphic novel *Coma*.[1] She recalls:

> There was a moment that I woke up in the dark—this is really early on before the coma—and a medieval skeleton was spiraling across my line of sight. So I can only imagine that they were opening my eyes and shining bright lights to see if I was conscious. But I couldn't see beyond my peripheral vision.
>
> I had this level of consciousness. The one I have now. And I knew it wasn't a dream but I knew I wasn't fully awake. And I was just trying to figure out what I'd woken up into. Then I saw the nurses at the end of my bed. And I knew there were medics, but they were half skulls and half faces. And my whole inside, my entire body, just flipped into absolute, abject fear. This was real. They were at my bedside. Anybody would be frightened! But I was in extreme pain. At this stage, I wasn't deeply sedated. And it was like that cast the die. From then on, it was cast in fear.
>
> I was very disturbed by being looked at all the time. I was very, very ill. I had two nurses with me all the time. And I was seeing eyes everywhere, like seventy pairs! Even the Keep Out sign on the curtain

looked like a big, red eye. I couldn't bear being looked at but, of course, they were monitoring me constantly.

I was conscious of my children coming to see me. So I do think I wasn't so deeply down. I was aware of them coming in. And I knew that I had to save them from the seismic emotional trauma that I couldn't quite locate. All I knew was that this was an extraordinarily dangerous place, that I was being held and tortured. And I needed to get my children out of there; they had to be got away.

For Janine, whose story about lying paralyzed but awake was shared earlier, the doctors had to keep increasing the sedatives as she repeatedly fought her way out of the coma. She recalls:

Eventually sedated, I slipped into somewhere between sleep and reality. Sometimes you can hear what's being said in the room and it gets twisted into part of the nightmare. Then the ICU starts to fade and an entirely different reality begins to take hold.

I was being held by an invisible force in an open-top wooden box on the back of a horse and cart. I tried to shout but I couldn't speak. I struggled to move but I felt tied to the bottom of the box, hands above my head and my legs apart. We went down a long, cobbled road, which got darker the further we went down it. At the top of the hill, the light faded into the distance. I was naked and felt totally vulnerable. I constantly fought to get free, but I was getting so tired. I was still determined to get back to my family.

After a torturous journey of interminable length and duration, Janine arrives at her destination.

I was taken into what appeared to be an old theater. Standing on the stage was a bent, twisted-up woman like an old hag . . . a hooded, skeletal woman wearing a black cape, holding a hooked cane that she held by the end, hitting the floor over and over. The noise was so loud it echoed around the whole room. There was a small Gollum-like man beneath her cape who crept around the floor on all fours. She beat and slashed him over and over with the end of her hooked cane, shouting to look away from me, that I was hers and so was he.

I began to feel invisible hands touching me all over in an intimate way. It makes me still feel sick now. I couldn't believe this was happening. I hadn't even said goodbye to my family, so I fought with everything I had left in me, over and over, but I remember thinking that all this pain would go away if I just gave in; maybe just rest for a bit.

Now I found myself totally exhausted, weightless, drifting in nothingness. Not aware of anything really, except the need to stop fighting and it would soon be over. Then I was aware of my partner's father who passed away months before. He was telling me to pull myself together, to fight it. He was telling me not to give up even when I needed to rest. Pull yourself together girl, they need you.

That was it. I wasn't going to give in. I would keep fighting, determined to get back. I was physically fighting, pulling the tubes out of my nose and throat, the arterial lines out of my neck and groin and the internal tubes, too. I believe I may even have punched a nurse, but she was too polite to say afterward. Then everything went in reverse like an old movie played backward and I was going back up the hill toward the light, back to the land of the living. I was going back to my family.

This was not like any dream or regular nightmare, insists Janine. What she experienced was "another level of reality entirely." And, unlike regular dreams or nightmares, these ghastly, otherworldly visions stay firmly implanted in the memory, refusing to fade over the years.

"Coma is the deepest form of unconsciousness," maintains Arnold Mindell, a psychotherapist and the author of more than twenty books, who has worked extensively with coma patients.[2] "If consciousness stands at one end of the awareness spectrum, then coma stands at the other end, with many forms of altered states in between."

He says the time has come to take a fresh look at what consciousness means and what levels of consciousness are attainable by the human mind, because we need to question "the belief that comas are unconscious, inaccessible states" and understand that human beings are not "merely machines whose central nervous systems—stimulated by extreme physical states—produce haphazard hallucinations and visions."

The thing to really remember is these are real memories to me. In my mind they all really happened to me.

This is Rory Atherton, survivor of a seven-day coma who found his coma experience far more harrowing than the actual home invasion he experienced that led to him being airlifted, unconscious, directly to emergency surgery. Rory was bleeding out from a near-lethal stab wound to his abdomen. One of his hands was hanging by a thread from a machete slash. He insists his coma experience was worse.

I think the hardest part for me is that no one in my life will ever understand just what I went through. It was a complete parallel universe. There was no escape. It was hell. My psychologist thinks it was so traumatic because of the horror I went through right before.

I was awake inside a glass bubble in a big, empty room with huge glass windows. I was inside what looked like a big, luxurious house somewhere like Spain. Lots of beautiful people around a pool having a party. I was very confused. At the back of my mind, I knew something had happened to me and I knew it was bad, but I couldn't quite work out what.

Then this very large, Black woman who appeared to be in charge came into the room surrounded by younger White men, and they appeared to be discussing me. This woman had purchased me and wanted me for sexual pleasure.

Not unlike a film sequence, the scene suddenly changes and Rory finds himself in the lounge room of a typical suburban house.

I was still in this glass bubble and the large Black woman was talking with some men, saying how she didn't want me anymore. Her children were running around playing, and I was just observing everything and being ignored. Now, all of a sudden, three other women are surrounding me. They're comforting me and rubbing my hands. I believe I'd opened my eyes briefly and seen the nurses, or I was in surgery. They soon went away.

The scene then changed again. I was in an abandoned, creepy-looking building. The large woman was again present along with about thirty children who were practicing a dance. Then I heard her very clearly telling these children how she was going to kill me or how she wanted me dead, and she was convincing these children it was the right thing to do.

The scene then changed again. I was on a hospital bed and not in a bubble and there were sinister-looking male nurses holding me down and this large woman was discussing with an Asian doctor how best to kill me.

Then the scene changed again and I was alone on this hospital bed, and this little, effeminate doctor with a big, black mustache was wiring me up to something. He was telling me, Don't worry, this won't hurt. It will be over soon. *He then pulled a lever and I felt my body leap off the hospital bed. My body then began to grow and swell in size, massively swell and start to turn orange and grow huge spikes until I was the size of a car. And then these doctors were laughing, saying it should've killed me and how strange the side effects were.*

Then they left the room, and naked teenage boys started stabbing me with knives, trying to finish me off. It didn't work, so they began to drink my blood from the wounds. Now, at this point, I believed I was actually dying because my vision was fading in and out, and all I was seeing was a very bright light.

This was never a dream. It wasn't anything like a dream. It was one hundred percent real to me. It was really happening.

"IT'S ALL IN THE HEAD"

It's a nice, crisp, sunny morning in April 1944, and the world-renowned Swiss psychologist Carl G. Jung is out for a stroll, enjoying the spring weather, when he takes a tumble on the Alpine ice and seriously hurts his foot. Rushed to the nearest hospital by horse and cart, he suffers a heart attack in the kerfuffle. Try as they might, the doctors and nurses are powerless to prevent one of the most influential psychiatrists of all time from slipping into a spontaneous coma. One nurse reports that his body appeared to glow. What Jung experienced next would change his life.[3]

> It seemed to me that I was high up in space. Far below I saw the globe of the Earth, bathed in a gloriously blue light, the reddish-yellow desert of Arabia. I could also see the snow-covered Himalayas.
>
> And then something strange happened. . . . I had the feeling that everything was being sloughed away; everything I aimed at or wished for or thought, the whole phantasmagoria of earthly existence, fell away or was stripped from me.
>
> I would know what had been before me, why I had come into being, and where my life was flowing.

Jung also had a premonition while in the coma that the doctor treating him would soon die. He actually did die a few days later of septicemia. Jung's coma experience would stay with him for the rest of his life as an occurrence both real and eternal.

From a modern medical perspective, the Swiss psychologist lauded for his razor-sharp perception and attention to detail would be considered delusional with a false psychotic belief regarding the self or persons or objects outside the self that is maintained despite indisputable evidence to the contrary.

But Jung thought otherwise and used the experience to expand on the concept of collective unconscious. He also kept his eyes open for similar accounts from other patients who had, for whatever reason, slipped into a coma. In a lengthy thesis, Jung introduced the case of a young woman "whose reliability and truthfulness I have no reason to doubt" who fell into a coma from blood loss during a botched forceps delivery. This patient, he wrote, "was in a coma and ought to have had a complete psychic black-out and been altogether incapable of clear observation and sound judgment."[4]

Not unlike Corey's experience of seeing the ICU and everyone around him from an entirely different and impossible viewpoint, Jung's patient described viewing events from the ceiling, looking down on her own body with her eyes shut and watching the flustered doctor pacing the floor and her mother and husband fraught with alarm.

When she came to, she described everything she had seen and eventually forced one nurse to admit that the doctor had been hysterical. She also recounted flying off to "a glorious park-like landscape shining in the brightest colors, and in particular an emerald green meadow with short grass, which sloped gently upwards beyond a wrought-iron gate leading into a park."

The way Jung saw it, this young woman had been tapping into the collective unconscious, "the deepest level of the psyche, containing the accumulation of inherited psychic structures." Along with his contemporary, Sigmund Freud, Jung came to the conclusion that the unconscious can be divided into two layers—the personal unconscious, where memories are suppressed or forgotten, and the collective unconscious, which contains "material of an entire species rather than of an individual. The whole spiritual heritage of mankind's evolution, born anew in the brain structure of every individual."

Jung was amazed to realize he had stumbled upon a seemingly unexplored level of consciousness. But he was by no means the first. Similar accounts go back to the dawn of time. One of the earliest recorded accounts, from 375 BCE, is in the story of Er, as recounted in Plato's *The Republic*.

Er was a Greek warrior who had died in battle. His body lay on the battlefield, along with hundreds of others, for ten days before it was recovered. Curiously, Er's body—while seemingly dead to the world—had not begun to decompose. Two days later, while stacked among the bodies of his fallen comrades, Er opened his eyes to find that he was on a funeral pyre that was just catching fire.

It's fair to assume that many at the funeral jumped out of their skin when they saw Er scramble off the rapidly catching pyre, but what Er recounted next was stranger by far. He told of traveling with his fellow warriors to an "awe-inspiring" place where two holes led into the ground and two led into the sky. From one sky opening came "clean souls" beaming love and joy, while from the ground came a haggard procession "crying in despair [and] recounting their awful experiences." Er spent seven days resting up here before traveling toward a vividly bright, distant rainbow. When he arrived, everybody was offered the choice of a new life based on lottery tokens that they were given. Everyone was then obliged to drink water from the River of Forgetfulness and lie down to sleep before being reborn. For some reason, Er missed out on the drink. He lay down, and when he next opened his eyes he could smell smoke.

Was Er delirious—suffering a false psychotic belief—or was he experiencing something that has been long understood? The Hindu vision of the afterlife, which goes back to around 800 BCE, shares certain similarities with Er's vision. Death is not the end of life. There is a resting period where minds are erased before souls return to earth, reborn. The soul or spirit must be reborn time and again for lessons to be learned, which in turn enriches the whole spiritual world.

Buddhists believe in a cycle of death and rebirth called samsara. Through karma and eventual enlightenment, they hope to escape samsara and achieve nirvana, an end to suffering.

The Buddha, who lived in the fifth or sixth century BCE, taught his disciples not to fear death but to seek nirvana and see the world as it really is. Nirvana means realizing and accepting the Four Noble Truths and being awake to reality. Some Buddhists believe that enlightened individuals can choose to be reborn to help others become enlightened. Others believe that when nirvana—the completed cycle of *samsara*—is achieved, all suffering and further existence for that individual ends.

Go back even further to around 2600 BCE, and the Egyptian *Book of the Dead* points to three known levels of afterlife: an underworld, eternal life, and the rebirth of the soul. The book also depicts a paradise where the recent dead are expected to rest and recuperate. This is the Field of Reeds, a lush and plentiful vision of Egyptian life at its best.

Early Christians, perhaps influenced by Plato, believed in reincarnation but dropped the idea in 553 CE at the Second Council of Constantinople. Anyone teaching the idea had their works banned because the notion clashed with the belief in Christ's corporeal (physical) resurrection. Many Islamic scholars have accepted the theory of life after death but tend to limit their beliefs to spiritual rather than physical resurrection.

Such views of the soul or spirit departing the body and taking off on their own adventures during severe illness or as the result of an accident are common globally, across cultures and centuries. They can be found being recalled in Aboriginal cave painting in Australia, carried by word of mouth among the indigenous peoples of the Americas and Africa, and discussed as fireside topics among the Celts, Persians, and Romans.

"In the past these kinds of experiences were known under names that reflected the worldview or religious beliefs of the day," says Dr. Pim van Lommel, a Dutch cardiologist and author of numerous books on the near-death experience (NDE). "At the time, people spoke of enlightenment experiences, mystical experiences, religious experiences, or visions. In antiquity, these kinds of experiences were described as a journey to the underworld or a sojourn with the gods, and, in the early Middle Ages, as a visit to paradise. These kinds of experiences were primarily ascribed to heroes, saints, and prophets, but sometimes also to normal people, as we see in Plato's story about the soldier Er."[5]

So why do we think differently now? Today, we think the way we do because science has not really progressed much in its worldview since the days of Sir Isaac Newton and the Enlightenment, which brought forth a new worldview based on the understanding of what can be witnessed. This science limited itself to subjects in the physical world that can be weighed and measured. Consciousness—as something not visible, not perceptible or tangible, that cannot be measured nor verified—managed to defy all scientific explanation. The tendency in the modern, enlightened world is to ignore it.

"The problem is that neuroscientists do not know what consciousness is and have no theories to explain its nature," maintains Dr. Peter Fenwick of King's College London's Institute of Psychiatry, Psychology and Neuroscience. "That's because our science is the science of the external world, a hangover from the time of the Renaissance, and it does not deal with subjective experience or with consciousness."[6]

Ask people today where their mind is or where the seat of consciousness is, and most will point to their head, saying they are products of the brain's activity. But this has not always been a universal belief. Aristotle believed the brain's sole function was to produce phlegm with which to cool the heart. Traditional Chinese medicine held that the brain was simply a nourishing marrow, which they called "kidney essence," while the ancient Egyptian word for brain translates as "skull offal." Philosophers such as Alcmaeon, who predated Socrates, believed the brain produced sperm which then travelled down the spinal cord.

And, while none of these have been proven to be correct, the current theory that the brain produces consciousness and houses the mind may turn out to be equally wrong. Despite vast amounts of money and research targeted at the brain in the quest for artificial intelligence, the precise location of either consciousness or the mind remains a mystery. Ancient civilizations from the Babylonians to the Greeks and Romans believed the mind, along with the soul, was located within the liver, the center of consciousness. One current theory has it that consciousness is not within the body at all but is received and processed by the brain rather in the same way a radio processes electromagnetic waves. Simply put, two and a half thousand years of medicine and we still do not know where the mind is, what it is, or even what it is capable of.

"A human being undergoing an NDE or psychedelic trip, for example, may well see and even participate in a three-, four-, or even five-dimensional, ultrareal world of unconditional love, pure terror, bizarre beings, and neon colors," explains Jeffrey J. Kripal, chair in Philosophy and Religious Thought at Rice University in Houston.*

---

*Unless stated otherwise, all quotations from Kripal are from interviews.

But under current scientific and medical thinking, "none of this bears any relationship to reality itself," he says. "It's all 'imagined.' It's all 'in the head' or it's nothing more than a hallucination of a dying or drugged brain." And this, as he points out, "often contradicts the actual experience of the human being.

"They just presume that if something occurs during a pathological state, it is due to the pathology. What if the pathology opens one up to influences and presences that are always there but not accessible? They just assume that consciousness is produced by the brain instead of filtered or reduced by it. I find this easy medicalization of the experiences so frustrating and, frankly, so dumb. My eyes roll," he grimaces. "I cannot think of a more pathetically inadequate term than *ICU delirium*."

As a modern phenomenon, "the occurrence of bizarre hallucinations and delusions in ICU patients has been virtually unknown outside of medical circles," explains Liverpool University's Intensive Care Research Group, which has noted "ICU psychosis" in over 70 percent of patients. It was first noticed by modern science in the 1950s, when recovery rates from coma began to improve. "Despite the consensus on its occurrence, however, the question of what might actually cause these strange experiences has never been satisfactorily addressed," says the group.[7]

"Interestingly," says Dr. Christina Jones, one of the leading lights on the clinical side of coma care in the United Kingdom, during an interview, "deep sedation has been associated with these kinds of memories, and that is likely to be because a patient has to come out of that sedation. As their sedation is lightened, they may misinterpret what is going on around them or become delirious because of withdrawal symptoms. Identifying where in a patient's ICU stay these memories are from is impossible at the moment."

"A major problem is determining exactly when supposed memories occurred," Nick Franks, FRSB, FRCA, FMedSci, FRS, professor of biophysics and anesthetics at Imperial College London, told us. "Apparently, long-lasting experiences can materialize in the blink of an eye during wakening, for example, so I am very wary about firsthand 'experiences' of consciousness during coma."

Another part of the problem is that many patients recovering from the grueling aftereffects of coma are in no position to talk for some time. Often, by the time they regain control of their vocal cords, they have been moved on, and nobody wants to pay much attention to what would appear to be the ramblings of someone who, until recently, had been drugged senseless.

The drugs, of course, figure large in the medical explanation for the experiences of coma patients. But the drugs employed by most hospitals to render patients sufficiently unconscious do not in themselves produce the peculiar effects of flying back in time or of living other lives that span decades.

"Most common drugs for sedation are propofol, Versed, fentanyl, morphine, and ketamine," explains Pusateri. Psychoactive benzodiazepines are also routinely administered, as is the sedative dexmedetomidine. "Usually a combination of these drugs are continuously infused. Most commonly, it will be a combination of a sedative like propofol or Versed with a sedative analgesic, a med that sedates and controls pain, like fentanyl, morphine, or ketamine. Ketamine is usually only used in very severe cases and is less common."

Of all these drugs, only ketamine is known to produce hallucinations. It also has value as a street drug because of its pleasant, subjective effects when employed in small doses. Ketamine works by blocking certain receptors in the brain, such as NMDA. Small doses produce a sense of detachment from the body and a tunnel effect. In a number of medical trials, subjects reported frightful and bizarre images, and many asked not to have the substance administered a second time. Ketamine does not, however, produce out-of-body experiences or other common effects reported by coma survivors.

"Opiates, given almost routinely to ventilated patients, have been shown to interfere with REM sleep by reducing the levels of acetylcholine in the brain," explains Dr. Jones. "Patients receiving several days of opiates will become REM-sleep deprived."

And it is this lack of sleep, says ICU nurse practitioner Kali Dayton, that lies behind the distressingly high instances of ICU delirium. "Let's make it clear: sedation is not sleep. When patients are unresponsive and in a medically induced coma, they are not free from anxiety, pain, or fear. They are trapped in it alone and unable to express what they're suffering. We have left them psychologically maimed with wounds they will spend the rest of their lives trying to heal."

Lack of REM sleep is known to have a serious impact on memory. It is used universally as a means of torture, driving people to the point of insanity within days. One study on rats showed that just four days of REM-sleep deprivation hindered brain cell development and scrambled long-term memory.

Conversely, for coma survivors, these memories are firmly implanted, and, unlike conventional dreams, nightmares, or even hallucinations, coma memories tend to last decades and have the emotional impact of life-changing events, such as falling in love for the first time or the birth of a child. These are memories for life. Additionally, the brain is in stasis and in no position to process memories, begging the question of where, then, are they stored?

Another explanation most often cited is the apparent lack of oxygen that some patients experience. "Many scientists assume that an NDE is caused by oxygen deficiency in the brain. This used to be my own firm belief," says Dr. van Lommel. "However, in the case of oxygen deficiency in the brain (hypoxia), the result is not unconsciousness but confusion and agitation."

"Lack of oxygen usually causes panic and anxiety. So the extreme calm and peace for most is not explained," insists Andrew Elkan, a veterinary assistant in San Diego who underwent a twenty-eight-day coma. "The growth and change that occurs spiritually cannot be explained. The common experience of connection to all and, for some like myself, a recollection of events in the hospital are unexplained."

Once Andrew was on the slow road to a degree of recovery, he found that other survivors were left equally as baffled by the experience as he was. He decided to set up the Facebook Coma Survivors' Group and also a foundation to help bring understanding. "I do what I can to help guide others new to the situation or help families of coma survivors. I try to find programs to assist with finance or therapy. I've only encountered two survivors that didn't have a life-altering, spiritual experience. Most are profoundly changed, like myself. I was extremely logical and an atheist prior. Now I'm very spiritual, not to any religion, just spiritual. I know there's a universal connection and more to this existence." At one stage during his coma, Andrew felt "connected to everything."

As if far away in the universe but, at the same time, everywhere. Pure energy connected to all time and all energy and yet still a sense of self. I could see things on a subatomic level, I could see things on a grander scale, all at the same time. And then you can see into other galaxies and see how everything's connected.

Andrew also has a very clear recollection of standing next to his body.

Watching everything. I recall last rites from a priest and a prayer of healing from a rabbi. There were all sorts of procedures and visitors. My perspective on everything changed.

While all this was going on, Andrew was undergoing status epilepticus, a single seizure lasting in excess of five minutes without regaining consciousness.

I recall watching as I was moved down the hall and into a room to the left. I recall two medical personnel as they struggled to insert a stent, a tiny tube that, once inserted, allows blood to flow to the heart. But they missed and punctured the wrong area.

Eventually, they did get it right. Andrew had witnessed the entire event while comatose and was able to corroborate it all with his parents and with hospital records. "Some things can be explained by medical reasons, [but] many of the specific memories that survivors come back with cannot be explained," he says.

The biggest problem here, as Dr. Fenwick, the neuropsychiatrist, puts it, is that neuroscience has "come up against a block" and has absolutely no convincing evidence to explain the experiences of coma survivors and others experiencing an NDE. "Neuroscience maintains that conscious experience is not possible during physical unconsciousness," he underlines. The events recounted here were never due to medication, he insists. "So something interesting is going on."

Nicky: I Am the Pope and I Did Go to the Oscars

Nicky Marcos was a high-powered union negotiator in the midst of tense strike talks when they all decided to take a break. She stepped out of the building and was crossing the road on her way to get a sandwich when her heart suddenly stopped beating. According to a doctor who attended her at the scene, her heart stopped for an unbelievable forty minutes. She was eventually rushed to one of London's best teaching hospitals, University College (UCH), where she was described as the sickest patient there. Nobody expected Nicky to live.

• • •

I'm told I was more or less dead. So I was intubated [where a tube is inserted into the airways]. They put me in a coma, to keep me down, to keep me unconscious, to recover. I was in the coma for ten days. Apparently, they tried to bring me up a couple of times but quickly put me back under again. They said to my daughter, Start thinking about power of attorney. When she comes out—if she comes out of it—it's very unlikely that she'll be able to walk or talk again.

My daughter said that at one point I opened my eyes and that my eyes were blue, which they're not, they're brown. But she said my eyes were just blue. I shut my eyes and that was it. Next thing I know, ten days have passed and they're bringing me round. The whole thing was a blank. I hear them telling me, Don't fight the tube. *Then I remember thinking,* What the fuck! Where am I?

What am I? *That's when I got it into my head that I was the pope.*

They started asking me lots of questions. I thought it was that day when I woke up but it was four days later. There was this weight of expectation from everybody; everybody's waiting on my words, my loved ones, the doctors. I was told I went very powerful—super, super powerful. And I was kind of propped up on a red scarf, so I really thought I was the pope. It was so vivid.

And I also knew that I'd been to the Oscars. People humored me but I knew I'd gone to the Oscars. They asked, Did you sit at a table? *And I said,* No, it was just seats. *I remember walking up the red carpet. I was wearing a gown. And I remember my friend Adam was there with me, and I saw him give Prince Harry a blow job. When I was more conscious, I warned him,* Watch out the Daily Mail don't get hold of it! *And he was like,* WHAT!!?

When I went to the postcoma care thing at UCH, they said, How did you feel when people contradicted you? *And I said I didn't mind them contradicting me because I knew I was right. I knew I had gone, so it didn't make me distressed.*

Otherwise, my memory was shot. I don't remember anything about having my fiftieth birthday party three months later. I didn't really remember much for the next few months.

I was basically dead. And the thing about being dead was I didn't have any bright light or relatives or anything. But I do find it incredibly comforting, that I just went and didn't actually know anything about it. I don't believe in God. I'm very, very logic driven.

Isobel: Put Me Under. I'm Ready.

"Isobel Wells" is a health care professional working in one of South Africa's top hospitals in Cape Town. She prefers that we do not use her real name because the experiences from within her two-month coma simply baffle her colleagues.

• • •

I was six months pregnant and I got COVID on Christmas Day 2019. My mother was already in hospital having chemotherapy, and my father had diabetic hypertension, and eleven of us in our family all got COVID at the same time. So my father and I both ended up in hospital. I went into labor prematurely. The baby got COVID and died. My husband couldn't visit me in hospital because you couldn't get a COVID test in South Africa then and vaccines didn't exist. As soon as my baby was born, my stats dropped and I was rushed to the ICU. I was there for about seven days. At first they gave me a breathing mask (CPAP), but I just couldn't get any oxygen and started to suffocate.

The nurses kept telling me, You're fine. *But I knew there was something really wrong here. It turns out I was going into sepsis. I started to get pissed off with the nurses and I said,* Listen here. I'm in trouble. Big trouble. I'm going to die if you don't help me. *We had a big discussion with my colleagues and the doctors. They wanted to avoid putting me in a coma. But by the next morning my stats dropped so low that I needed to be put on life support. So they said,* You're going to go to sleep. *And much like everybody else at that time, I thought intubation and induced coma were the way to go. So I was like,* Put me under. I'm ready.

So I was put into a coma. And my reality changed. I woke up in an organ-harvesting facility. And I thought my doctor father had done surgery on my lungs and fixed them, but suddenly they were hot property on the organ-harvesting market because mine were the first lungs to have survived COVID.

So they found a way to kill me and regrow my organs over and over again. And that went on for four years, and I was kept in a coffin. All of my organs were harvested over and over again. And each time I was murdered, I woke up into a different life—die, wake up, have another life, then die again and wake up. Each time I was murdered, I was raped and my organs harvested. Sometimes I starved to death.

In one lifetime, there was a father and the family, and they were all murderers, and another one where I lived in the hills and there was a butcher who kept chopping people up. And, I mean, they were just countless, these lives. There was another with a big lawsuit and I was being defended because I killed my bosses. And in every reality I was paralyzed.

In one life, I woke up in the Arizona desert and I was being raped by a serial killer in front of my bosses at the hospital and he murdered me. In another life, they wanted to remove my uterus, so they did lots of gynecological procedures, about seven. And each time they did that, I thought I was being raped. In one, it must have been around the early 1900s, the Age of Steam. I was being held by this crazy women who was trying to take my husband from me. She wore a high collar to her blouse with a brooch on the front. She held me for a long time. In another life, I was fighting apartheid in Simon's Town, and I was murdered on a train track because I was trying to protect someone.

I had another reality where I spent one hundred thousand years on the top and bottom levels of existence. On the upper levels it was all ones and zeros. And on the bottom was the sediment and different layers of life throughout the years. And you switched between the two.

In another one, I thought this awful kidnapper had melted the top of a toothbrush and inserted blades to cut deep into my teeth. Obviously, the nurses were, in reality, cleaning my teeth, but they didn't realize what I was experiencing, that on some other level, which they weren't trained to understand, I was altering it in my mind into something evil.

When they did the tracheotomy, I thought that a nurse was sticking an apple core into my throat to send a chain through my throat to chain me to the bed. When my nasal feeding tube was being put in, I thought they were cutting my nose off to disfigure me so I wouldn't try and escape.

You know, people like to think these are just like dreams. But I remember it as a memory. I can give all kinds of detail. These are clear memories. I can't help but wonder what I was really seeing, or why did my mind take that route? Was it because of the things I've seen in my past or read about? But I just feel that it was real.

Apparently, I did die four times, and each time I was resuscitated. It's just been a very rough journey for me with sepsis. Every organ in my body failed, full life support and paralyzed and no voice. I was in hospital for four and a half months, two months in a coma. They would bring me round, and I kept thinking I'm brain damaged. I kept getting agitated, so they kept putting me down.

But the portion where I was awake was far more bearable than the horrors that my mind created—very sick, delusional, just horrific. The worst thing you can imagine, whereas being in hospital is super traumatic but at least you know what's going on.

Deborah: An Encounter with Willie

Deborah, who wasn't expected to last the night, shares the following story. She has absolutely no idea why the maverick Irish airline executive Willie Walsh—former CEO of International Airlines Group, Aer Lingus, and British Airways—should feature so prominently in her coma, but he does. "I couldn't pick him out of a crowd, then or now," she says, begging the question: Where exactly did he come from?

. . .

Losing sixteen days of my life is so strange. I don't fear death like I used to but I fear hell. I think my nightmares were my personal hell.

I dreamed I was in hospital on oxygen and was awaiting transport to Bristol for a lifesaving operation. I sat in air traffic control on my bed, watching all the controllers. A kind nurse negotiated for me to hitch a ride on Willie's personal jet to Bristol, something he occasionally did if he had the space. He was escorting his heavily pregnant daughter to Bristol hospital and his mum was very poorly, too. So I'm wheeled out onto the tarmac and curtains are drawn around me for privacy. I'm on a lift, a moving platform, and I am raised into the plane.

Inside Willy's executive jet is a small hospital with six beds and two isolation rooms. One bed had his daughter in, one his mum, one was an illegal immigrant family with a baby on the way, one was a footballer with a broken leg, one was a man whose wife was in a coma—why?—and that left one space for me. Only I needed my husband to get on the plane with me. Adam had gone to get a sandwich, as he needed to eat—he's type 1 diabetic.

I was crying my eyes out, imploring Willie and his mum to wait just five minutes for my husband. Willie's mum said I should have more respect for myself and not to beg, that it was embarrassing for her and her family and they were under no obligation to help me. I was screaming to let me fly with them but I was wheeled off the platform and back onto the [Leicester hospital] ward. In my coma I was apparently crying at times.

The next thing I know, a nurse is pulling a lever, turning the hospital ward ninety degrees on its side. She then pulled down loads of sheeting and the ward turned into a bar! It was called the Old Airport, and we sold all kinds of beers, martini, etc. She said, as I had no family and couldn't move, did I fancy earning my keep by being a real-life mannequin in her pub? It was going to be a serial-killer-themed bar and she needed victims to lie still.

Nick: Frozen Feet and Daiquiris

To this day, Nick likes to check his feet for the frostbite scars that are no longer there. His missing toes have come back, too. Before he ever chose to settle down in the town with the pink ice cream, Nick lived a chaotic and fairly screwball life. At one stage, he recalls feeling desperate to get out of the hospital and was urgently trying to grab a ride.

• • •

At one point, I was in the hospital because I had frostbite on my feet. I remember my feet were all bandaged up and I kept watching this Ovaltine commercial over and over again.

The hospital people kept telling me they couldn't let me leave because I didn't have a confirmed place to stay. My mom and her boyfriend came, but they wouldn't let me stay with them for some reason, so I couldn't leave the hospital. I remember thinking the hospital people were evil.

Even my Aunt Jackie, everybody came and saw me, but they wouldn't help me. It was shitty. I was also able to close my eyes and create chaos, able to blow shit up with my mind power, which is part of the reason they were strapping me to the bed, I think.

Sometime later, I found myself waiting in a dentist chair for what felt like twenty-four hours and no progress on my teeth cleaning. I had to keep going to the front desk and asking the woman if I could leave. Of course, she said no every time.

The next time I went to ask her, the whole office complex was abandoned. I make my way through the deserted corridors, past empty offices and consulting rooms. When I finally make my way outside, a beautiful, black, fifties-model Cadillac is waiting for me. I met up with my girlfriend and she proceeded to talk me into joining her on a Bonnie and Clyde killing spree.

I did all the driving, like Woody Harrelson in Natural Born Killers. *The pigs were on our ass, we had to make a move.*

I figured the best thing would be to sell frozen food to large chain stores, like Costco. So next thing you know, I am on a cruise ship selling this frozen food. It was just one color in clear bags. Each color was a different flavor. I actually remember having a good time on the cruise ships in the sun, drinking daiquiris and margaritas. To say a piece of me is left with the void, I mean, how could it not be? I'm dealing with some heavy scenarios in this parallel universe.

Stephen: Bargains and Scales

For Stephen the statistician, his time in a Belgian hospital is coming to a grateful end. All departing patients must now take part in a splendid "graduation" ceremony. Stephen takes up the story as he stands just outside the atrium doors, feeling the heat bounce back off the thick granite walls. Beside him stands his blue-suited nurse. She shares a warmhearted smile.

. . .

On the midday grass lawn, patients with relatives, nurses and doctors, smart suited men, summer-dress ladies. Light breeze fluttering pennants and banners. But something is wrong. Across the sun-bright, green lawn, with grim demeanor, administrators stride up with shock-surprise news: I am not to be discharged! I must remain in hospital for the foreseeable future. Dismay! Disbelief! Angry tears. This cannot be right. Blackness.

Change of scene, and Stephen's wife is sitting in a darkened room, illuminated by a desk lamp to one side. Across the desk sits a doctor, intransigent, impassive. Stephen's wife is forced to negotiate for his release. In front of her, she has laid out a number of small brass weights of the kind that balance scales. As they attempt a bargain, the stack increases in size. Eventually a pyramid of brass weights covers the desk, but still the doctor is not impressed.

My wife argues for my release from hospital, but the doctor is adamant and shakes his head, No. He will not relent. It's too soon to be released. No more to be said. Hopeless despair. Three or more nurses are struggling to restrain me. In cloaking black dark, desperate struggle. Violent pushing and pulling. I fall to the floor with nurses standing over me. I slowly curl up, fetal-folded, defeated.

Suddenly, I am leaving the hospital but not by the atrium door. Beneath, a gaping, yawning wide, whirlpool mouth opens; violent colors spiraling, pouring into abyss, sucking me down; winding up, tightening, throttling. . . .

2

Fantasies, Dreams, and Lucky Guesses

Or Something We Have Known All Along?

I t's a moment we've all seen on TV: a hospital ward with every-body going about their business, when suddenly an alarm goes off and nurses quickly draw the curtains around a bed. The camera cuts to the monitor beside the unconscious patient. The electrocardio-gram is flatlining. One of the nurses starts CPR—cardiopulmonary resuscitation—by thumping on the man's chest. Another nurse swiftly reaches for the resuscitation trolley and grabs the defibrillator that will send a powerful electric shock to the heart. Gel is quickly smeared over the device's paddles, the patient's chest is bared, and somebody shouts *Clear!* Except this is the Netherlands in 1969, so they probably shouted something like *Blijf weg!*

This is the first time that junior doctor Pim van Lommel has seen a myocardial infarction (heart attack). He is fresh out of Utrecht University with just one year's cardiology training under his belt. He watches as the powerful electric shock has no effect. The nurse resumes pounding the chest, another tries artificial respiration, and young

Dr. van Lommel swiftly pumps more medication into the IV drip. And then a nurse shouts again. They all stand clear and watch.

The last thing they are expecting when the patient finally opens his eyes is such deep anger and annoyance. "He was extremely disappointed," Dr. van Lommel recalls. "He was also extremely emotional. He spoke of a tunnel, colors, a light, a beautiful landscape, and music."

The patient was seriously annoyed at being brought back from what he clearly viewed as his entry to paradise. Stranger still—given that the man was technically dead for four minutes—was that he had any recollection of anything.

"I had never heard of people remembering the period of their cardiac arrest," Dr. van Lommel recounts in his absorbing book *Consciousness Beyond Life*.[1] "While studying for my degree, I had learned that such a thing is in fact impossible: being unconscious means being unaware. The same applies to people suffering a cardiac arrest or patients in a coma. At such a moment it is simply impossible to be conscious or to have memories because all brain function has ceased."

The events of that day led Dr. van Lommel to spend more than two decades studying something that had no name at that time. Dr. van Lommel made a point of talking to every survivor of a cardiac arrest that he could find, and he discovered that his original patient—and the clear events and images he described—was being echoed by around one-fifth of the people he spoke to. Something very strange was going on, he concluded. It wasn't until six years later that Dr. Raymond A. Moody, Jr., philosopher, psychologist, physician, coined the phrase *near-death experience* or NDE in his best-selling book *Life after Life*.[2]

There are numerous theories as to what causes an NDE. Some think that the lack of oxygen kills off brain cells, bringing about physiological changes in the brain, while others point to the possible release of endorphins. Those who experience one say that such a close brush with death points to a deeper spiritual significance that ultimately proves life changing. To this date, there has been no serious, scientifically designed study to explain the content of an NDE.

However, a range of studies over the years have concluded that memories from NDEs are in fact far more detailed and have greater emotional impact than other forms of memory, with the overall conclusion that NDEs should not be considered imagined events, as they contain more perceptual information, such as colors, smells, and sounds, and more contextual information, such as time and place, as measured using the standard Memory Characteristics Questionnaire (MCQ). These findings were confirmed in a 2020 study, "Near-Death Experience Memories Include More Episodic Components Than Flashbulb Memories."[3] A flashbulb memory is a vivid, long-lasting memory, such as watching 9/11 unfold live on the TV news.

Another study in 2020, "Near-Death Experience as a Probe to Explore (Disconnected) Consciousness," concluded that far more research needs to be conducted in this important field. "Because this raises numerous important neuroscience and philosophical questions," the report noted, "the study of NDEs holds great promise to ultimately better understand consciousness itself."[4]

To get a grip on what constitutes an NDE, in 1980 the American psychologist Dr. Kenneth Ring devised a list of the most commonly reported experiences around what he termed the core experience. These are: an overwhelming experience of peace and well-being and the absence of pain; a sense of detachment from the physical body, progressing to an out-of-body experience (OBE); entering darkness, a tunnel experience with panoramic memory and predominantly positive effects; an experience of light that is bright, warm, and attractive; and entering the light, meeting persons or figures. Outside of this there are, according to Moody, the noncore experiences that include: reviewing one's life, encountering a presence, encountering deceased loved ones, and deciding to return.[5]

Dr. Eben Alexander is an American neurosurgeon who experienced such a profound NDE while in a coma that he has devoted his time since to telling everyone about it.[6] Neurosurgeons typically study for around fourteen years and specialize in disorders of the central and peripheral nervous system, including infections of the brain.

Dr. Alexander was born in Charlotte, North Carolina, in 1953 and brought up in a deeply Christian family. Early one November morning in 2008, he awoke with a shocking headache. He had acute bacterial meningoencephalitis, an infection so rare in adults that it usually kills them. His chances of survival were put at 10 percent.

He found himself on an "irreversible death spiral, failing to respond to triple antibiotics" and spent the next seven days comatose on a ventilator. "If one had asked me before my coma how much a patient would remember after such severe meningitis, I would have answered 'nothing' and been thinking in the back of my mind that no one would recover from such an illness, at least not to the point of being able to discuss their memories."

So, he says, "imagine my surprise at remembering an elaborate and rich odyssey from deep within coma." And while his recall of the coma events is crystal clear, all memory of his life before appeared to vanish. This included all "language and any knowledge of humans or this universe." What he terms a scorched-earth intensity was the setting for a profound spiritual experience that took him beyond space and time and back to the origin of all existence.

The first thing he remembers is "a slowly spinning, clear, white light associated with a musical melody that served as a portal up into rich and ultrareal realms. The Gateway Valley was filled with many Earth-like and spiritual features: vibrant and dynamic plant life, with flowers and buds blossoming richly and no signs of death or decay; waterfalls into sparkling crystal pools, thousands of beings dancing below with great joy and festivity, all fueled by swooping golden orbs in the sky above; angelic choirs emanating chants and anthems that thundered through my awareness."

Dr. Alexander, a Christian well-versed in the faith, had met his God but not necessarily the God he knew or expected. "God seemed too puny, a little human word with much baggage, clearly failing to describe the power, majesty, and awe I had witnessed," he insists.

"My coma taught me many things. First and foremost, NDEs—and related mystical states of awareness—reveal crucial truths about the nature of existence. Simply dismissing them as hallucinations is convenient for many in the conventional scientific community, but only continues to lead them away from the deeper truth these experiences are revealing to us."

Dr. Alexander, along with many others, believes we are entering a new period of awakening. "NDEs such as mine represent the tip of the spear in a rapidly progressing enlightenment of the scientific community around the mind-brain relationship and our understanding of the very nature of reality," he maintains. "The world will never be the same."

"I'M YOUR SISTER. I DIED A MONTH AFTER I WAS BORN."

In December 2001, the medical journal *The Lancet* published Dr. van Lommel's results from a thirteen-year study covering ten Dutch hospitals and 334 patients who had been successfully resuscitated after suffering cardiac arrest. They were all interviewed in the immediate aftermath and again up to eight years after the event.[7] The article caused an immediate outcry from many in his profession, but it also sparked massive worldwide interest. It even ran on ABC's flagship evening news, which, in turn, sparked a flood of letters and calls to the station from people wanting to share their own NDE experiences.

Dr. van Lommel found his email inbox swamped, "including a lot from physicians who wrote to me about their own NDEs!" One GP, Colorado physician Dr. Pam Kircher, who read the findings and herself had undergone an NDE, commented soon after, saying the landmark article should be read by every doctor because she now realized that "NDEs really are life transforming. They create much greater changes in a person's life than does simply having a cardiac arrest or being near death."

She also stressed the vital importance of getting survivors to discuss their experiences with their doctors, rather than simply accepting them as delusions caused by the meds and lack of oxygen, because "people with NDEs will be able to adjust more easily to the changes that occur in their values if they have some assistance with that from immediate caregivers while still in the hospital setting."

During the trial, Dr. van Lommel's team assessed patients' attitudes to key factors of life to see if their views had changed. This included their thoughts on the fear of death, their interest in spirituality, and their acceptance of others. The team found significant differences between those who had undergone an NDE (around 18 percent) and those who had not. Those with the NDE experience became much more empathetic and accepting of others and had become much more appreciative of the ordinary things in life and far less fearful of death.

But not everybody was convinced. The editors at *The Lancet* felt the need to include a commentary arguing that the highly detailed and remarkably similar accounts could most likely be put down to "prior knowledge, fantasy or dreams, lucky guesses . . . details learned between the NDE and giving an account of it, and false memories." The editors concluded that the mind was trying to retrospectively "fill in the gap after a period of cortical inactivity."[8]

All well and good, some might say, but this does not account for the experiences relayed by many children who underwent an NDE or experienced events within coma—many too young to have preconceived ideas about any afterlife, let alone events outside of their personal experience. "It seems inconceivable that children without any prior knowledge could fabricate a story that is entirely consistent with the NDE reports of adults," as Dr. van Lommel likes to stress. "Young and uninhibited, children will talk about what really happened to them."

One study at Guy's Hospital in London found a number of children willing to talk about their experiences inside coma. One four-year-old boy, who eventually recovered from a severe meningococcal infection, told Dr. Dan Shears that "a man with wings came to see me while I was in hospital. I could see him out of the corner of my eye." The boy then went on to describe leaving his body and seeing his grandmother beside his bed and how he wanted her to stop talking but that he "couldn't tell her to shut up."

One boy of three and a half years described how two angels came to fetch him—one an adult, the other a little boy angel—to come and play with his granddad in a beautiful environment with other children and plenty of toys. "Then the angels came and took me back," he told Dr. Shears, explaining what an absolutely wonderful time he had. What the toddler could not have known was that his grandfather had died nine days after the boy was rushed to the hospital.[9]

Dr. van Lommel tells the story of a five-year-old Dutch boy who fell into a coma after contracting meningitis. The boy insisted to the doctor that he had actually died, before drifting to a black void where he felt safe, with no fear or pain. He felt at home. The boy recounted years later:

> I saw a little girl of about ten years old. I sensed that she recognized me. We hugged and then she told me, I'm your sister. I died a month after I was born. I was named after our grandmother. Our parents called me Rietje for short. She kissed me, and I felt her warmth and love. You must go now, she said.
>
> In a flash, I was back in my body. I opened my eyes and saw the happy and relieved looks on my parents' faces. When I told them about my experience, they initially dismissed it as a dream. I made a drawing of my angel sister who had welcomed me and repeated everything she'd told me. My parents were so shocked that they panicked. They got up and left the room. After a while they returned. They confirmed that they had indeed lost a daughter called Rietje. She had died of poisoning about a year before I was born. They had decided not to tell me and my brother until we were old enough to understand the meaning of life and death.

"A PLACE OF DELIGHTS AND GOODNESS"

It is thought that in the last fifty years, twenty-five million people around the world experienced an NDE. Not surprisingly, hard data is not easy to come by, but recent studies in the United States and Germany put the number of people reporting NDEs at over 4 percent of the population.

Across the globe, NDEs are remarkably similar, but cultural and religious differences tend to give color to the individual accounts. In the West, we encounter tunnels and absorbing white light. People meet with dead relatives who are all in the prime of life, usually around thirty-five years of age, and, if they were missing a leg in this life, it has come back to them in the next.

In Japan, they enter caves, which are perceived as entrances to a new reality, and often come across a dark river where they need to negotiate with a boatman. In ancient Greece, the ferryman carried the dead across the River Styx, receiving the coin in the corpse's mouth as payment. Hunter-gatherers in the Amazon must hop aboard a canoe and travel for three days before arriving at an otherworldly realm. The Inuit people of the far north were slow to take on Christian beliefs because the idea of heaven they were being sold contained no seals or walruses. They had a clear vision of the next life.

"Life continues after death on two levels," explains anthropologist Frédéric Laugrand in his essay, "The Beauty of the Afterlife Among the Inuit of Nunavut." He continues: "While the *tarniq*—the double-soul—joins the world of the dead, the *atiq*—the name-soul—is passed on to a newborn child and recycled. The dead thus live on, as much in the world of the living as in other worlds."[10]

When Christian missionaries tried to convert the so-called heathen on the American continent from 1500 onward, they were regularly met with amusement and derision. The stories the native peoples were being told of a Christian God and heaven and hell were just parables, they believed. Why accept the curious beliefs of strange foreign folk when you had seen the afterlife yourself?

In his essay, "The Sun Told Me I Would Be Restored to Life," Gregory Shushan, PhD, tells how the NDE formed the basis of Native American afterlife beliefs across the continent. "Individuals who had such experiences often returned with knowledge or instructions given to them ostensibly by spirits in the other world, sometimes leading to a change in existing religious belief or practice, including new ritual songs or dances, decreasing funerary offerings to the dead, moral strictures such as ending wife-beating, and accepting or rejecting elements of Christianity or other colonial influence,"[11] he explains.

In 1875, the ethnologist Hubert Howe Bancroft undertook the largest study of Native Americans of that time and repeatedly noted the widely held belief that the spirit lives on after death. He cataloged meetings with deceased relatives, encounters with deities, an afterlife judgment, an idealized mirror-image of Earth, and reincarnation and transformation into heavenly bodies, not to mention feelings of joy and bliss.

"The other realm was frequently characterized as a place of dancing, music, and happiness, with unlimited supplies of food and drink," says Shushan. "The dead feared living visitors such as near-death experiencers and shamans, as if they were ghosts and found them to be offensive smelling."

In common with the ancient Greeks and many others, the souls of Native Americans "had to wait for a new life to be assigned to them," says Shushan. "More often, they were given the choice of whether or not to reincarnate and, if they so chose, which society and even which parents.

"Around the continent, Native Americans believed that shamans were able to travel to the other world in spirit form to retrieve the soul of a sick or apparently dead person," he writes. "Such journeys were achieved by deliberately inducing altered states of consciousness through practices such as smoking, fasting, extended graveside vigils, and continuous, repetitive drumming, dancing, and singing."

Those who returned from the dead brought with them a "spiritual renewal or transformation with a change in values or purpose" and told of a "place of delights and goodness, without evil, where people danced and feasted in villages and fields."

The Fang people of Gabon and Cameroon use the psychedelic root bark of the *Tabernanthe iboga* plant to bring about a state resembling the classic NDE that they describe as "breaking open one's head."

James W. Fernandez writes in his enlightening book *Bwiti: An Ethnography of the Religious Imagination in Africa*, "Their understanding is flooded with illuminations from the world beyond. They will come to the knowledge of how things really are based on journeying to that world."[12] Fernandez catalogs over twenty firsthand accounts that he collected from people who had taken the drug *eboga* as part of a Bwiti religious ritual. Here is the account of Mendame Nkogo, a middle-aged cocoa planter from the district of Oyem:

I saw in the mirror that they had set in front of me a great crowd of Black men. They were then changed to a great crowd of White men. I found myself in a garden surrounded by a crowd of people whose color I do not know. I was surrounded by eboga bushes and by two chapels of Bwiti.

Then I saw my grandfather at the other end of the garden in a hollow in the rocks. And I saw myself as a child sitting between his legs. Then that child which was me changed into a ngombi *[the cult harp], which my grandfather was playing. And now, whenever I play the* ngombi, *I know it is my grandfather playing through me.*

My grandfather told me to look at the sun. It blinded me. I saw a path to Eyen Zame [the father of all the spirits]. I knocked against the door but Eyen Zame said I could not enter. This was because I still had Black skin. All the dead are White. When I die, I will become White. My father of eboga saw that I was already gone too long with eboga. He brought me back. He gave me sugarcane to eat. Now, whenever I eat eboga, I see or hear my grandfather.

From those he interviewed, Fernandez noted three elements that repeatedly cropped up. They are contact with the dead, where all the visions involved visual contact with some dead relative or a group of relatives; experiences of visionary excursion, where fifteen of the visions involved a prolonged excursion up a long path, usually in the company of a relative or relatives; and experiences with greater powers, where in twelve instances the visionary encountered one of the greater supernatural powers. Other common features included crossing rivers, life reviews undertaken by men at desks, flying or floating through space, changing color from black to white, and being told to return. A number also reported gaining the ability to play the *ngombi* cult harp.

In an address to the International Association for Near-Death Studies (IANDS) in 2004, Dr. Peter Fenwick told the audience that of the people he had interviewed, some 76 percent told of delightful, pastoral landscapes. Sixty-six percent reported an out-of-body experience, while nearly 40 percent reported seeing deceased relatives or friends, 12 percent went back in time to experience events from earlier in their lives, and 72 percent had been given the chance to return home and had taken it.[13]

"I was particularly interested in the pastoral landscapes," says Dr. Fenwick. "The landscapes have always been described as very beautiful and usually include wonderful flowers. We had two botanists among our respondents and they said that the colors were most exciting but, interestingly, they saw no new species, only species they already knew." Curiously, just 4 percent reported what he termed hellish experiences.

"The great majority of NDEs reported publicly over the past four decades have been described as pleasant, even glorious," maintains Dr. Bruce Greyson, professor of psychiatry and neurobehavioral sciences at the University of Virginia School of Medicine. "Almost unnoticed in the euphoria about them has been the sobering fact that not all NDEs are so affirming. Some are deeply disturbing."[14]

This, he believes, is because fewer people are likely to want to talk about these. "They hide, they disappear when asked for information."

He recounts the case of a man with heart failure who felt himself falling into the depths of the earth. "At the bottom was a set of high, rusty gates, which he perceived as the gates of hell. Panic-stricken, he managed to scramble back up to daylight."

He also gives the example of a woman who attempted suicide and felt her body sliding downward into a cold, dark, watery environment. "When I reached the bottom," she told him, "it resembled the entrance to a cave, with what looked like webs hanging. I heard cries, wails, moans, and the gnashing of teeth. I saw these beings that resembled humans, with the shape of a head and body, but they were ugly and grotesque. They were frightening and sounded like they were tormented, in agony."

Too often, he says, physicians prescribe medication to block out the memories and they dismiss the NDE as fanciful or pathological. The reluctance to report a distressing NDE may lead to long-lasting trauma for individuals and limit the data on occurrence. "Therapists will not address the matter, or they leave the client feeling blamed or [they] romanticize spirituality and cannot deal with its dark side. Clergy have no idea what to say or reject the experience outright."

While fewer hellish experiences are reported in NDEs, coma survivors more often report horrendously dark and terrifying encounters. James Morrall barely remembers his ICU experience, but the coma "nightmares" proved all too real, leaving him to struggle with the experiences years on and with a diagnosis from his doctor of a hefty case of PTSD. Once placed in a coma, he found himself trapped in a cycle of death and dying. He told us:

I lived a whole other life while in the coma, spanning many different eras. I was a Spitfire pilot, and I crashed in the Thames and drowned. I was locked in a box as punishment, and it was filled with water and I drowned. I was a fisherman and was involved in an accident while unloading fish, and I drowned. I was flying a really, really old plane over what I assume was the Caribbean when we lost power and crashed into the sea. I spent a couple of days looking for the people from the wreck, but they had died. I was involved in a terrorist bombing in Manchester that killed many people, including my partner, but there was no body. I remember spending what felt like weeks looking for her. I was involved in a robbery where I was shot in the chest and spent many weeks in hospital with people visiting me. And then I had a recurring one where my partner passed away during childbirth.

This all began in 2016 when James came down with a staggering cocktail of illnesses, including an earlier variant of a coronavirus, swine flu, Australian flu, and then sepsis. The first thing he remembers is being outside of his body and staring through a one-way glass or mirror.

My family were looking for me. They were calling my name and asking where I had gone, and I could see them. They were upset. I was telling them that I was there but they couldn't hear me. Then a doctor told them I had gone and they were crying. I was banging on the glass, shouting, and I watched them walk out and leave me.

James told us how he was left abandoned until he felt himself being steered away.

I was led down a very badly lit corridor, like a prison. There were hands coming out through bars in the walls, hundreds of arms and hands, and shouting. If you could imagine lots of different voices calling all different names. Some sounded panicked, like they were desperate to find someone, others were just calmly saying names.

For James, what came next was no meeting with his deceased loved ones, all in the prime of their lives and overjoyed to greet him. James stumbled onto a delegation clearly waiting for someone else. He describes encountering a "frigid, old woman," clearly disappointed to see him.

She asked who I was. I said James, *then she looked me over.* Who's James? *she wanted to know. And she started to shout,* Who's James? Who's James? *Then I heard someone say in a really calm voice,* Calm down, Edith. *The old woman then started to sob in disappointment.* I want Dotty! I want Dotty! Go away, go away! I want Dotty. *She got quite irate. Then I slowly started to back away and that was the end of that.*

We asked James if he had any idea who Edith or Dotty might be.

Dotty was the nickname for my grandma, Dorothy. And Edith was a distant relative. I'd never met her in this life, but I gave a full description and my Mum was gobsmacked.

By this time, my grandmother was going downhill fast with dementia. I told my mum to tell her that Edith was waiting for her Dotty. She told her and it seemed to give great comfort. She couldn't remember any of her children's names by this time—they were all just strangers to her—but she started to say she was going to be with Edith. The name just seemed to stick with her.

Dotty died a few days later.

Chiara: Lost in Time

A few days after her fifteenth birthday, Chiara, from Piedmont in Italy, pulled to a halt at stoplights on her tiny moped. That was when she was hit side-on at considerable speed by a car. She was thrown across the road, hitting her head and breaking her pelvis.

• • •

I don't have any recollection of this. But according to the people who were there, I was very agitated. No one can tell me if I was conscious or not. I don't remember being conscious. As far as I know, I went into a spontaneous coma. I was in that coma for one and a half days. And when I woke up in the hospital, they said I was agitated again and I was moving so much they had to sedate me. They put me in a coma for ten days. I'm told I had a cardiac arrest in the first thirty-six hours. But I don't remember any of this.

It's really difficult to explain, to even try and rationalize it for myself, but before I started to dream within my coma, I just remember pitch black, like I was there but not really there in pitch dark. And then I woke up inside the coma.

And I'm in my mother's room, which is on the second floor, and the light was yellow. And there was another light coming from the window, a really bright, blinding, white light. So I approached the window, and I remember getting into this light and it was a kind of star tunnel, so many stars of different brightness. I traveled thousands of light years. It felt a bit like in films where you're seeing something that's going at the speed of light but you're seeing it in slow motion.

I went through the light and found myself in an alpine meadow. It seemed like a very early summer morning, the skies super clear, and the light was very strong, making all the colors seem more vivid. And it's so beautiful. There was just grass, no flowers. I couldn't tell if there were trees or mountains around, just the grass, not very high. And there in front of me were these three mushrooms, but they were huge, abnormally huge. The first one must have been as tall as a man, the second much larger still, and the third as tall as the ceiling. And they were the classical red and white. And on the last and tallest mushroom was the Mad Hatter.

Now, for the record, I'd been watching a lot of films before my coma and one I watched a lot was Alice in Wonderland *with Johnny Depp. So, to get a precise idea of who I was seeing, I was seeing that guy and he was looking at me. And he was standing totally still. And it was like he was frozen but conscious, and there were his eyes looking at me. And this lasted for quite a while. I can't say how long, I was just there witnessing all this.*

With time, fog started to rise up out of the ground. And as it grew, there were no more colors, just gray and black. And I couldn't see anything anymore, except the eyes of this man, just looking at me. They were yellow and glowing, but I wasn't afraid of him.

This dream is lasting so long. I've been sleeping for so long. Mommy's gonna come wake me up in a while. *But she didn't, and I kept saying to myself,* Oh, she's not come yet but she's gonna come wake me up. *The fog is rolling in and I'm thinking,* Why is nobody waking me up? Now I'm worried. I don't like this. It's not normal. I've been sleeping too long. Like forever. I cannot wake up.

So, apparently, during my coma they tried a couple of times to wake me up but I was all agitated, so they put me back down. And I think in one of these instances when they were lowering my dose I started to gain consciousness. I was aware of my head lying on my chest and I realized that I'm in this room, but it's like I had a pair of yellow-filtered glasses on, everything felt really filtered. And I can see this IV in my chest.

So I'm thinking to myself, You're awake. Back awake! And I thought, I need to cling on to this world, on to anything of this world that I can cling on to. So I grabbed the IV and I ripped it off and, because it was so close to the heart, blood started pumping out. I remember watching this blood pour all over me and it was actually so sweet. I felt guilty after to have thought that way.

After the accident, when I started to live again and was back at high school, I felt very angry with the world, angry that I couldn't remember what happened in those missing bits. I was lost in time. I felt like I needed to know, and that made me so angry. At school we have all different workshops, so I signed up for a hypnosis workshop. There were about fifteen of us. And this guy is talking, trying to hypnotize us. It's basically a meditation state. You close your eyes and breathe a certain way.

In a matter of a second, I find myself on the road that goes to my house. And it was a lovely, early summer day, and I can see myself in front of me, the younger me, dressed as on the day of the accident, my Hard Rock turquoise T-shirt, my short hair, and I walk toward myself. I was looking at me, my younger self. Then we hugged, and it was very weird because I could feel my hair, I could smell my smell. We stepped back and she says, Now it's time to let go.

And then I woke up and I was never angry again. I'd been feeling like I was in the wrong life, the wrong time line. And I never feel like this anymore.

Rory: Death by Fire Extinguisher

Rory survived a horrendous home invasion and then felt that he was dying a second time in his coma when naked teenage boys stabbed him and drank his blood.

. . .

That's when the bright light was finally absolute. I knew in my head that I had died. All of a sudden, I was a jet-black sperm inside a giant, pink chamber, surrounded by other sperm. All I could think was that I'm now being reborn and I'm going to forget my son and my family and be born again. That's when it ended, and I woke up in the second "dream."

I was in a communal area of a care home, sitting on a reclining chair. My mother and uncle sat with me, talking, telling me they loved me. That's when a tall, Asian doctor or male nurse came into the room. He was very nice and caring and chatted pleasantly with my family. My family then left and I was alone with him.

He asked me what I would like to eat. I told him, Nothing, *as I was still feeling terrible. He then got suddenly angry because I didn't want food. Then, as sometimes happens in dreams, there appeared a canteen-like area in the corner of the room. And it was filled with women, all busy cooking.*

Then the male nurse called over a very large, scary-looking woman who appeared to be in charge. He told her that I didn't like her food, that I thought it was disgusting. I panicked and pleaded that I didn't say that. She gave me the evilest look I've ever had in my life, and the nurse, smiling and laughing, left the room saying, It's your fault. You've done this to yourself. I'm now leaving you alone with her. Good luck!

Then this woman pointed to a huge menu on the chalkboard and started listing off absolutely everything I was going to be force-fed. I was terrified. I was bedridden, unable to move, totally vulnerable. Then the male nurse reappeared and asked how I was doing. I pleaded with him and begged him to help me, but he just laughed.

At this point, a really nice, young, female doctor came into the room and asked me how I was. I grabbed her arm, screaming and crying, Don't leave me alone with these people! Help me!

She strokes my hair and assures me everything is fine. I begged her not to leave. Suddenly, she seems to realize that something is wrong and quickly tries to get me out, but the woman and male nurse quickly chase her out of sight. I saw the male nurse pick up a fire extinguisher, and I could hear the doctor screaming and being smashed and murdered with the fire extinguisher. Then the other canteen women followed out of sight with black trash bags.

Now I could hear my mum and uncle outside, banging on the door to be let in. The room was filling with thick, black smoke, and I could also hear sirens. Then I was outside and watching this small wooden shack burning, and I was slowly moving away from it. It was on a coastal road with high cliffs, and I was happy and crying in relief.

That's a real memory for me, not a dream memory. I remember that as vividly as I remember my son being born.

Stephen (Continued): Cowgirls and Gangsters

Stephen the statistician wakes up to find himself seated in a dark corner of a bistro bar. Other customers sit around quietly, drinking, while the barman polishes glasses with his back turned. Stephen gets up and walks toward the brightly illuminated door at the far end of the long bar.

Outside, brilliant sunlight illuminates the cobbled street. He is still in Belgium. He stands at the top of the steps leading down to the street. Flags and colored pennants are strung everywhere and festoon the medieval shops. Tourists stroll around, gazing at souvenirs through the windows. But Stephen is stuck. He cannot move down the steps and onto the street. Reluctantly, he returns to his seat while the barman eyes him furtively before slipping quickly down the wooden staircase behind the bar.

From the dark, down below, Stephen is aware of heated voices and whispers. "He's got what we want," says one voice. "Let's kill him and take it," says another. "We can't take it, he's got to give it," explains one more. Stephen senses flicking knives that flash in sweaty hands.

Stephen moves to peer into the bar hidden below the stairs. The real action is here.

· · ·

Thundering thousands cheering and shouting. Seated in dark-enclosed stadium, high encircling dazzle-white spotlights. In floodlight-bright ring, dancing, color-starched pugilists trade punches. At ringside, a gold 'horse-goat' trophy sits blank-eyed, demon-horned, sinister grinning. Within the shadows, the gangsters place bets and argue.

Stephen is now inside the basement bar, the hazy dark, loud jukebox music, neon strip lights, and beeping games machines. He takes in the beer cask smells and works his way through the throng to order a drink. The new barman, bathed in yellow light, ignores him. Stephen turns and takes in the view.

Swishing through the reveling crowd, from ceiling-suspended chains, two glitzy cowgirls seated on horse saddles, competing in a bar game; swinging between gnarly tree stumps, catching hold of rough bark with crampon-spike boots.

Now it is morning already, and a watery sun slowly seeps into the dim basement. Stephen finally has a drink in hand. Suddenly, a silver-rhinestone white boot with sparkling red star slams down inches from his face.

Looking down from her saddle with icy-blue threatening eyes, a cropped- and ginger-haired cowgirl issues a threatening warning that means that was meant for you!

Stephen finds himself on the floor, crouching low beside the bar, anxiously scanning the smoky darkness for signs of the gangsters.

But shock and surprise, opening beneath me, floor melting away, a yawning-wide whirlpool; violent swirling, pouring, cream, chocolate colors, sucking me in; winding up, tightening, throttling. . . .

Nick (Continued): Rain and Romance

When Nick looks back on his time in "Coma World," he recalls a different pace of life. The town with the pink ice cream was part of a bygone era where the cars guzzled more gas and people had more time for one another. "Coming back online and being thrown back into this life has been difficult," he recalls. "The world we live in today is so fast, and it doesn't stop to let you catch up." The life he experienced there resembled an alternate United States circa 1960. It even had its own alternate Southeast Asian war.

• • •

I remember listening to the radio and I heard my number called, so I knew I was gonna have to go overseas. It was sort of like Vietnam but it wasn't Vietnam, but it was constantly raining the whole time. I remember the boots I had on were just soaking wet and my feet were so wet and wrinkled it was ridiculous! We were in these little trenches, in puddles of water with the constantly pouring rain. We were waiting for the next move, orders from the general.

Nick returns to his obsession with selling frozen food—the same one-color, one-flavor variety that was funding his leisurely life on the cruise ships.

The whole time we were in that little trench, I was thinking about how I could turn the situation to my advantage, getting some sort of importing and exporting deal for my food business. Getting past customs was extremely difficult.

Next thing you know, I heard an announcement and we were going back home. So I got to get out of my water puddle, and I remember the ride home; my feet and hands were wrinkled the whole time and never got better.

Once Nick makes it back to the States, he remembers embarking on a series of often stormy relationships around the country. First stop, California . . .

I moved to a neighborhood with a lot of famous celebrity types, including some professional wrestlers and NBA players. My girlfriend was a hot Black chick, but she bitched all the time and had her mom around all the time, and her mom had little, annoying dogs that shat everywhere.

I also remember that I was about to get married to a Latina girl, sexy but very old-fashioned. Her parents owned a bar and a sewing shop next to each other, and I worked in the kitchen, mostly frying chips. That's how we met.

We flew down to the Caribbean somewhere together and partied on the beach all weekend. The night before the wedding, we were supposed to meet at a restaurant, but I was late getting there because I was snorkeling and saw the restaurant manager under water, ripping this red coral up from the ocean floor and taking it to the kitchen to serve. I was angry and refused to eat in the restaurant, which then pissed off everyone in my family and my future bride's. Next thing, the wedding was off.

But I ended up meeting this girl with blonde hair, really cute. I saved her from this guy at a gas station. Somehow, I got into a hotdog-eating competition with this guy and kicked his ass.

I wanted to stay in that small town with her. I wanted to be a dairy farmer, which probably had something to do with the pink ice cream that they sold there, so I tried that for a little bit, and then that led me into starting a garden business. I taught people how to grow all kinds of shit.

Next, I remember my girl was having a baby and we went to this New Age midwife place, and she has a baby in a bathtub, just like a hot tub. I remember going there to get ready for the baby. I would also get into the bath with her, and I remember peeing in the bath a couple times. Ha, ha, ha!

Putting this into words here doesn't even do one bit of justice as to how much more detail there was. I just don't know how to explain it all.

3

Blinded by Science
And an Awakening to Other Possibilities

Picture the scene: a young but rather serious scientist has a guilty secret. He knows that he must finally open up to his wife but is embarrassed to do so. He is scared stiff that she will think him a fool or worse, so he employs the assistance of specialist counselor Kimberly Clark Sharp to help soften the blow. They are all sitting down in the couple's comfy lounge. The husband cannot bear to look his wife in the eye. She is also a serious scientist. He looks at the floor as he reminds her about his recent myocardial infarction, or his MI, as they refer to it. And then he lets it drop. "I had an NDE," he blurts out. "The full-on thing. The meaning of life, the universe, and everything!"

Kim the counselor is keeping a close watch on the wife and sees her jaw drop. And then she speaks for the first time, or rather, she almost shouts: "*Stop a minute! Stop a minute!*"

"Believe me, your husband is quite sane," explains Kimberly.

"That's not it," exclaims the wife. "This happened to me ten years ago. I was afraid to tell anyone because you'd all think me nuts!"

This is the story, more or less, that Kimberly likes to tell when she talks about the "awakening of the scientific mind." Having experienced a particularly remarkable NDE herself after her heart suddenly stopped beating while she was out shopping, the former critical care social worker went on to write her own account in the book *After the Light*.[1] Her entire worldview had changed in the blink of an eye.

"I'm not a theologian," she says. "This had nothing to do with religion, but it had everything to do with life." Kim had the sense that all her questions were spontaneously answered. "But this wasn't new information," she says. "It was like, oh yeah, oh yeah, I get it. I had known this all along."

Without such epiphanies, the majority of psychologists, neuroscientists, and even philosophers today still limit their understanding to the classical physics of the age of Newton, where facts are ultimately determined by physical evidence alone and human beings are seen as little more than complicated biological machines.

According to this view, known as materialism, everything we do is explainable by our biology and chemistry and by physics, while the mind and consciousness are no more than neurophysiological processes occurring in our brains. We have no free will because all our actions are dictated by chemistry and the firing of synapses. We are no more than "moist robots," as the artificial intelligence pioneer Marvin Minsky (1927–2016) liked to put it.

Thinking of this kind permeates all levels of scientific understanding and society generally, fueling an increasing disenchantment with our modern world—a sense that something is clearly lacking in our lives. The broadly accepted view is that life has no meaning. We live. We die. Full stop. This thinking is effectively self-perpetuating and forms the basis of our educational system and media. And yet this modern, scientific worldview is regularly at odds with everyday human experience shared across cultures and faiths, time and distance.

This mechanical way of thinking became known as the Enlightenment and took a firm hold in 1660 with the founding of the world's first academy of science, Britain's Royal Society. This was a period of political and religious extremism, beginning with the Reformation of the Protestant Church a century earlier, when many ancient festivals and the traditions of pilgrimage were banned and price-less artworks held in churches and cathedrals destroyed. These actions are not dissimilar to those of the Islamic State, or Daesh, with their destruction of historic sites in the ancient Syrian city of Palmyra, or the Taliban's reducing of Buddhist shrines to rubble. Yet today it would seem nonsensical to base our understanding of science on the mindset that drove those actions.

These rigid views held by scientific academies, says the biologist Rupert Sheldrake, created "a system of authority within science which has become stronger and stronger as Science has become more profes-sionalized." Science found itself under state patronage, a firm part of the establishment, with "no separation of Science and State, creating a system of authority within Science."[2]

Such bodies shape careers and decide where billions of dollars of funding go. Only approved scientists are published in the most presti-gious peer-reviewed journals. The result is an extreme, dictatorial ortho-doxy that marginalizes or excludes alternative views.

Until very recently, cultures across the Americas were ridiculed for believing that plants possess intelligence and consciousness. Now we learn from rapid advances in botany that plants actually do possess sophisti-cated intelligence and interact with their environment much in the same way as animals do. During our Enlightenment, the state, church, and sci-ence have all argued that not only animals but plants, too, lack any com-parable intelligence or even feelings, let alone a soul or spirit.

And yet, says Sheldrake, it is ridiculous to consider the universe, the earth, and every living thing simply as machines. "All traditional societies have treated the world as alive; the Earth is a living organ-ism. Animals and plants are truly alive, the whole Universe is a kind of organism," he points out.

The most ancient of all faiths, animism, held that objects, places, and creatures, from rivers to rocks, all possess a distinct spiritual essence and are all as equally alive as we are. Quartz crystals may resonate at frequencies ranging from four to six MHz, but any hint of life is dis-missed by materialistic science as fantasy. Now, in quantum science, the integrated information theory of consciousness (IIT) holds that electrons—subatomic particles found in all atoms and the primary carriers of electricity—are conscious in their own right.[3]

"We think it requires astonishing hubris to dismiss summarily the collective experience and wisdom of our forebears, including persons widely recognized as pillars of all human civilization, and we believe that the single most important task confronting all of modernity is that of meaningful reconciliation of science and spirituality," says Edward F. Kelly, professor of perceptual studies at the University of Virginia's Department of Psychiatry and Neurobehavioral Sciences.

"We believe that emerging developments within science itself are leading inexorably toward an enlarged conception of nature, one that can accommodate realities of a spiritual sort," he adds in the foreword to his book *Consciousness Unbound*. "Under the surface we and the world are much more deeply and widely interconnected than previously realized."[4]

Kelly and others believe that our fate as humans, both individually and collectively, "ultimately hinges upon wider recognition and more effective utilization of the expanded 'states of being' that are potentially available to us, but largely ignored or even actively suppressed by our struggling postmodern civilization."

However, more optimistically, others already see evidence of movement toward these other levels of understanding. "In the past ten years, medical professionals have gone from looking upon spirituality with a skeptical if not cynical eye, to embracing it enthusiastically," says NDE researcher Dr. Peter Fenwick.[5] In 1995, only three American medical schools taught courses on spirituality in medicine. Today, only 10 percent of schools fail to.

Over the years, there have been a number of studies into the power of prayer using double-blind, randomized, and controlled trials, seemingly with very positive results. One of the major journals of cardiology recently suggested that every hospital should have prayer groups for patients. Such a thought would have been unthinkable a few years ago.

Today, the Association of American Medical Colleges, the World Health Organization, and the Joint Commission recommend that spiritual issues be addressed in clinical care and the education of health professionals. To that end, Professor Kelly has been working with others for many years to expand the remit of modern science. But in order to swing the balance, science still requires data of some sort. He says:

> We focused initially on various forms of evidence suggestive of postmortem survival. Because survival beliefs are common to traditional faiths but cannot be true if the physicalist worldview is correct. Moreover, there already exists—largely unknown to believers, skeptics, and the general public alike—a sizable body of high-quality evidence suggesting that survival in personal form does at least sometimes occur.

Examples of paranormal or psi evidence, he maintains, include religious stigmata and hypnotically induced blisters, prodigious forms of memory and calculation, genius-level creativity, near-death and out-of-body experiences—including those occurring under deep anesthesia or cardiac arrest—and mystical experiences, whether spontaneous or brought about by psychedelic substances. All of these, he insists, defy any scientific explanation but are simply "perfectly ordinary, everyday properties of our conscious mental life."

"It is fairly uncontroversial to state that psi is almost invisible in contemporary mainstream consciousness, neuroscience and cognitive studies as well as philosophy of mind," writes Hannah Jenkins of the University of Tasmania in her paper "A Catch-22: PSI and Explanation."[6]

"It is also fairly well accepted that the evidence for psi has the potential to inform the understanding of how the mind functions. However, there appears to be a gap between the continued buildup of evidence for psi . . . and the use of psi in mainstream investigations of the mind. For those who are conversant with the evidence for psi, the situation is absurd," she says. "And yet it continues."

The catch-22, she maintains, is that mainstream science "will not accept psi until it is explained; but psi is unlikely to be fully explained until it is incorporated into more inclusive scientific problem-solving." As a result, the mainstream is missing out on the "potential to use anomalous phenomena to further explain the workings of the mind because of ingrained and outdated beliefs about the status of psi."

The French educator, translator, and author Hippolyte Léon Denizard Rivail was up against similar resistance back in the mid-1800s when he tried to have the study of the paranormal taken seriously as a science, specifically, "a science that deals with the nature, origin, and destiny of spirits, and their relation with the corporeal world." He was the first to coin the term *spiritualism*, a word that held broader meaning back then and encompassed pretty much everything that went without scientific explanation, including telepathy and reincarnation, out-of-body experiences, and psychic visions.

He did not see these things as supernatural or miracles but assumed that everything that happens in nature must have a natural explanation and be part of a yet-to-be-explained natural law; this at a time when most mediums and anyone acting "spiritual" outside of the church were legally considered insane and confined where possible to mental institutions.

Not to be deterred, writing under the nom de plume of Allan Kardec, he published five books known as the *Spiritist Codification.*[7] Kardec wrote in his first work, *The Spirits' Book:* "When an extraordinary phenomenon is produced, the first thought should be about a natural cause because it is the most frequent and the most probable."

He interviewed ten mediums, none of whom knew each other, and put to them over one thousand questions covering the nature and workings of spirit communications, the reasons for human life on Earth, and various other aspects of the spiritual realm. He concluded that they were able to provide accurate information about deceased individuals by communicating with personalities that had survived death and whose consciousnesses existed in another realm.

"I foresaw in these phenomena its key issue, so obscure and controversial; the past and the future of humanity, the solution of what I've searched through all my life," he told his followers. "It was, in one word, a revolution of ideas and beliefs."

Despite selling millions of copies of his books around the world, Kardec was not taken seriously for the usual reasons; namely, that he could not prove any of the things he claimed by established scientific means. "Scientists deceived themselves when they attempted to experiment with spirits as they experiment with voltaic batteries," he wrote. "What does a naturalist do when he wishes to study the habits of an animal? Does he command it to do a certain thing, so as to observe it at his will? No, because he knows well that the animal will not obey him. He observes the spontaneous behavior of the animal and records them when they take place."

One possibility for tangible evidence of the continuation of life after death comes from the accounts of children reporting memories of previous lives, many of which are impressively detailed and borne out by verifiable facts and personal testimonies. These children are usually very young when they first start to describe a past life, and they often show unusual behaviors that appear appropriate to that life, such as fear of water when the previous personality died of drowning, or they have skills or talents that cannot be explained. Some also display extremely unusual birthmarks or birth defects that correspond to fatal wounds suffered, apparently, in a previous life.

The University of Virginia's Division of Personality Studies has collected in excess of six thousand such cases and, so far, has managed to investigate nearly half of them. They found that children who recollect past lives generally start talking about them between the ages of two and four and generally stop once they reach the age of eight. The university recorded numerous instances of children correctly identifying names, places, and people associated with their past lives, more than half of which ended violently.

Reincarnation forms the basis of numerous world religions and goes unquestioned by millions globally and across time. Also known as transmigration or metempsychosis, it formed part of many ancient Middle Eastern and African religions and is widely believed in South and East

Asian faiths today, including Hinduism, Jainism, Buddhism, and Sikhism. They also believe in karma, meaning what we do in this life reflects in all the others. Some believe that we relive a form of human rebirth, while others believe we also take turns as animals and even plants.

The Reincarnation Research Centre in Bangalore, India, was probably the first body to systematically catalog and research reported instances of child reincarnation. One of the first cases they studied was that of Shanti Devi, who was born in a small village near Delhi to a traditional Hindu family in October 1926. From the age of three, she started to tell of a previous life cut short. She claimed to have died one year before she had been reborn and that she lived in the town of Muttra, some sixty miles away. Her name had been Lugdi and she was married to a cloth merchant called Kedarnath Choubey. She had died ten days after giving birth to a boy.

Finally, the family in question was tracked down. Shanti could not only recognize them all but could also provide intricate and often intimate details of their lives, much to everyone's utter astonishment. When she came face to face with her previous husband and her young boy, she broke down in tears. After a few minutes, the husband was not only dumbstruck but utterly convinced. As the researchers reported at the time: "In the face of such accurate experiences, Pundit Kedarnath was not only overwhelmed but acknowledged that Shanti Devi was certainly his life partner and companion in her previous existence."

But things took an even stranger turn when she toured her former village, pointing out key landmarks and small details mostly known only to locals. Finally, she stopped before a tree and started to scratch away at the earth until she revealed a bundle of banknotes wrapped in cloth, totaling one hundred rupees. She explained that she had hidden the money while pregnant as her blessing to the god Krishna.[8]

Elsewhere in the archive is the account of Giriraj Soni, a Hindu boy born in March 1979 in Madhya Pradesh. By the age of two, he insisted on being called by the Muslim name of Subhan Khan and would face Mecca to pray five times a day. He told his vegetarian parents that he needed meat and showed them how to cook it. He correctly located the house of the former Subhan Khan and told of a "despicable" life that ended in his murder, aged sixty, in July 1978. Stranger still were the deformities he had been born with. The left side of his chest looked like it had been battered in and he also had a number of birthmarks that clearly resembled head wounds that would never entirely heal. He was also born fully circumcised, a Muslim, not Hindu, practice. Unusually, he had been born with four adult teeth.

The murder of Subhan Khan had created a considerable stir at the time. The details of his killing and of the wounds he sustained were recorded in detail. His chest had been staved in but he had died from multiple head wounds. He had been left with just four teeth. There are hundreds upon hundreds of similar cases in the Bangalore archive.

"LIKE STUDYING THE STARS AT MIDDAY"

The flip, says Jeffrey J. Kripal, is when the penny drops and a new understanding takes hold. "It's that moment of realization beyond all linear thought, beyond all language, beyond all belief," he explains. "Such a flip is often sudden, unbidden, or traumatically catalyzed. It is also beautifully, elegantly simple." He liked the term so much that he chose it as the title for his book.[9]

He insists that contemporary neuroscience will continue to fail spectacularly to explain consciousness if it persists with the materialistic model and continues to deny that events like a child recalling a previous life or a coma patient experiencing an alternate existence are mere imaginings.

"I simply want to call out those who want to claim that they do not happen. They do," he says. "I also want to suggest that such strange signs could guide us on our way, if only we would listen and look and not turn away." If we find ourselves staring down at our bodies from the ICU ceiling, then it is far easier to entertain the idea of a separable, immortal soul, he explains.

"The professional debunker's insistence, then, that the phenomena play by his rules and appear for all to see in a safe and sterile controlled laboratory is little more than a mark of his own serious ignorance of the nature of the phenomena in question," writes Kripal in his book. "To play by these rules is like trying to study the stars at midday, and then claiming that they don't exist because they do not appear under those particular conditions."

We are, he insists, "in the fantastically ridiculous situation that conscious intellectuals are telling us that consciousness does not really exist as such, that there is nothing to it except cognitive grids, software loops, and warm brain matter. If this were not so patently absurd, it would be very funny."

Kripal demonstrates in his book how various luminaries from the past have experienced a form of the flip and how it changed their thinking forever. Alan Turing, the great British mathematician, codebreaker, and computer pioneer, believed wholeheartedly in telepathy, clairvoyance, precognition, and psychokinesis. "These disturbing phenomena seem to deny all our usual scientific ideas. How we should like to discredit them!" he wrote. "Unfortunately, the statistical evidence, at least for telepathy, is overwhelming."

Marie Curie—two-time winner of the Nobel Prize, one for Physics and the other for Chemistry—was a firm believer in the spirit world and regularly attended seances, while Albert Einstein wrote: "The most beautiful thing we can experience is the mysterious. It is the source of all true art and science."

One of the founding fathers of modern science, Francis Bacon (1561–1626), believed that consciousness could be divided into two zones: the personal, including dreams and religious ecstasy, and another that received inspiration from "disembodied spirits."

"There is much more to life than what we see, hear, smell, touch, and taste," says Dr. Eben Alexander, the neurosurgeon with the life-changing NDE. "Conventional science has limited reality to the proof of our external senses. But consciousness underlies all of existence, and the spiritual realm is a collective truth that can no longer be dismissed— and that can be accessed by each of us."[10]

In summing up *The Flip*, Kripal writes:

What we need is a new way of knowing, a new metaphysical imagination that does not confuse what we can observe in the third person with all there is. . . .

We should remember that early science arose in what were essentially private clubs and confidential social spaces outside the university,
the church, or any other official structures, mostly because the origina-
tors knew perfectly well just how heretical and incompatible their new
knowledge was vis-à-vis the reigning forms of knowledge. . . .

If the past is any measure, the future of knowledge, too, may
emerge from the margins.

REJECTING THE BLINDINGLY OBVIOUS

In 2020, the British Parliament refused to accept that animals are
sentient beings. The dictionary defines *sentient* as having feelings
and sensations. They did so largely because they did not want to
accept European Union animal welfare laws after breaking from the
trading bloc and because they wanted to clear the path for so-called
Frankenstein meat via gene editing. This, as *The Guardian* reported at
the time, means, "There's no law that ensures the feelings of these animals in decision-making."

If decision-makers in the self-proclaimed mother of parliaments
cannot accept that animals are alive in the same sense that we are,
many fear there is scant hope that the establishment will accept that
the planet and all the creatures on it are more than the machines the
materialists would have us believe. This, when most people would consider the question of animal sentience blindingly obvious. One wonders
how many members of Britain's two Houses of Parliament ever cared
for a cat or dog.

It is worth stopping to reassess many of the things we believe in or
take as fact because so much of what we assume to be true or accept as
fact is often little more than a theory. In scientific terms, a theory—
defined by the dictionary as no more than "a rational type of abstract
thinking about a phenomenon"—is accepted as a valid explanation,

meaning that a theory is taken as fact until it can be proven otherwise. This is not the same as an actual proven fact, such as that Earth revolves around the sun.

Gravity, as most people understand it, is the result of centrifugal force and the spinning of our planet, which prevents us all floating off into space. But it turns out to be a whole lot more complicated than that. In fact, we know little more now about gravity than Newton did when he watched the apple fall from the tree.

A visit to the NASA website will tell us this: "Gravity is the force by which a planet or other body draws objects toward its center. The force of gravity keeps all of the planets in orbit around the sun." Dig somewhat deeper into the information that NASA shares online and, in answer to this particular question, we read: "We don't really know. We can define what it is as a field of influence, because we know how it operates in the universe. However, if we are to be honest, we do not know what gravity 'is' in any fundamental way—we only know how it behaves."

Time is another example of something we assume we understand but never stop to question. We can measure it, but we have no idea what it really is or why, for that matter, it behaves the way it does, like slowing down as it nears a black hole. Everything we thought we knew about time is no more than a few unproven theories. Theoretical physicist Carlo Rovelli believes time is little more than an illusion because our naive perception of its flow does not correspond to physical reality. Albert Einstein wrote: "People like us who believe in physics know that the distinction between past, present, and future is only a stubbornly persistent illusion."

Some believe that time is in fact speeding up as the universe expands. It does not just seem that the days go by faster as we grow older—they may actually be doing so. As an experiment, open the stopwatch on a smartphone, set it going, and start counting *one Mississippi, two Mississippi,* and so on. Count to ten, then look at the screen. It is likely that fifteen seconds will have passed in that time, not ten. Counting this way used to work. It now no longer appears to.

Ask anyone on the street whether they think most scientists have a grasp of DNA—the molecule that contains all the instructions an organism needs to develop, live, and reproduce—and the answer is likely to be yes. But they would only be partially right—less than 2 percent right, to be precise. It transpires that scientists know very little about this molecule that effectively makes us who we are.

This may seem strange to anyone who read in April 2003 that the Human Genome Project had been declared complete with the final mapping of the genes of the human genome, our entire genetic material. What they did not appear to report was that they had uncovered yet another mystery because they could not explain what more than 98 percent of DNA does. Rather dismissively, they call these mysterious parts junk DNA, and yet there is generally a reason for most things found in nature. New theories surface regularly but, as yet, there is no definitive answer. This would be like mapping Africa but missing all the towns and cities and giving yourself a pat on the back. In short, materialistic scientists barely know anything about DNA but they let us think they have it all worked out.

In the 1960s, one CIA operative opened another can of worms with a series of peculiar experiments. Cleve Backster spent a lot of his time submitting plants to polygraph tests, commonly known as lie detectors. He discovered that plants not only feel pain but have a form of extrasensory perception. And then he did something very strange.

Backster removed white blood cells via oral swab from a living human subject and transported them twelve miles away, keeping them alive in a culture medium. He then showed the subject horrific and sexually arousing images and noted that the cells instantaneously reacted, even though they were a good half day's walk away and encased in a Faraday cage shielding them from electromagnetic signals.[11]

Backster had found proof that human cells, regardless of distance, react to their owner's specific state of mind. Science may have numerous theories but it has no definitive answers to this one. This, then, begs the questions: What does science think is happening when one human donates a body part to another human and how does it explain the phenomenon of transplanted memory when we have been told all along that memories are stored in the brain?

Personality changes following organ transplantation have been reported for decades. French actress Charlotte Valandrey received a heart transplant in 2003 and soon after began to have a recurring nightmare of being in a car crash, blinded by headlights in driving rain. She also developed a taste for wine that she never had before. In her memoir, *Of Heart Unknown,* she maintains that she experienced cellular memory from her donor.[12] She eventually took things a stage further by falling in love with the husband of her donor.

Or there is the case of seventeen-year-old Amy Tippins, who received a new liver in 1993. Soon after, she developed an unhealthy craving for hamburgers. She also found herself wandering unbidden into hardware stores, discussing DIY projects in depth, and carrying them out competently herself, having never done so before. It turns out her new liver was donated by U.S. marshal Mike James, who had a big thing for hamburgers and was halfway through renovating the bathroom when he died.[13]

Stephen (Continued): The Cushioned Room

Medical statistician Stephen wakes to find himself in a large hotel room; the walls and even the ceiling are covered in cushions of different sizes. He recalls the scene.

• • •

Red and crimson, colored patterns, overwhelming, stifling, oppressive. Try to get up, cannot, wriggle, squirm, can't get up. Something slip sliding beneath me, refusing any purchase, so lumpy, hundreds of cushions. And facing, on opposite wall, a huge, square, center-buttoned cushion exudes a grim malevolent threat to engulf and smother.

Escape thoughts suppressed by fearful anticipation of imminent suffocation. But then hear noises behind and to the right; an open doorway, leading outside. Now a yard, along one side and facing the

*door, a long, low pen holding small animals: goats, pigs, chickens; all
gray, dirty and grimy.*

Salvation is at hand. Stephen sees three or four workmen in
bright orange vests. With strong metal pliers they snap the metal
strips that somehow keep him trapped in the Cushioned Room.

*The work is hard; some workers tire and want a break. Me,
pleading.* Please, please don't stop! Help me. It's suffocating
in here; please help me escape. *Then, there before me, the pen;
head-height low roof; inside, dirty, muddy, filthy, gray listless animals.*

*Turning from pen, face a frowning new sight: standing atop
plateau of Liverpool Metropolitan Cathedral, looking over from top
steps to Mount Pleasant and Hope Street. But all is gray, desolate,
buildings in ruins.*

*And now, looking across to Brownlow Hill, the University,
city center and the distance beyond; wasteland, oppressed under
crouching, brooding gray clouds. As far as I can see, a vast industrial
vista: sprawling railway sidings, shacks, sheds, warehouses, slag
heaps; polluting smoke, grinding grit and grime for miles around.
Desolation. Void.*

*From afar, a distant sound, growing louder, coming closer: car
engine power, roar racing the rubble roads.* The gangsters! They're
coming and there's no escape. I cannot see them, but they're coming.
All around, desolation. Hopeless. No escape.

Deborah in Amber (Continued)

Have you ever seen that show Preacher? *They go down into hell
and the punishment is a repeated loop of the worst thing that's ever
happened to them in their life. And it's played out over and over
again. And that's how it was for me.*

*Now I get them as flashbacks—the smells, the sounds, the
feelings, the emotions—and then I'm back there, and that's how I
experienced my coma: the same dreams looping and looping. It was*

just horrific, such as remembering being in a hangar waiting for my flight to Bristol with Willie Walsh and his daughter and mother. I was assaulted. I was raped. I was cast in fiberglass. I was abandoned. I was placed in a water tank with my dad's decomposing corpse. I was told my husband didn't love me anymore by two actors employed by the nurse, who was actually the angel of death in disguise. I had to send Morse code with my pelvic floor to control the lights on the Embankment because I was drowning in the Thames. And they are all so vivid and they stay with me. Which is real? Am I awake or still in my coma? This is my loop, my hell.

For the longest loop, I was in this serial-killer-themed pub, and they decided that they wanted it to be totally realistic and use real people as murder victims, and I was one of the living murder victims because I was in a coma and they could do whatever they wanted to me.

Throughout the years, they would spray me with lacquer or a cotton candy type of fiberglass to keep me preserved. I remember the smell even now. And they kept me alive with tubes and stuff. There was a guy on the door taking money, a tour guide, several actors, and me—a big, fat nothing, a slob lying in a bay window with no memory of who I was or where my family were.

And they kept making it more and more realistic. So they went from having actors and actresses playing these serial killers to then having real-life serial killers, actual people released from prison, to reenact some of their murders on me and on the other people, the other bodies being kept alive. I was raped, which was just horrific. I had three children.

Without the kiss from my true love, I would never leave the bar. Years passed, decades. I became encased in so much fiberglass it was like golden rock, like amber. But the pub was due to be demolished and they didn't know what to do with me. I'd been there eighty years.

They thought the man at the bar was my true love, but he loved the barmaid. They realized I'd had kids and tracked them down through DNA, thinking their father might be my love, but he was the Indian guy whose wife was in a coma, and he'd raped me in my glass cocoon. My three children didn't want to know me, as they were mixed race and they were ashamed of their White mother.

I spent the first two months after my coma convinced I had died. And still, I have to check I am actually alive. I tell people I was in my coma for eighty years because that's what happened. I think my nightmares were my personal hell. I know it was in my head but it was as real as I stand here today.

Nick the Repairman (Continued)

It's weird, but I now know how to do things I learned there. I had new skills when I woke up that I didn't have before. Well, let me rephrase that—I had a perpetual urge for learning new skills when I woke up. I was able to fix my fiancé's old-school HVAC (heating, ventilation, and air-conditioning) system at her house. I can't really tell you how I did. Somehow, I just knew it was the fuse. I found the fuse box, took the fuse out, went to Home Depot and got a new one, went home and popped it in, and bam! Fixed it. Similar story with the neighbor's push mower and my car. So that's eerie.

Before coma—I call it BC—I wouldn't have even looked at it. I would have just called someone to come fix it, pay them a shitload of money to come and replace a fuse. Seems silly, huh? But just because I tried, I was able to figure it out. I never did stuff like this before, so why could I now? Was it stuff I learned in my other life and was now applying here?

It didn't stop there. I was able to fix a 6 x 6 walk-in cooler that was not cooling after a heating and cooling company came and said they couldn't fix it, scrap it. I watched them repair a line that had a small leak in the top, and they kept stuffing Freon in the unit. After they left, and the cooler was at sixty degrees, I remembered from somewhere that it's possible to add too much Freon and that can actually cause adverse reactions. I walked up, simply let some Freon escape. Now it's thirty-eight degrees. Fixed! Perfect!

I'm now taking on bigger issues, like my car, and was successful in fixing it a few times. Now, I'm not like a newfound prodigy or something. I can't just walk up and fix whatever; it still takes a little bit of effort. But at least now I always try. I kind of enjoy it, actually.

PART 2

Shining a Light on the Dimensions of Consciousness

4

The Chattering Monkey

And the Strange Things That Happen When Parts of the Brain Switch Off

Here is an interesting experiment. Remove the queen bee from her hive and take her about ten miles away. Now study the hive and we see that life goes on as normal. But kill the queen, and immediately anarchy and chaos break out. It had been thought that the queen controlled her hive by releasing certain chemicals, but that probably would not work at such a distance. Something else is surely going on.

Very occasionally, a queen will just pack it all in and give up. No one appears to know why. Ben Oldroyd from the University of Sydney is one of the few to have witnessed the event. He told *New Scientist:* "The queen ends up in a corner of the colony surrounded by a few loyal workers, and the rest of the colony goes berserk just laying eggs."

Eventually workers become disoriented, barely able to feed themselves, the magazine explained. Oldroyd has even seen them trying to rear queens out of male larvae. At that point, he says, total social collapse is inevitable.[1]

The most likely theory is that the queen maintains control over her hive using a collective consciousness, which by its very nature is likely to be external to the body and something that each creature can tap into. We see similar social structures among wasps, ants, and termites. Dr. van Lommel, the NDE expert, sees this as the only possible explanation. "These colonies are examples of living and self-organizing systems composed of animals with different tasks but with a collective consciousness coordinated by the queen," he says.[2]

The particular conundrum of consciousness—collective or otherwise—has baffled both science and philosophy through the ages. It is generally defined as the state of being aware of and responsive to one's surroundings. And we believe ourselves to be conscious because we assume that we are here, having first-person experiences that feel like something; we assume that those around us feel much the same; and we assume that inanimate objects like ladders, paperclips, and loaves of bread have no consciousness. The jury would appear to be out on plants and animals.

Consciousness is especially hard to define because there appear to be so many different levels to it. There is the consciousness you feel right now, which changes profoundly during a good night's sleep, and you can experience totally different levels when you take psychedelic drugs or find yourself sufficiently sedated to the level of coma.

In 1976, the American psychologist Julian Jaynes suggested that early humans were not conscious as we know it today and that the stories of gods speaking to people were actually no more than the voices inside their heads that most of us experience throughout the day.

In his book *The Origin of Consciousness in the Breakdown of the Bicameral Mind*,[3] he suggested that the mind was divided into two zones, which he termed bicameralism, with one part of the mind responsible for speaking and the other for listening and obeying. He maintained that the brain underwent radical changes toward the end of the Bronze Age, leading to modern consciousness, and that people experiencing schizophrenia today retain vestiges of this primitive brain. He even suggested that if we had a time machine and could go back around three thousand years, the majority of people we might meet would be diagnosed as schizophrenic by today's standards. Not surprisingly, Jaynes was laughed at by his contemporaries.

Fast-forward to the twenty-first century, and there still appears to be no clear understanding of the relationship between the brain and consciousness. In philosophical terms, this is known as the Hard Problem, a term coined by philosopher David Chalmers to distinguish it from easier problems that can be explained by science, such as hearing and eyesight.

As Edward Kelly writes in *Consciousness Unbound:* "We have no understanding whatsoever of how consciousness could be produced by physical events in brains, and recent theoretical work in philosophy of mind has convinced many that we can never achieve one."[4]

"It has generally been assumed that consciousness and memories are localized inside the brain, that the brain produces them," writes Dr. van Lommel in his paper "About the Continuity of Consciousness." He continues, "According to this unproven concept, consciousness and memories ought to vanish with physical death, and necessary[il]y also during clinical death or brain death. However, during an NDE patients experience the continuity of their consciousness."[5]

How then, he asks, can somebody experience a clear consciousness—in many cases with an ultravivid clarity to the consciousness—with a flat electroencephalogram (EEG), as happens in deeper coma states? "Such a brain would be roughly analogous to a computer with its power source unplugged and its circuits detached. It couldn't hallucinate; it couldn't do anything at all," he insists.

After years of research into NDEs, Dr. van Lommel is a firm believer that consciousness is independent of the body and that we are capable of experiencing other dimensions where all past, present, and future events exist and can be observed simultaneously and instantaneously. This effect is known as nonlocality—the apparent ability of objects to instantaneously know about each other's state, even when separated by large distances—and has been a feature of all enduring world religions: that the soul exists outside the body unhampered by the constraints of time.

"The conclusion that consciousness can be experienced independently of brain function might well induce a huge change in the scientific paradigm in Western medicine," he writes. "And could have practical implications in actual medical and ethical problems, such as the care for comatose or dying patients, euthanasia, abortion, and the removal of organs for transplantation from somebody in the dying process, with a beating heart in a warm body but a diagnosis of brain death."

In February 2006, Anita Moorjani slipped into a coma in a Hong Kong hospital. She was dying of N-stage lymphoma and her entire body was shutting down. At one moment, she felt her consciousness connect with all those around her. In her uplifting TEDx talk she says:

I was aware of every single thing that was happening. It felt as though I had a 360-degree peripheral vision. I could see everything happening all around my body. But not just in the room where my body was, but even beyond. And it was as if I had expanded out of my body.

I felt I was in a realm of clarity, where I understood everything. I understood why I had cancer. I understood that I was much greater; in fact all of us are much greater and more powerful than we realize. I also felt as if I was connected to everybody, like all the doctors that were treating me, the nurses, my husband, my mother, my brother, and everybody. I felt as though we all shared the same consciousness. I felt as though I could feel what they were feeling, I could feel the distress they were feeling, I could feel the resignation of the doctors. It's like we all share the same consciousness . . . we're all expressions of the same consciousness. That's what it felt like.

Anita likens our everyday experience to wandering around a warehouse with just a small flashlight, illuminating only tiny parts of the whole that she experienced within her coma. She prompted her TEDx audience:

Just imagine that right now, you're in a warehouse that's completely pitch black, and you use just the beam of that little flashlight to navigate your way in the dark.

Now imagine if the beam is shining over there, all you see is what's over there. Everything else is in darkness. Now imagine one day big floodlights go on so the whole warehouse is illuminated, and you realize this warehouse is huge. It's bigger than you've ever imagined it to be. And it's lined with shelves and shelves and shelves of all kinds of different things. Every kind of thing you can imagine, and things you can't even imagine, all exist on these shelves, side by side by side.

Some of these things are beautiful, some not so beautiful, some large, some small, some things in colors you've never ever seen before, colors you've never imagined to exist, and some things that are strange and funny-looking, all exist side by side, and you've seen some of them before with your flashlight, but many of them you've never seen before because your flashlight had never shone on them.

Now imagine if the lights go back off again, and you're back to one flashlight. Now, even though all you can see is what you see with the beam of one flashlight, at least you now know there's so much more that exists simultaneously.

She adds that it was this knowledge that enabled her to expel the cancer from her body and come back from death.

You now know that just because you cannot see it, you cannot experience it, doesn't mean it doesn't exist. You now know that because you've had that experience. That's what it feels like to me.[6]

Anita is far from alone in believing that consciousness connects us all. Some hold that the universe itself is consciousness in the form of an all-pervading energy that every single thing is plugged into. The connection with an all-encompassing energy is a recurring theme reported by those seeking other obtainable levels of consciousness, from ecstatic dance through to magic mushrooms. Many returning from a near-death experience or emerging from coma report the same. In turn, it is thought that this energy is decoded rather in the way a radio receives its particular program and that we each receive different frequencies pertinent to ourselves, our own individual consciousness.

This argument gains traction when you think that the world around us is largely made up of electromagnetic energy and that it flows through us in much the same way that Wi-Fi signals and radio transmissions do. Our cells conduct electrical currents, and this energy powers our nervous system. The average person taking it easy on the sofa produces around one hundred watts of power an hour, while a jogger may clock up over two thousand watts.

The electrical pioneer Nikola Tesla (1856–1943) spent much of his life trying to tap into the electromagnetic energy that surrounds us as a free source of universal power. And while he never achieved his goal, he did set the scene for virtually every other type of electrical device in use today as well as predict the application of email and Wi-Fi. "If you want to find the secrets of the universe," he famously said, "think in terms of energy, frequency, and vibration."

It is worth noting that the first law of thermodynamics says energy can neither be created nor destroyed—that it is everywhere around us and that we only release and utilize it. That we are all part of the same universal consciousness—the same energy source—is a view shared by multiple religions and held by those who have experimented with psychedelic substances or achieved deep spiritual awareness.

Reporting the effects of the psychedelic compound 1P-LSD, one respondent told us:

I had a clear sense that I was connected to everything around me by the same energy. As I watched bees buzz about and the birds flying from tree to tree, I knew that we are all connected by this energy. It was abundantly self-evident.

It became clear to me that the planet—the entire earth—is actually an infinite powerhouse running off this same energy. And then I understood why we need all the storms and wars, the heartache and anger. When a bird kills and eats a bee, it sparks and releases energy that powers the motor. This essence gives life to everything, and the love and compassion we share feeds the motor, too. The beauty, the wonder of the connectedness of all, the ecstatic joy, all run on the same energy. And the dark side, together with the love we generate, these power the dynamo that keeps the whole universe turning. We each take turns at living and feeding the engine because we all share in the energy. This energy is what we call love.

A common feature of those recounting an NDE—when they have met with dead relatives and learned the meaning of everything—is the feeling that all the suffering we experience in this life makes sense, that they finally understood, although another common feature is that any understanding learned there cannot be brought back. And yet the knowledge of such a secret persists.

No matter which particular level of consciousness we happen to be experiencing, they are all equally impossible to fathom or define, so can we actually be certain that anyone else is truly conscious? How might we test for it? And what of ourselves, for that matter?

One day, PlayStation might take us to a level so fully immersive, so utterly vivid and convincing, that it may be impossible to distinguish the game from reality. Top of the charts may be the virtual reality game *Pandemic,* set in the early twenty-first century against a backdrop of wars, refugees, soaring prices, cataclysmic climate change, and species extinction, leaving us to hope it will automatically pause soon because the table is being laid for supper.

If that concept appears far-fetched, it is worth noting that much of reality as we know it is up for question. It is fair to say that the majority of people tend to believe in many things that do not actually exist in any permanent, physical sense but only within the imagination. A fan may be committed body and soul to a particular football club, but change all the players and all the managers, as happens naturally over time, and you have an entirely different entity, and yet the fans continue to love the club because of the way they perceive it in their minds.

Across the globe, people believe that particular political parties will improve the quality of their lives when easily accessible evidence rarely shows this to be the case. Others have faith that one politician or another will prove honest and care deeply for each and every constituent, while ignoring the likelihood that his or her persona is a carefully crafted fiction to gain favor in an election.

Teenagers regularly fall in love with pop stars, but these are not actual people, just two-dimensional images in light and color, and the person they purport to represent is in reality the construct of a music industry executive. Hearts are easily broken, especially on social media, where reality is distorted as a matter of course. Worldwide, people continue to defend beliefs that may die within a generation, and they continue to lay down their lives for concepts conjured up in the minds of other people that change erratically over time, depending on the mood of the moment.

Much of the news we take in is a fiction, based on preloaded cultural, political, or national biases. There is no one Truth that any media outlet can peddle, because all truth is subjective and entirely different, depending on one's perspective.

"Over the years, people have woven an incredibly complex network of stories," says Yuval Noah Harari in *Sapiens: A Brief History of Humankind*. "The kinds of things that people create through this network of stories are known in academic circles as fictions, social constructs, or imagined realities. An imagined reality is not a lie," he says, and "unlike lying, an imagined reality is something that everyone believes in, and as long as this communal belief persists, the imagined reality exerts force in the world."[7]

Harari believes that we are all living a dual reality. "On the one hand, the objective reality of rivers, trees and lions; and on the other hand, the imagined reality of gods, nations and corporations. As time went by, the imagined reality became ever more powerful, so that today the very survival of rivers, trees and lions depends on the grace of imagined entities such as gods, nations and corporations."

LESS IS MORE

We all have memories—from early childhood right through to what we had for breakfast—yet such a vast amount of data would be nigh impossible to store by any conventional, electronic means, let alone retrieve at will. According to current medical understanding, memories are stored in various parts of the brain alongside our consciousness. But by what means can so much knowledge be crammed into our skulls when the brain is constantly active on other, more immediate tasks? There are various theories but little else.

"Different types [of memory] are stored across different, interconnected brain regions," says the Queensland Brain Institute. "For explicit memories—which are about events that happened to you (episodic), as well as general facts and information (semantic)—there are three important areas of the brain: the hippocampus, the neocortex and the amygdala. Implicit memories, such as motor memories, rely on the basal ganglia and cerebellum. Short-term working memory relies most heavily on the prefrontal cortex."[8]

However, evidence of this is truly hard to come by and on closer inspection this, too, turns out to be nothing more than an unproven hypothesis, but one that continues to be taught as fact in virtually every Western medical school.

It is easy to see just how doctors have got stuck on the notion that memory resides in the brain. When using functional magnetic resonance imaging (MRI), they see changes in the brain's hippocampus when the subject is asked to conjure up old memories. This is generally accepted as showing just where certain memories are stored. But it can be equally argued that the MRI detects brain activity simply when memories are accessed or processed, from whichever source. And, as Simon Berkovich, professor of engineering and applied science at George Washington University, has proven, a lifetime's memories cannot be stored in the brain alone and there simply is not enough space for the body to retain all the data it requires, from detailed memories through to the blueprint of ourselves said to be stored in our cells and DNA.

Other theories abound. Karl Pribram's holographic hypothesis has it that memories are not stored in the brain itself but in the electromagnetic fields of the brain, and these fields, which exist in the space between the brain and skull, are capable of storing almost infinite amounts of data.[9]

"[Science] cannot account for the physical limitations of brain structure," says Professor Berkovich. "The amount of information in the human genome—about thirty thousand genes—is supposed to be the 'blueprint' of human development. In the digital world, this amount of information would be hardly enough to portray a blurry digital picture of a living being," he says.[10]

In comparison, worms have more than half as many genes as humans. Plants have more DNA than animals, while oak trees have around fifty thousand genes—twenty thousand more than us. "It is readily apparent that the way genes are constructed, they simply cannot hold all the information necessary to explain the human body," stresses Berkovich.

Others maintain that memory is stored within the gaps in DNA, the so-called junk DNA, which in turn are filled with electromagnetic energy. Other theories maintain that memory is shared among the cells of the body, which would go some way toward explaining transferred memory among transplant patients. And yet these cells, which are seen as our very building blocks, are constantly dying and being reborn.

"During our life, 500,000 cells die each second [and] each day about fifty billion cells in our body are replaced, resulting in a new body each year," points out Dr. van Lommel. "Each living being is in an unstable balance of two opposing processes of continual disintegration and integration. But no one realizes this constant change."[11] We experience our body as a continuity. How can we explain this experience of continuity of the ever-changing body? Van Lommel says, "Consciousness cannot be stored in our DNA, rendering a cell in our body and brain a highly unlikely producer for consciousness."[12]

The information contained in our DNA may be little more than a form of bar code, according to many theorists, because it cannot contain all the necessary information so must therefore obtain it elsewhere. "If the barcode theory holds and memory is stored elsewhere," insists Berkovich, "then the way we look at consciousness when separated from the body has some profound implications on the way society and religion [are] organized."

And, in the same vein of consciousness existing separately from the body, memories might behave in the same way and be stored in the vast sea of electromagnetic energy surrounding us. Memory may simply resemble the cloud. Rather than storing data in our personal device—everything from childhood recollections and recipes to plans for the future—store them in the instantly accessible and seemingly infinite data bank that surrounds us. This concept is easier to accept once we realize that most of us already store many of our memories this way when we upload photos and videos.

If such a theory could be proven, it would likely revolutionize the treatment of various memory disorders, such as Alzheimer's. The amyloid plaques that collect between the neurons and the tangled bundles of fibers may simply be hindering reception.

Neurologist professor John Lorber (1915–1996) said memories can still be retrieved even when the brain is missing large sectors or is simply shriveled to the size of a walnut. He cited the case of his student with a high IQ of 126 and a first-class honors degree in mathematics who appeared socially well-adjusted. The only thing that appeared odd about the boy was his larger-than-average head.

"When we did a brain scan on him," Lorber told the magazine *Science,* "we saw that instead of the normal 4.5 centimeter thickness of brain tissue between the ventricles and the cortical surface, there was just a thin layer of mantle measuring a millimeter or so. His cranium is filled mainly with cerebrospinal fluid. This boy has virtually no brain."[13]

Similar evidence was uncovered back in the 1920s when psychologist Karl Lashley began systematically to remove parts of the brain from rats and discovered that no matter which parts were removed, or actually how much of the brain was removed, the rats were still able to perform the tasks they were set before their brain operations.[14]

Not only can rats and people function with only a limited portion of the brain but actual brain injuries have been shown to be beneficial in a number of rare cases. Derek Amato, a thirty-nine-year-old sales trainer, was paying a visit to old buddies in his hometown of Sioux

Falls, South Dakota, when they all decided to go swimming. Derek, unfortunately, managed to dive headfirst into the water and smash his head with considerable force on the pool's concrete bottom.

When they managed to fish him out, blood was gushing from his ears. He drifted in and out of consciousness. When he finally became coherent, he told everyone that he was a professional baseball player and he must dash because he was late for spring training in Phoenix.

Later, while recuperating with friends, Derek stumbled out of bed after a mammoth four-day sleep and made his way to a makeshift music studio in the house where he was staying. He ignored his friends, who sat there chatting, and went straight to the electric keyboard. Derek had never touched a piano before, but for the next six hours he gave his buddies a virtuoso performance. He has now given up his job training sales staff and concentrates full time on composing and performing on the piano.[15]

Wisconsin psychiatrist Darold Treffert (1933–2020) studied the subject of brain injury savants for many years and collected well over three hundred accounts. He thought the sudden onset of remarkable skills, from music and art to mathematics, was the result of what he termed "genetic memory" and that the injuries can unlock levels of consciousness that most of us never have access to.[16]

In a separate study of the degenerative brain disease frontotemporal dementia (FTD), Bruce Miller, professor of neurology at the University of California, San Francisco, discovered that a number of his patients had gained "incredible artistic abilities" that only improved as their condition worsened.[17]

Researchers at the University of Missouri decided to see what other effects there were after traumatic brain injury and began to discover a large number of apparent spiritual experiences. "People with injuries to the right parietal lobe of the brain reported higher levels of spiritual experiences, such as transcendence," one researcher said, adding that feelings of unity and oneness with the universe were associated with decreased activity in the right parietal lobe—*as opposed to increased activity*—a part of the brain associated with visual-spatial perception.[18]

Similar results were found after studying head wounds sustained in combat. "We investigated mystical experience among participants from the Vietnam Head Injury Study," explains Irene Cristofori, associate professor at the Université Claude Bernard in Lyon. Analysis, she says, clearly "showed that lesions to frontal and temporal brain regions were linked with greater mystical experiences."[19]

Robert Mentzer was injured in Vietnam when the truck he was riding in ran over a landmine in April 1969. He suffered minor injuries but was knocked unconscious by the blast. At the time, he underwent an out-of-body experience, but nearly a year would pass before he had a full mystic experience.

He recalled for us that he was sitting at home with his wife when suddenly:

> *I was above myself, looking down on my body sitting in the chair. I saw my wife across the room sitting in her chair. Just as suddenly, I went up and outward into space. I could see stars in the distance. I did the same thing when I was blown up. I checked my senses and realized I could see. I could sort of hear. I realized I was without any of my usual pain, and I realized I did not bring my body along with me.*
>
> *I traveled a long, long distance in a very short time. I went to a place that had no stars, just blackness. Suddenly, I went through what seemed to be a fabric of sorts by what I describe as osmosis. Again, suddenly, I realized I was standing in the center of what I would describe as a coliseum of pure white. There was no other color. But I could make out every detail of the people seated in the coliseum, even though everything was bright white.*
>
> *Then an extremely white light was above me. I didn't look up. I knew who or what was above me. I had a conversation with the light. After the conversation was over, suddenly I was going back through the fabric by osmosis again, and was again traveling in space, seeing a few stars off in the far distance as I travelled back the way I came.*

I stopped when I got back to my apartment, hovering right above my own body sitting in the chair, looking over at my wife. Suddenly, I was back in my body, looking through my own eyes again. I was completely stunned by what I just experienced. But what was even more stunning was the fact that I could not remember the conversation. I speculate the only thing I remember was the question, Do you want to go back? *and I said,* Yes.

I told several people over the next few months what I experienced, and their reactions made me stop telling any others of the experience.

"Clearly, there is a broad and consistent pattern associating impairment of brain function with extraordinary scientific, artistic, and spiritual insights," says computer scientist Bernardo Kastrup. He adds that reduced brain function has been shown to lead to "expanded awareness and self-transcendence." The implications of this hypothesis for both neuroscience and neurophilosophy, he says, are far-reaching.[20]

Neuroscientist Andrew Newberg scanned the brains of Tibetan Buddhist monks and clearly found decreased activity in the parietal lobe during meditation, when the monks were experiencing transcendence and a oneness with the universe.

"For those individuals who want to go down the path of arguing that all of our religious and spiritual experiences are nothing more than biological phenomena, some of this data does support that kind of a conclusion," Newberg says in his book *Principles of Neurotheology*. "But the data also does not specifically eliminate the notion that there is a religious or spiritual or divine presence in the world."[21]

"Even more intriguingly," says Kastrup, "it is well known that psychedelic substances induce powerful experiences of self-transcendence. It had been assumed that they did so by exciting parts of the brain. Yet, recent neuroimaging studies have shown that psychedelics do largely the opposite. A person lying in a vegetative state could be having indescribably rich inner experiences and we would be none the wiser."[22]

Professor David Nutt is a neuropsychopharmacologist and former British government advisor on the safety of drugs. In a series of tests, he administered the psychedelic substance psilocybin to a number of subjects and monitored their brains for signs of activity. He says:

> What we found was completely surprising and exactly the opposite of what we predicted, because we found that psilocybin turned off blood flow in the key parts of the brain such as the prefrontal cortex, the posterior cortex, and the thalamus.
>
> When you look at those parts of the brain, you realize that they are actually the parts of the brain which control and integrate the way in which the brain processes information. They are the kind of gatekeeper regions which regulate what you do and what you feel and by switching those off, we can kind of liberate the rest of the brain so that it can do other things and that's why you get the expansion of consciousness.[23]

Simply put, the less going on in the brain, the greater expansion of consciousness.

THE MONKEY HAS HIJACKED THE SHIP

It's 1892 and the young German astronomy student Hans Berger is getting nowhere with his studies so decides to take a year off and join the horse artillery for a bit of fun and fresh air. Then one day, while on exercises, his horse is spooked, he is thrown from the saddle, and he lands with a thump directly in the path of a thundering horse-drawn artillery team. As luck would have it, the driver manages to steer clear of the prostrate Berger, which turns out to be a very good thing for the world of brain science.

Later that evening, Berger was handed a telegram from his sister who had become overwhelmed that very morning by a feeling that something terrible had happened to her much-loved brother.

"It was a case of spontaneous telepathy in which at a time of mortal danger I transmitted my thoughts while my sister who was particularly close to me acted as the receiver," Berger wrote in his diary.[24] The event and the telegram caused him to change tack and study medicine, specifically psychiatry and neurology, in a quest to understand psychic communication. What he ended up discovering was the electroencephalogram or EEG, a means of recording the electrical activity of the brain, our actual brainwaves.

He then went on to propose the idea that the brain never shuts down but is kept constantly busy, even when the subject is seen to be staring vacantly into space. But, true to form, Berger's ideas were ridiculed by other scientists, who firmly believed that the brain spent most of its time inactive and only sprang into action when given an activity to focus upon. It turns out they were wrong and Berger was right.

But it was not until 2001 that Marcus Raichle, a neurologist at Washington University, had a lucky stumble himself. While carrying out MRI scans and trying to establish a resting state baseline by getting volunteers to sit quietly doing nothing, he was surprised to discover that certain areas of the brain suddenly became very excited precisely when the subjects were doing nothing. He had discovered an area of the brain he termed the default mode network (DMN)—the place where daydreams reside and the ego has voice, home to the chattering monkey of our internal monologue.

In simple terms, the DMN links parts of the cerebral cortex to deeper and older structures of the brain thought to involve memory and emotion. This is the bridge of our ship, the control center that acts as a filter to ensure we are not overloaded with information, allowing us to keep focused on the tasks of the day.

Dr. Raichle discovered that the DMN keeps order in an otherwise chaotic brain, preventing the anarchy of mental illness by acting "as an uber-conductor to ensure that the cacophony of competing signals from one system do not interfere with those from another."[25] But the DMN is also a bit of a nag.

"It's the part of your brain most connected to the ego which contends that you can't do anything right," explains Diana Raab, author of *The Empowerment Diary* blog. "It's also the part of you that stifles creativity and prevents you from moving forward with your passions. The monkey mind insists on being heard, and sometimes it takes a lot of self-control to shut it down. It is also the part of your brain that becomes easily distracted so, if you want to get anything done in life, your challenge will be to shut down the monkey mind."[26]

This is something that Buddhists have known for around two and a half millennia, since the Buddha himself coined the word *kapicitta* to describe the agitated, easily distracted, and incessantly active behavior of ordinary human consciousness. It has been the goal of every guru and mystic since to find the off switch.

The DMN will spring into action whenever the brain is at wakeful rest and we are not focused on the outside world or on a particular task. This allows the mind to wander and opens the way for daydreams. The network goes into overdrive when we start thinking about ourselves and our relationships with others and when we remember the past or plan for the future. It would not be a stretch to say that the DMN is actually the producer of almost all the stress we experience in our daily lives. While preventing one form of mental anarchy, the DMN appears to be sparking another form of mental illness, the ever-present stress that is such a hallmark of the modern world. The monkey has hijacked the ship.

"I call this automatic habit of intense self-talk the 'thought torrent,'" explains Laura Maciuika, psychologist and author of *Conscious Calm: Keys to Freedom from Stress and Worry*. It's when "we don't notice we've headed into an internal stream of thought, which gains more and more force as we add thoughts and feelings to the internal stories. The thought torrent can leave us even more stressed and tired by the end of the day."

Maciuika also came up with the term *motor minding* to explain the underlying chatter that seems to most of us perfectly normal and runs on an internal loop without our really noticing. "In modern life in general, this endless random thinking is rarely discussed," she says. "We act as if thinking without ceasing is normal."[27]

"This voice might seem like a nagging parent or spouse," says Raab.

"The ego has the ability to create false thoughts, which is the inner chatter we hear most often. In fact, it is the voice in our heads that we sometimes tell to shut up. Otherwise, we can become overwhelmed by these thoughts or even lose touch with reality. Sometimes this voice turns dark and can lead to feelings of fear, guilt, anger, sadness, envy, and resentment."[28]

"When someone goes to the doctor and says, *I hear a voice in my head,* he or she will most likely be sent to a psychiatrist," explains Eckhart Tolle, spiritual teacher and author of the best-selling book *The Power of Now: A Guide to Spiritual Enlightenment.* But, he says, "Virtually everyone hears a voice, or several voices, in their head all the time: the involuntary thought processes that you don't realize you have the power to stop—the continuous monologues and dialogues."[29] We are all, he maintains, little different from the mad people we occasionally see in the street, incessantly talking or muttering to themselves, "Except that you don't do it out loud," he says.

"It is not uncommon for the voice to be a person's worst enemy," he writes. "Many people live with a tormentor in their head that continuously attacks and punishes them and drains them of vital energy. It is the cause of untold misery and unhappiness, as well as of disease."

If you have ever found yourself reading a book and then realized you have not taken in a single word for the past few minutes, that is what psychologists and neuroscientists call a lapse in meta-awareness. The same thing often happens when we drive. The monkey wants attention. Most of us would then snap out of it and turn our attention back to the book or the road. If any of this sounds familiar, that's because this constant soundtrack has been running most of your life, but it also shows you can switch it off for short periods.

"Unlike other animals, human beings spend a lot of time thinking about what is not going on around them, contemplating events that happened in the past, might happen in the future, or will never happen at all," say the authors of a report, "A Wandering Mind Is an Unhappy Mind," in the journal *Science.* "Many philosophical and religious traditions teach that happiness is to be found by living in the moment, and practitioners are trained to resist mind wandering and 'to be here now.' These traditions suggest that a wandering mind is an unhappy mind," say the authors, who tried to find out if this were true.[30]

In a series of experiments using a smartphone app to capture people at precise moments, they concluded that mind wandering is truly negative, that we do it regardless of other activities we may be engaged in and that the ability to think about what is not happening is a cognitive achievement that comes with a heavy emotional cost.

"Although negative moods are known to cause mind wandering, time-lag analyses strongly suggested that mind wandering in our sample was generally the cause, and not merely the consequence, of unhappiness," reported the authors, who found that the only exception to the rule was when people made love.

Sometimes the incessant, negative chatter will drive people over the edge. There was a time, before Eckhart Tolle was a best-selling author, when he was an extremely unhappy young man toying with the notion of suicide. *I can't live with myself* was a line constantly running through his mind. And then a strange thought occurred to him. "If *I* cannot live with *myself*, then who is this *I* and what is this *self* that I can't live with? Are we talking of two separate entities here?" he wondered.

"I was so stunned by this strange realization that my mind stopped," he says in the introduction to his book *The Power of Now*. "I was fully conscious, but there were no more thoughts. Then I felt drawn into what seemed like a vortex of energy. I could feel myself being sucked into a void. It felt as if the void was inside myself rather than outside. Suddenly, there was no more fear, and I let myself fall into that void."

Tolle believes that he achieved a level of enlightenment because his mind could not take the constant nagging a moment longer. "I knew, of course, that something profoundly significant had happened to me, but I didn't understand it at all. It wasn't until several years later, after I had read spiritual texts and spent time with spiritual teachers, that I realized that what everybody was looking for had already happened to me," he told his readers.

"People would occasionally come up to me and say, *I want what you*

have. Can you give it to me or show me how to get it? And I would say:
You have it already. You just can't feel it because your mind is making too
much noise."

The DMN is now the most-studied part of the brain, but still a lot
more needs to be learned. The network has been implicated in a number of psychiatric disorders, including autism and Alzheimer's. Tests on
animals have left scientists believing the DMN is unique to humans
and specifically to adults. In children, the network does not begin to
develop for several years and continues to expand and gain more control
as the child reaches adolescence.

In the paper "Disruptions of Functional Connectivity in the Default
Mode Network of Comatose Patients," doctors found by examining the
DMN in fourteen patients with brain damage and varying levels of consciousness "that DMN connectivity decreased in proportion to the degree
of consciousness impairment."[31] In other words, the further they drifted
from a wakeful state of consciousness, the quieter the network became.

Also stating what may appear obvious, another paper, "Resting
State Networks and Consciousness," noted that "DMN connectivity is
reduced under altered states of consciousness, such as sleep, sedation/
anesthesia, hypnotic state, and clinical states of disorders of consciousness [including] coma and brain death."[32]

One neuroanatomist working in Boston found to her shock and
surprise just what it feels like to have the network suddenly switched
off. Dr. Jill Bolte Taylor was studying how brain cells communicate
with each other as part of her research into mental illness when one
morning in December 1996 she awoke with a shattering headache. She
explains in her TEDx talk:

> I woke up to discover that I had a brain disorder of my own. A blood
> vessel exploded in the left half of my brain. And in the course of four
> hours, I watched my brain completely deteriorate.

Dr. Taylor's brain had done a *Ctrl+Alt+Del*.

I couldn't walk, talk, read, write, or recall any of my life. I essentially became an infant in a woman's body. And in that moment, my left hemisphere brain chatter went totally silent. Just like someone took a remote control and pushed the mute button. Total silence. And at first I was shocked to find myself inside a silent mind. But then I was immediately captivated by the magnificence of the energy around me. I felt enormous and expansive. I felt at one with all the energy that was, and it was beautiful there.

Because I could not identify the position of my body in space, I felt like a genie just liberated from her bottle. And my spirit soared free, like a great whale gliding through the sea of silent euphoria. Nirvana. I found nirvana. And I remember thinking, there's no way I would ever be able to squeeze the enormousness of myself back inside this tiny little body. I am the life-force power of the universe. I am the life-force power of the fifty trillion beautiful molecular geniuses that make up my form—at one with all that is!

I affectionately refer to this space as la-la land. But it was beautiful there. Imagine what it would be like to be totally disconnected from your brain chatter that connects you to the external world? So here I am in this space, and my job, and any stress related to my job—it was gone. Oh! I felt euphoria—euphoria. It was beautiful![33]

Ted's Dad and His Idea of Heaven

Ted's Dad, the composer Stephen Watkins, had a good coma as comas go. "Now that I've come back, I accept that it wasn't reality," he says. "But if somebody asked me, do you want to stay there? I would say yes."

• • •

In every scenario I was in, I was seriously ill. There was no question about that. I was never leading an alternate life where I was perfectly healthy. But within most of them, I had the expectation of getting better. But I was traveling all over the place. I was convinced I'd been in the West Indies, in New Zealand, Hanover, and Rotterdam. But I didn't know what was happening. I knew everybody was trying to be nice to me. I'm very, very lucky in that.

I imagined I was in the West Indies. The weather, the accent, all the people. And I was in hospital there with lots of very nice, caring nurses and some real characters. I loved it there. I knew my wife would like it, too. And it was all set, as soon as I got out of there, I was coming back to work as a volunteer porter. I thought, well, I've got enough money to buy a little house here and live on the beach, which isn't that different from where I live, anyway. It really was nice.

I don't know where we were exactly, but we were by the sea. There were people in Hawaii Five-0 canoes, and there was a sign warning about saltwater crocodiles. I knew I wanted to stay there. I'd love my wife to come here, all my family. I think it was because I really like that TV show Murder in Paradise. Yeah, I really like that program. Perhaps that's what it is. I like the characters. I like the fact there's a good story. And it's a lovely place. Other than the Alps, it's my idea of heaven.

When I was in the coma, I was still me. I still had all the same reactions that I have to everything. I had the same interests, the same abilities. I'm interested in sailing and I was doing that while I was there. As a musician, that's how I identify myself. All of those things were just the same.

But I never had a meal. I knew I'd never had a meal. And I'd never been to the toilet. And this didn't make any sense. In my coma world, I wasn't intubated and everything else. There was no need for that [inside the coma]. But when your mind is more awake than your body, you try to make sense of what you know hasn't happened.

"Debbie": The Guiding Hand

I was a staff nurse on a children or babies ward in a hospital in London. The beds were empty. I was dressed as English nurses used to dress in the 1940s. It was wartime but it was modern in my mind. Then it got bombed to ruins and the Nazis were coming. I had to protect this special kind of incubator. It was groundbreaking, and I think there was a baby inside. It wasn't just any old incubator but a lifesaving one that made people and children completely better and was extremely advanced for the 1940s. I was desperate that the Nazis didn't get hold of it, getting its secret design. It was the only one of its kind, but it was extremely heavy and almost like a small iron lung or something out of an old sci-fi film. It was fixed to the wall partly but its feet were on wheels. There was rubble everywhere.

There was a special type of helicopter hovering above me. I could hear it. They were trying to winch me and the incubator out but the rope was too short. The helicopter was designed by my uncle, a distant uncle from the past. He doesn't exist in real life and he had also designed that groundbreaking, lifesaving incubator, too.

The helicopter could take us back to the future. It was a very modern-day helicopter. It was a time machine. It could take us away to before the hospital was bombed. It could change the outcome, but to do so, it needed the incubator.

The hospital ward was being bombed around me. Walls were crumbling, dust was everywhere, bricks and mortar blown onto the beds in the ward. Things everywhere, blown out by bomb blasts. I could hear rubble falling, war sirens, machine-gun fire. There were abandoned green army tanks that had crashed through the wall, covered in dust and debris. I could hear the bombs, the ceiling was partly collapsed. I could hear German Nazi soldiers coming toward the big double doors.

I wasn't afraid and didn't feel in danger. I was just dumbfounded by the war zone in front of my eyes; that an actual war was going on and that I was in the 1940s and a nurse in a bombed, almost demolished, ward.

There were dead bodies on the ground that were trying to come back to life, twitching on the floor. Zombies pretending to be dead but they weren't. The Nazis were going to be got by them once they pushed through those doors. The zombies didn't look like zombies, just clothed humans covered in dust and rubble, dead on the ground but twitching, coming back to life and not horror-movie style. It was sad. The ward was in ruins, metal beds covered in dust. The noise was so loud. I ended up in a hospital corridor with huge windows either side; the lighting the whole time was dim but not pitch black, just no lights on and lots of dark shadow. In the corridor, it was silent. I was looking ahead of me.

Then a hand with a very long arm appeared; a hand and arm I recognized but couldn't place. It pulled me behind it as I ran down a passageway and pulled me away from that ward fast, before I got killed. I realized sometime after my coma that the hand and distinctive long arm belonged to a very close friend of mine who had died in real life. I recognized her hand, her long arm, but couldn't in my confusion place it and never saw her face properly. But after the coma, I remembered a birthmark on the arm and the hair, plus the height and a blurry fast-moving face. The strength in that hand and long arm I recognized as that of my friend, who had often grabbed my hand as we ran upstairs or to catch a bus, taxi, lift, anything. And I was lagging behind. She had my hand, pulling me behind her but not so I would fall.

That's all I remember about that. It was all very realistic. I could feel myself there and it all made sense.

Stephen (Continued): Swish, Swish, Swish

Stephen the statistician finds himself back in the bistro, sitting in a dark corner. Yellow sunlight creeps in through the door at the far end of the long bar. There is no barman. He gets up and makes his way behind the bar, peering down the wooden stairs into the nightclub below. He walks down the steps but quickly catches the eye of a ginger-haired cowgirl sitting at a copper-topped table. She gives him an icy stab of a stare that says, *You stay put*, which roots him in place. Listless gangster girls sing while they drink bottled beer amid the detritus of the night before; dancing dust beams of warm morning sun filter through; he smells the dank odor of wooden beer kegs and makes his way back to the street.

• • •

Outside, soft morning sunlight, quiet stores, sleeping cars, cobble street gently winding beneath lime-green tree canopy; leafy colonnade climbing to Hospital Hill Road. Now, terraced street and bright sunlight. Inside a house, small front room, sun outside. Young wife with baby in nearby cot talking to female friend, discussing something serious.

Later now, wife with husband, parents visiting, sitting on sun-warm front doorstep. Smiles, talk, laughter. Sunlit green hillsides bask beyond town. Nearby, a small corner shop. Blazing hot, high sun. I'm down low, just above the pavement, beside open display boxes of fruit, greens, groceries; I peep around the corner and see the family approaching; at shop front, water, bottled water! Cool thirst refreshment, just beyond reach.

But dismay, surprise, gray manhole cover opens. I fall away into yawning, pouring whirlpool of creamy dark colors; pulling me in; winding up, tightening, throttling.

Surface into rural car park; small, empty, isolated; dusty cracked concrete. Chicken-wire fencing all around; one single entrance, the only way out. Here, a narrow, single-track, white gravel road; beyond, fir tree forest, dark, ominous, still, quiet.

Suddenly, silence split: roaring through dust clouds, white, gold, gangster cars in relentless pursuit; charge toward entrance, then hard brake, wheels lock, crunching gravel scatters. Doors fling open, shadow shapes emerging; entrance blocked, fence enclosing . . .

Waking now, lying prostrate, looking around into gray-blue daylight. Bright window at my right, the light washing into the room. And a swish, swish; constant swish, swishing like a window blind, inducing vague feeling of irritated anxiety. Time seeming interminable; interminable hours.

And, occasionally, movement round about: blurry, slender gray creatures with elongated heads, bobbing, gliding by; ignoring me, drifting past. But now one hovers near, looms over, then glides away. And swish, swish, goes the swishing blind.

Anxiety. I've been here before, I know this, I've been here. But when? Why am I here again? Why? Why does nobody help me? When will it end? Another creature drifts by. Anxious. I want this to stop, the interminable swish, swish.

Rory (Continued): No Escape

I remember the feeling of being encased in a glass bubble. I could feel how solid it was, but that's the only recollection I have of any kind of texture. Also, in the bubble I was very, very hot. I remember that very clearly. It was almost unbearably hot. I was always thirsty but never drank anything.

I absolutely felt like I was being observed from inside a dome, but I might add that this glass bubble was very small and I was squashed inside. I honestly couldn't tell you why my mind put me inside that dome, but it was very confusing and very scary.

I think I was slowly coming out of the coma. I knew I was in hospital by this point but still didn't have a clue what was going on. However, the hospital was a wooden castle with tall battlements and flags and banners flying. I was in a huge room with a very high ceiling, and at the end was a giant wooden wall that had lots of small trapdoors that were constantly opening and closing. The people in charge were hiding behind these trapdoors. I heard them whispering things to me, saying I was going to die soon, and laughing.

My uncle then went down there to go fight them, but he collapsed. Then, next thing I knew, he was leering over my bed, his eyes were unfocused, and he was grinning an insane grin. The people behind the wooden doors had hypnotized him. I then looked over and saw my mum right across the room, sitting on a hospital bed. There was a big machine shining green lasers into her eyes. The Asian doctor sat *holding her hand, talking in her ear. I tried to scream for help but my uncle told me to be quiet or I'd be next.*

This went on for what seemed like a very long time before the scene changed to something else entirely, a mixture of totally bizarre short experiences. I was on a paddle boat. I was having fire thrown at me by my American cousin. I was forced to take heroin. I was flying around a farm with animals and people. I was cooking and I heard someone calling my name. Then everything went very dark. In the middle of the room there was a big hot tub with a cover over it. It was now almost pitch black but I could see this hot tub. I walked over to it and slowly slid the cover off. Suddenly, hands started grabbing at me, trying to pull me inside.

I remember it all vividly, like it was really happening. There was never anything good or anything positive. It was traumatizing and frightening, and there was no escape. I think the hardest part for me is that no one in my life will ever understand just what I went through. There's no help for this, it's there now forever.

5

Delirium, Hallucinations, and Something Else

Other Realities and How to Obtain Them

Conjure up an image of a magic carpet and it's likely that you will envisage a turbaned prince from *One Thousand and One Nights* soaring above glittering minarets while sitting cross-legged on an oriental rug. And while that may be the stuff of fantasy and legend, it turns out that magic or flying carpets really did exist, at least according to author Wretch Gunk in his wonderfully odd paper "Magic Carpets, Sensory Deprivation and Entheogenic Ceremonial Magick."[1]

"As with most myths, people have taken this at face value as a fantastical legend with no basis in reality," he writes. "From the occult, however, we can learn of the true spiritual practice which inspired these legends."

The ability to enter other levels of reality—and to peer behind the curtain at what may lie beyond—has fascinated humans since the first caveman nibbled on a magic mushroom. While mystics and magicians have pushed themselves to the very edge of death with potions and poisons in their search for altered states of consciousness, others have sought answers by a variety of different means. Archaeological and paleoanthropological evidence points to the use of mind-altering substances as far back as two and a half million years to the early Stone Age in diverse locations worldwide.

At other times, apparent mystic experiences and inexplicable hallucinations occur spontaneously or are the result of illness or injury. They can be induced in solitary confinement and have been recorded by polar explorers and solo voyagers. Given their reported frequency, they would appear to be a fairly common occurrence, and yet we live in a world where they are regularly dismissed as fantasy or the imaginings of deranged minds, where few ever stop to question just why the mind would wish to play such tricks. We may know what triggers some of these events, but we do not understand why the mind should conjure up such beautiful and bizarre images when they form no part of our material world.

Our understanding of these phenomena changes by the century. Some argue that the ancients—who saw them as part of the fabric of life—knew more than we might ever know and that by the loss of these arts we know less about ourselves now. If such thinking had persisted across the ages, doctors today might not be so swift to diagnose mental illness. But as a subject for scientific study, delusions, delirium, and hallucinations have taken on a new importance in the twenty-first century as scientists and computer engineers struggle to get a grip on the workings of the mind.

The way we perceive life today may just be one big hallucination and the fabric of our lives simply an illusion conjured up by the brain as it attempts to process incoming data alongside its own ideas of how things should be. This, more or less, is the view of Anil Seth, professor of cognitive and computational neuroscience at the University of Sussex. "All perceptions are acts of interpretation. They're acts of informed guesswork that the brain applies when it encounters sensory data."

In his TED talk, "Your Brain Hallucinates Your Conscious Reality," he says the world we experience comes as much, if not more, from the inside out as from the outside in:

Instead of perception depending largely on signals coming into the brain from the outside world, it depends as much, if not more, on perceptual predictions flowing in the opposite direction.

If hallucination is a kind of uncontrolled perception, then perception right here and right now is also a kind of hallucination, but a controlled hallucination in which the brain's predictions are being reined in by sensory information from the world. In fact, we're all hallucinating all the time, including right now. It's just that when we agree about our hallucinations, we call that reality.[2]

He says that we don't just actively perceive the world, we actively generate it.

The way Gunk tells it, to begin any magic carpet ride you first need a concoction of plants and herbs and often esoteric parts of a toad that you roast above a brazier. The carpet is then placed over the head while the rider inhales deeply. The carpet doesn't actually fly, he says, but the magician has an out-of-body experience and altered states of consciousness are achieved.

These carpets functioned as a means of sensory deprivation, blocking all stimulus from the outside world, which allowed the mind "to create its own visions" by putting "thought to sleep," while excluding all exterior light "so that we may pay attention to the interior light alone."

These intoxicating substances, in combination with sensory deprivation, he recounts, will take the practitioner to the "nonphysical realm of existence," and "by the same means, spirits may be terrified and disturbed. [These] cause a man to see secret visions and secret mysteries concerning the whole use of the world."

Gunk provides various recipes, many containing scopolamine, a highly poisonous chemical found in mandrake, henbane, and datura. These, he says, were also used in "flying ointments," which witches would rub all over to induce astral projection, a voluntary form of OBE.

"I must stress that these chemicals are very dangerous and it is very easy to fatally overdose," he cautions. "But even when administered correctly, they can induce long-term psychosis and open a person up to the spirit world far more permanently than they may wish."

Most of the concoctions and potions that Gunk reproduces in his paper go back to King Solomon (970–931 BCE) and his fabled book of spells known as the *Key of Solomon,* which has undergone numerous rewrites over the centuries as people sought to recreate the mystic journeys of the ancients. Typically, these include floating free of the body and traveling to mystic realms of bucolic beauty, bird-like flight, and feelings of oneness and deep understanding of the universe, together with the absence of time and space, and visions of majestic or mythical beings including—for those who appear to take a wrong turning—the hellish zones of monstrous demons and sadistic devils.

These are all features that have been reported during near-death experiences and by a large proportion of coma survivors—who are themselves undergoing an extreme form of sensory deprivation, devoid of all external stimulation. But in our modern, scientific world these are the imaginings of the deranged and the hallmark symptoms of ICU delirium.

Equally, by modern medical understanding, those sufficiently sedated to qualify as being in a deep coma state are effectively dead to the world. When Dr. E. Wesley Ely of Vanderbilt connected coma patients to an EEG machine and ran the raw data through a bispectral index, he was astonished by what he saw.

"Some sank all the way down to zero, which was far beyond the threshold for coma," he reported. Instead of the rapid on-screen scribbles of an awake patient, he noted less and less brain activity as they lost consciousness, "Moving beyond the point of being arousable, until there was just one long line of minimal electrical activity: a burst suppression. Flat line. Like a heart with no pulse. Now I knew where my patients were when they were unconscious, and it was near death."[3]

As such, coma patients cannot be delusional or delirious nor can they hallucinate because these are conscious states. And yet their minds are often far from inactive. The level of detail and the extreme clarity of vision experienced by those in coma would not appear to resemble any conventional forms of delusion, delirium, or hallucination. Nonetheless, it is by these seemingly vague terms that the coma experience is defined by most doctors. Even so, there are no clear definitions of these terms. A person lost in the desert seeing glimmering water on the horizon might be suffering any of these—or all three.

Delirium derives from the Latin *deliro-delirare* (*de-lira*, "to go out of the furrow"), which means "to deviate from a straight line, to be crazy, deranged, out of one's wits, to be silly, to dote, to rave," and is usually defined as "an acutely disturbed state of mind characterized by restlessness, illusions, and incoherence, usually as a result of intoxication, fever, and other disorders."

As a word, it first turned up in medical literature in the first century CE but did not enter English medical texts until 1592, when delirium was defined as "a weakness of conceit and consideration and a notable forgetfulness of all things almost that heretofore a man hath known."

"Despite the three millennia of delirium research, delirium remains hard to define and difficult to study," explain the authors of the paper "A Brief Review of the History of Delirium as a Mental Disorder." They go on to say: "Delirium is usually assumed to be an acute, fluctuating, transient and reversible condition caused by physical illness," but can also be seen to be irreversible, as in the case of Parkinson's. "The term 'confusion' as a synonym for delirium is in widespread use in all countries to this day," they add.[4]

The word *delusion* comes from the Latin *delusio* and is defined in most dictionaries as "an idiosyncratic belief or impression maintained despite being contradicted by reality or rational argument, typically as a symptom of mental disorder." It can, however, take many forms. A person who sees a twelve-foot pink rabbit at the foot of their bed would be considered delusional, but so might someone who believed a politician's promises. Imaginary friends—a common delusion—are often a feature of early childhood but are only considered a problem if they persist into later life.

Generally, delusions fall into two types. Nonbizarre delusions concern things that could realistically happen, like being followed or being conspired against. Bizarre delusions are less likely to happen, such as thinking one's thoughts are being broadcast on TV or imagining yourself to be the pope.

The word *hallucination* is derived from the ancient Greek *alucinari,* which means "to wander in mind or roam," and is usually defined as "a false or distorted sensory perception that appears to be real." Today, the American Psychiatric Association does leave a little more room for maneuver in its *Diagnostic and Statistical Manual of Mental Disorders,* which defines an hallucination as "a sensory perception that has the convincing sense of truth or a true perception but that occurs without external stimulation of the specific sensory organ."[5] The word first started to appear in medical textbooks in the sixteenth century, and by the mid-twentieth century it was firmly equated with mental illness.

"Originally, the term *hallucination* was applied solely to the experiences of the mentally ill," says Dr. Mitchell Liester in the paper "Toward a New Definition of Hallucination." He continues: "Now, it is applied to a wide range of phenomena. Vivid mental imagery, religious revelations, inner voices, psychotic symptoms, as well as other types of unshared sensory experiences are all subsumed under the definition of a hallucination."[6]

The fact that the term is so broad has not gone unnoticed. "I am not suggesting that we should purge the word hallucination of its association with mental illness," wrote Dr. Ian Stevenson of the University of Virginia School of Medicine back in 1983. "But we should not apply it indiscriminately to all types of sensory experiences for which we cannot immediately identify an external physical stimulus."[7]

Paranormal is generally defined as "denoting events or phenomena such as telekinesis, spiritualism, or clairvoyance, as well as a belief in ghosts and UFOs and all things that are beyond the scope of normal scientific understanding." It first entered the English language around 1920 and consists of the two words *para* and *normal,* meaning the world around us is *normal* and anything contrary to that is beyond or *para.*

The meaning of *spirituality* has developed and expanded over time but is generally considered to be "a subjective experience which is interpreted within a religious framework and comes from the Latin *spiritualitatem*." The difference between *spiritual* and *mystic* is that *spiritual* is said to relate to the spirit or soul as defined in religious terms, while *mystical* simply relates to mystics or mysticism, and a mystic is a person who seeks by contemplation and self-surrender to obtain unity with or absorption into the Deity or the absolute, or who believes in the spiritual apprehension of truths that are beyond the intellect.

"A critical definitional feature of the mystical experience is a sense of unity, or the experience of becoming one with all that exists," explain the authors of the paper "Classic Hallucinogens and Mystical Experiences." They also list the loss of time and space, feelings of euphoria, and an inability—through lack of appropriate words—to describe the experience adequately. "Mystical experiences are not similar to the altered states of consciousness associated with intoxication of many common psychoactive drugs such alcohol or opiates," the authors point out. "Mystical experiences may be accompanied by spiritual insights, but the mystical experience is not, in and of itself, simply the experience of religious or spiritual insight."[8]

According to the 2008 U.S. National Comorbidity Survey, more than a quarter of the general population has at one time or another had an experience that would appear to qualify as mystical, although they prefer to use the term *psychotic-like experience,* which includes lucid dreaming and delusional ideas, OBEs, telepathy, extrasensory perception, and auditory or visual hallucinations.[9]

Most people who experience such events tend to keep them firmly to themselves or risk being labelled delusional or insane in a world that insists such things cannot happen. Roberta Moore is a retired college professor. When she was about twelve years old, she had a spontaneous out-of-body experience and found herself pressed up close to the ceiling. She recalled for us:

I was quite astonished, shocked, terrified. It was my first little hint that the world doesn't function in the materialistic way I'd been taught. So I just kept it to myself and didn't tell anyone. I certainly couldn't tell my parents. They'd say I was just dreaming. But I was wide awake. I knew that this was a real experience.

Events like these, says Moore, are far more common than people imagine.

Just start talking to friends and neighbors, and they turn up all the time. But people don't like to openly talk about it because it's a taboo subject. And when they do talk about it, they're shut down.

The event, and subsequent other spiritual experiences, set Roberta on a path of discovery that eventually led her to explore near-death experiences. Even though she had been nowhere near death—and says she has always been "perfectly healthy"—she eventually became vice president of IANDS, and today has her own YouTube channel devoted to NDEs, drawing visitors from all over the world.[10]

The real turning point, she says, was when she had an encounter with what she terms a being of light.

This light is really the heart of the NDE and the most transformative aspect of it. But it's also known as the mystical experience, the heart of all religions. I'd been praying, and I got the full-blown being of light. I was engulfed in the light! I began to research and found what I experienced came close to the NDE. So, really, an NDE contains the kernel of a mystical experience, which can happen and does happen, even when you're not in a near-death state. These things don't always happen in a discrete period of time. And once they start to occur, they unfold over time.

The first scientific attempts to understand spontaneous mystical experiences, simply seen as hallucinations, began in the early nineteenth century when pioneering French psychiatrist Jean-Étienne Esquirol defined hallucinations as "the conviction of perceiving a sense to which there is no external object." Although he believed that hallucinations were a disorder in their own right, by the end of the century—and the emergence of psychiatry as an independent branch of medicine—it was generally assumed that hallucinations were a symptom of a range of psychiatric disorders and little else.

In the late nineteenth century, the London-based Society for Psychical Research carried out the first scientific study of hallucinations in normal people. In all, more than fourteen thousand men and women were interviewed and those with any form of mental illness were excluded. They found that nearly 8 percent of men and 12 percent of women had experienced at least one vivid hallucination, which they generally interpreted as spiritual, mystical, or paranormal. Visual hallucinations were more common than auditory hallucinations.[11] The study was repeated soon after the Second World War with very similar findings.

Historically, they were in good company. Alexander the Great, Julius Caesar, Napoleon Bonaparte, Winston Churchill, Mohandas Gandhi, Martin Luther King Jr., and General George Patton all reportedly experienced hallucinations. When "Old Blood and Guts" Patton was pinned down by machine-gun fire during the First World War, he recounted in his memoirs seeing his grandfather and great-uncles looking down on him from the clouds. *Get up and fight!* they told him. He did and won the Distinguished Service Cross that day.

In 1760, Swiss philosopher Charles Bonnet wrote up the experiences of his grandfather, who suffered strange visual hallucinations following blindness due to secondary cataracts. He concluded that in the absence of fresh visual data, the brain filled in the blanks by recalling previously stored images. These included landscapes—such as mountains and waterfalls—animals, insects, and imaginary creatures—such as dragons—and people dressed in clothes from earlier times. But it was not until 1967 that Swiss scientist Georges de Morsier finally gave the condition the name Charles Bonnet syndrome.

"Hallucinations will occur more frequently with eyes open and will disappear when the eyes close or visual gaze changes," noted two Chicago doctors, Tiffany Jan and Jorge del Castillo, in their paper "Visual

Hallucinations: Charles Bonnet Syndrome," adding that while older people are more susceptible, the syndrome has been noted in all ages.[12]

The authors reported the case of an elderly woman with rapidly
deteriorating eyesight who turned up at the emergency department of
her local hospital complaining of curious, episodic visions lasting hours
at a time in which she would see household items, such as clocks and
plants, moving of their own accord or people and faces clinging to the
ceiling or hovering in the corners of rooms.

"Up to 60 percent of patients with Charles Bonnet syndrome are
hesitant to tell their physician about their visual hallucinations for
fear of being labeled with a mental illness or dementia," they noted.
"Misdiagnosis is also common as the syndrome is not recognized by clinicians and often labeled as psychosis, delirium or early dementia."

Other known causes of visual hallucinations include retinal disease,
migraines, acute stroke, drug-related side effects, neurodegenerative
disease, alcohol and/or drug use, toxic infections involving the brain,
and psychiatric illness. In psychotic conditions such as schizophrenia,
hallucinations have been linked with dysfunction of the DMN. These
hallucinations can be categorized as simple or complex. Simple hallucinations involve basic imagery, such as lights, colors, lines, and shapes,
while complex hallucinations include images of people, objects, or specific scenes.

People suffering from Parkinson's disease regularly report vivid hallucinations and forms of delirium that include seeing animals or people,
such as furry creatures running about or deceased loved ones sitting in
the room. People with Alzheimer's disease and other degenerative brain
diseases regularly experience delusions and hallucinations ranging from
visions of people and animals to delusions about themselves, often offering complex but highly inaccurate descriptions of their lives and past
occupations.

Patients recovering from open-heart surgery often report auditory
or visual hallucinations, and around 30 percent of these patients apparently go on to develop various forms of psychosis. A lack of visual stimulation is believed to play a major part, and "upon recovery these patients

described their postoperative environment as a major pathogenic factor in producing their psychiatric illness," concluded Dr. Donald Kornfeld in his paper "Psychiatric Complications of Open-Heart Surgery."[13]

Anecdotal accounts of shipwrecked sailors and others on solo voyages regularly include delusions and vivid hallucinations, often thought to have been brought on by sleep deprivation and fatigue, together with a degree of wishful thinking. Ancient mariners frequently reported false landfalls, sea serpents, and mermaids.

In his bestseller of 1900, *Sailing Alone Around the World*, Joshua Slocum recounted a dose of food poisoning that knocked him out. He awoke to find his sloop plunging into heavy seas. "And looking out through the companionway, to my amazement I saw a tall man at the helm. *I am the pilot of the Pinta come to aid you. Lie quiet, Señor Captain, and I will guide your ship tonight.*" Although in Slocum's recollection the line between hallucination and reality became blurred, he claimed to owe thanks to the pilot for keeping his little vessel on course.[14]

During the 1986 Solo Trans-Tasman Yacht Challenge, David Adams suffered a series of mishaps that led to a near-total lack of sleep. "By day eight, I discovered just what happens when you push yourself too hard. I started hallucinating. I still remember it vividly. There was a full crew on board with me. I didn't recognize any of the faces, and I wasn't quite sure how they got there, but there they were, sailing the boat. I was playing the traditional owner's role of standing down the back, adjusting the running backstays (though in reality I was steering), while these blokes were running around the deck doing all the work."[15]

In her 1933 memoir, *A Woman in the Polar Night*, Christiane Ritter recounted seeing monsters resembling the Mahaha, a demon that terrorizes the Arctic and tickles its victims to death, and spoke of "dissolving in the moonlight as though it were eating us up."[16] Such sightings are so common among the hunters of the far north that they have a word for it—*ran*, meaning "strange experiences."

At the height of the witch hunts of the sixteenth century, confessions were forced from women considered suspicious and others by depriving them of sleep for days, even weeks, at a time. They were then questioned about their delusions and hallucinations, and these were treated as confessions. This was known as "waking the witch."

Much of the witch hysteria of this period is thought to have been driven by hallucinations as a result of the diet at that time. From the fourteenth to seventeenth centuries, as the result of a succession of plagues, wars, and famines, and localized climate change, rye proved easier to grow than other grains and became a staple. But these changes boosted the ergot fungus, found in rye, which contains lysergic acid, the main component of lysergic acid diethylamide (LSD).

Those who claimed to be bewitched—or were seen to be acting in a suspiciously witch-like way—were possibly experiencing an acid trip, in which reality becomes distorted, frequently proving to be terrifying for the uninitiated. It was not until the Age of Rationalism in the mid-eighteenth century that these symptoms were reimagined by the church as religious ecstasy, mystical visions, devotional trances, apparitions of the Virgin Mary and other saints, and feelings of bliss, love, and oneness—in this case, with the Christian God.

Disturbing visual effects are reported by prisoners confined for lengthy durations to dark cells, a phenomenon known as the prisoner's cinema. In most cases, people are treated to dramatic light shows featuring fantastic geometric patterns, but the hallucinations can also include shapes, faces, figures, places, and visual excursions to other apparent realities. Such strange effects have also been noted by long-distance drivers at night, pilots, and astronauts.

During the 1950s and 1960s, numerous experiments were designed to induce hallucinations and other mystic phenomena in healthy individuals. Many of these involved the ingestion of hallucinogenic substances and different forms of sensory deprivation. The conclusion, in many trials, was that these anomalous experiences occur in "highly suggestible individuals" who have a tendency to mistake imaginary events as real.

"Hallucinatory experiences, such as hearing voices when no one is present, or seeing objects that are not really there, are commonly thought of as symptoms of severe mental illness, most commonly schizophrenia," says medical researcher Abdullah Alotaibi in his paper "A Neuroimaging Investigation into Hallucination Proneness in a Healthy Population." He adds, "However, research conducted during the past few decades has increasingly revealed evidence that these kinds of experiences are not confined to people who regard themselves, or are regarded by others, as mentally unwell. [They are] relatively frequent in the general population."[17]

In one recent study, the authors of "Predicting Psychotic-Like Experiences during Sensory Deprivation" reported that just fifteen minutes in a sensory deprivation room completely devoid of light and sound was more than enough to induce these effects in almost anyone, without the need for any drugs or potions, and that fantasy proneness played no part in the reported hallucinations.[18]

More than two hundred volunteers took part in the study and were tested beforehand for their predisposition for seeing things that are not there by completing the Revised Hallucination Scale, which asks participants to answer true or false to questions such as: *No matter how hard I try to concentrate, unrelated thoughts always creep into my mind; I have been troubled by hearing voices in my head;* and *On occasion I have seen a person's face in front of me when no one was in fact there.*

To see the effects across a range of individuals, participants were selected in both the upper and lower ratings. They were then placed in a padded room with a panic button nearby, and all lights and sounds were shut out.

"Both high and low hallucination prone groups responded to sensory deprivation in a qualitatively similar manner," they reported, adding: "Increased anxiety, fantasy proneness, and suggestibility were characteristics of the high-scoring group, but only anxiety was found to be a predictor of psychosis-like experiences in sensory deprivation."

They concluded that the brain has a need to create images where none exist and that hallucinations happen because the brain tries to make sense of the experience. This is termed "faulty source monitoring," in which the brain misattributes the source of sensory input. In a similar vein, amputees can experience itchy toes where none exist, and those with progressive hearing loss often report auditory hallucinations, such as doors slamming or the calling of their name.

Musical ear syndrome affects thousands globally and can mistakenly be linked with dementia. Sufferers report hearing a range of musical instruments, from solo performances through to full orchestras. Some hear simple melodies; others hear highly complex pieces of music. The effect generally accompanies profound hearing loss in later life and can cause breakdowns in relationships and feuds with neighbors. There is no known cure.

Turning it to their advantage, Mozart, Wagner, and Schumann all claimed they could hear music from sources unexplained but were lucky enough to be able to write down what they were apparently hearing, to the delight of audiences ever since.

Most healthy people are prone to the creation of alternative realities, says Professor Paul Fletcher, a psychiatrist at Cambridge University. "We are inherently pattern-seeking and we readily impose patterns based on our prior expectations and experience in order to make some sort of sense of things," he told us, adding that the narrative or pattern that we construct will be rooted in our own mental life and preoccupations. He went on to say:

> I tend to think of the whole brain-mind system as struggling to make sense of noisy, ambiguous sensory inputs and doing so by achieving a balance of what the inputs are telling us and what makes sense in light of what we already know. So we are always superimposing our expectations onto the world. This may result in things being combined in very novel and seemingly bizarre ways, constructing a very different picture of the world, and one that may be greatly influenced by prevailing emotions, such as fear or anger.

LETTING THE MIND DRIFT

In 1942, at the height of the Second World War, Japanese forces invaded the Indonesian island of Java. Amid the chaos, three Dutch civilians were captured and confined in near-darkness to a single room in a large, quiet house. They would stay there for nearly three years. They soon realized they might all go mad if they had nothing to occupy their minds, so they came up with a remarkable solution. They would each attempt to create something purely within their minds. Alan recalls the account from his own memory, as he has not been able to pin down the source where he read it long ago. Their story goes something like this.

The first man worked backward through the days, remembering each and every detail as he wound back the clock in his imagination, meticulously remembering his way in reverse through the minutes, hours, days, weeks, and months until he made his way back to happier times. And then he stayed there. He spent his days having picnics with his girl on the banks of the Dintel, drinking beer and *jenever* under the dappled shade of an elm, and kicking a ball about with his mates from college.

The second man, whose background was hospitality, decided to build and equip the finest hotel in the world. He selected the perfect location and gently modified the land around and then he began to construct his hotel brick by brick. Each room took up his full attention. He chose the wallpaper, the light fittings, the carpets, and all the furniture and then arranged all the flowers. Staff were interviewed and selected, then dressed in the finest livery that he had designed himself. He was in full flow, landscaping the grounds and stocking the botanical gardens, when the door to his cell was eventually yanked opened by nationalist militia.

The third man was a keen gardener who decided to imagine the most perfect rose possible. It got to the point where he could see his rose in stunning 360 degrees in every shade of light from sunrise to sunset. Just then, one of his companions spoke up. "*Godverdomme!*" he hissed. "Which one of you is it? Who's got the bloody soap?"

"Well, it ain't me," said the second man. "I thought I was going crazy. I've been smelling roses all damn morning!"

The chances are that there was nothing particularly special about these men; they just had the notion and the opportunity to alter their consciousness as a survival tactic. And it worked for them because they had determination and little else to interrupt their concentration. Through a form of self-hypnosis, they had created and maintained their own reality. Consciousness, they discovered, is literally a state of mind and one open to many means of alteration.

Not unlike Buddhist monks who meditate for hours each day, these men, by eliminating all possible distractions, had sufficiently enhanced their powers of concentration to bring other realities into clear focus. In the same way, a monk might focus on a single pebble for hours at a time to recall in exquisite detail scenes from past lives. The Buddha could apparently recall more than five hundred such lives this way.

In one sense, these men were lucky to be sharing their cell and not undergoing the experience alone. "Even a few days of solitary confinement will predictably shift the EEG pattern toward an abnormal pattern characteristic of stupor and delirium," says Dr. Stuart Grassian, a psychiatrist at Harvard Medical School for over twenty-five years.

Solitary confinement—which he defines as the confinement of a prisoner alone in a cell for all, or nearly all, of the day with minimal environmental stimulation and minimal opportunity for social interaction—can cause serious long-term problems. "Indeed, the psychiatric harm caused by solitary confinement had become exceedingly apparent well over one hundred years ago," he says.

During his career, Grassian had the opportunity to evaluate the psychiatric effects of solitary confinement in well over two hundred prisoners in various state and federal penitentiaries. What he learned, he says, is also of major concern for many groups of patients, including those in intensive care units, immobilized spinal patients, and those with impairment of their sensory apparatus, such as eye-patched or hearing-impaired patients. In his paper "Psychiatric Effects of Solitary Confinement," he maintains:

Most individuals have at one time or another experienced, at least briefly, the effects of intense monotony and inadequate environmental stimulation. After even a relatively brief period of time in such a situation, an individual is likely to descend into a mental torpor or "fog," in which alertness, attention, and concentration all become impaired.

Over time, the very absence of stimulation causes whatever stimulation is available to become noxious and irritating. In solitary confinement, ordinary stimuli become intensely unpleasant and small irritations become maddening.[19]

All manner of hallucinations, from geometric patterns through to vivid and complex scenes, are common among prisoners in solitary, often after only a few days. The lack of environmental stimulation together with social isolation "are strikingly toxic to mental functioning, producing a stuporous condition associated with perceptual and cognitive impairment and affective disturbances," Grassian writes.

During the Korean War (1950–1953), fears that the Chinese were brainwashing captured NATO soldiers and airmen by submitting them to sensory deprivation prompted a string of research projects in the United States, Canada, and Europe. In one such experiment, McGill University psychologist Donald Hebb was commissioned to see what happens when humans experience a complete lack of sensory data. The results astonished all concerned.

A number of college students were recruited and paid twenty dollars a day, a veritable fortune at the time. They were given a comfortable bed in a tiny cubicle and fitted with translucent plastic goggles, cotton gloves, and cardboard tubes extending beyond the fingertips to restrict all perception by touch. A faint air-conditioning hum filled their cell, masking all other sound. They could stay there for as long as they wished but, as it turned out, few could manage even a week.

At first, the students were content to sit in silence, thinking about their studies, but soon this became too much effort and they were "content to let the mind drift." What happened next surprised the researchers. "Many of them, after long isolation, began to see images," recalled a colleague of Hebb, the delightfully named Woodburn Heron, in a 1957 article for *Scientific American*.[20]

"One man repeatedly saw a vision of a rock shaded by a tree; another kept on seeing pictures of babies and could not get them out of his head," he wrote. But not until one of the research team went through the isolation experience himself "did we realize the power and strangeness of the phenomenon," said Heron.

At first, the students saw dots of light, lines, or simple geometric patterns. Then the visions became more complex, with abstract patterns or recognizable figures, such as "rows of little yellow men with black caps on and their mouths open." One subject reported a procession of squirrels with sacks over their shoulders, marching purposefully across his visual field. Another saw prehistoric animals walking about in the jungle, while another saw a procession of reading glasses marching down a street.

"Usually, the subjects were at first surprised and amused by these phenomena, looked forward eagerly to see what was going to happen next and found that the pictures alleviated their boredom," said Heron. "But after a while, the pictures became disturbing and so vivid that they interfered with sleep. They found sometimes that they could even scan the scene, taking in new parts as they moved their eyes as if they were looking at real pictures."

Not all the hallucinations were visual. One subject reportedly heard the people he was visualizing clearly talking. Another man repeatedly heard a music box, and another could hear a choir singing "in full stereophonic sound." Others felt particular sensations, with one recalling being hit on the arm by pellets fired from a miniature spaceship. Several reported bodies lying beside them. "My mind seemed to be a ball of cotton wool floating above my body," said one. "Something seemed to be sucking my mind out through my eyes," recounted another.

As to precisely what was happening to the students inside their minds, nobody could conclude. The researchers did note, however, that "prolonged exposure to a monotonous environment has definitely deleterious effects," and they speculated that visual perception becomes disturbed, prompting hallucinations as the brain waves change. "A changing sensory environment seems essential for human beings. Without it," they concluded, "the brain ceases to function in an adequate way and abnormalities of behavior develop."

WHEN SCIENCE BECOMES SURREAL

Maurice Jean Jacques Merleau-Ponty (1908–1961) was a hero of the French Resistance, a close friend of author Jean-Paul Sartre, and a phenomenological philosopher who was fascinated by the question of consciousness. He believed that anyone suffering a hallucination could distinguish it from reality but that they were misled by the hallucination all the same, so he set out to see if he was right.

Among his patients, he had a number with peculiar delusions that took hallucinogenic forms. One patient claimed to see a man wearing particular clothes and standing at the same spot in his garden every day. A female patient regularly heard voices, and one man, whenever he shook hands with his doctor, had the firm belief that the doctor's hand was in reality a guinea pig. Merleau-Ponty's bright idea was to present each patient with a real version of the hallucination. When he played the deluded woman a gramophone recording of a voice similar to the one she described, she immediately cottoned on, pointing to the gramophone and saying that these were not her voices.

The patient who saw the man standing in the garden was apparently "astonished" but he did point out that somebody entirely different was now standing in his garden, although he did not say whether he could now see two people. Sadly, Merleau-Ponty does not appear to have recorded how the gentleman with the guinea pig handshake reacted.

It is hard to say what anybody might realistically conclude from such experiments, but Merleau-Ponty came away believing that hallucinations were the mind's way of summoning up images in the absence of the appropriate worldly cues, which is largely where we are today. He did not, however, appear to know why. Almost a century later, and modern science is still struggling with the same questions and no nearer to finding the answers.

Komarine Romdenh-Romluc is a senior lecturer in philosophy and an author who has written extensively on Merleau-Ponty. She said in an interview that Merleau-Ponty concluded that "hallucinations are nevertheless akin to sensory experiences insofar as they result from the exercise of perceptual capacities." In other words, they seem real because the mind makes them so. According to Merleau-Ponty, the subject "makes use of his sensory fields and his natural insertion into the world to build up an artificial world." She says, "This is why hallucinating subjects describe their hallucinations in sensory terms."

In lieu of any other means, one may wonder how else they might describe a voice or the furry touch of a guinea pig? Every coma survivor that we interviewed described the experience in the same terms that they might describe any daily event, with the rich detail of sight, sound, smell, and touch, pain and pleasure. They tend to describe their experiences mostly in terms of delusion and hallucination because that is the diagnosis they have been given. But, when questioned, many will say their experiences were in every sense real to them and do not resemble hallucinations in any classic definition. These are memories of equal emotional impact to any in real life.

Often, another major difference is the duration of the experience, with many coma survivors recounting events that encompass not just days but decades. Hallucinations generally are fleeting affairs, with the experience rarely lasting more than a single day at most. And while there are numerous accounts of people hallucinating an alternative reality, there would appear to be no accounts in the medical annals of people hallucinating an alternate existence or another life that spans decades.

We contacted a number of the world's leading authorities on hallucination and showed them the account that follows, as told to us by Nikki Milne in Edinburgh. We asked if this account resembled any hallucination from their experience or if they thought it could be rightly considered a hallucination within the generally accepted use of the word. Not one answered in the affirmative.

"The chief difference," Professor Michael Tye of the University of Texas at Austin told us, is that the account "is extremely vivid and long-lasting."

"A basic part of the definition of hallucinations is that they occur in clear consciousness," Professor Charles Fernyhough, a developmental psychologist at Durham University, told us. "Since coma is defined in terms of the absence of consciousness, I wouldn't have thought that it would make sense to describe such experiences as hallucinations."

"Nikki relates an extraordinary story and one that is not clearly ICU delirium or hallucinations," says James Bernat, professor of neurology at Dartmouth's Geisel School of Medicine. "One point I have made to patients who later reported experiences they recalled from a time they were thought to be fully unconscious is that, in some unconscious states, consciousness may become restored gradually over time and a patient's awareness may resume at a moment before doctors know that the patient has regained consciousness. In that interval, it is possible for patients to have thoughts, feelings, hopes, fears, and dreams that later are memorable. Although I lack any medical details of Nikki's illness, obviously she recovered consciousness, and therefore it is possible that this process explains her memories. Her vibrant and intense account of them resemble vivid dreams that, as in her case, patients later may report in great detail and with profound emotional valence."

The theory that the mind somehow scrambles to make sense of the missing period of time during coma, by creating another possible reality, is one that numerous doctors have put forward. We asked one of the world's leading experts on false memories to give us her take on Nikki's account. Did it ring true as a genuine memory or as something that she or her mind may have conjured up?

Professor Elizabeth Loftus, who is an expert in human memory, did not see any immediate similarity with either and suggested that Nikki was simply dreaming. "Obviously, in dreams, all sorts of detailed events happen, but they really don't happen," she said. When pressed about the sheer detail in the account and that dreams do not generally have much lasting impact psychologically, Professor Loftus pointed out, "Some people have very detailed false memories, often after they have spent a lot of time rehearsing and thinking about them."

Additionally, we showed Nikki's account to Professor Fletcher, who expressed surprise, describing it as "utterly stunning" and adding he had "no idea it would be so detailed and vivid. It's the sort of thing we could see as an isolated, albeit amazing, one-off phenomenon but, from the sound of it, you're seeing a pattern of such experiences, which has to suggest some commonality to the mechanisms by which they arise." Conventional ideas, he concluded, "may be well off the mark and totally inadequate for explaining this."

Nikki's account of her time within coma does not appear to resemble other instances of delusion, delirium, or hallucination. Logically, it must be something else. Her story follows.

Nikki: The Baby with the Ice-Blue Eyes

I was in coma for thirty-four days, and I was a vegetable on full life support for several months after. Within the coma, I had continuous coma dreams and nightmares. I think about some on a daily basis, and they're now part of my long-term memory; so confusing, as I know they didn't happen in reality, but in my head and heart they are just as real to me as actual memories of real events.

I found myself on a maternity train in India. On the train, there were basic amenities, the walls were once white, the paint was peeling away, revealing the chipboard. The floor was old wooden boards, varnished originally but worn now, and recently polished but a little dusty. There were wooden blinds on the windows allowing some parallel bars of light into the carriage, thin curtains blowing in the tiny bit of breeze, which gave some relief from the intense heat.

There was a lot of hustle and bustle in the corridors, although I never saw anyone. I could hear other women groaning in pain, self-soothing in time with the rattling movement of the train.

Within the small carriage, there was a small wooden bench, a thin bed draped in a busy, faded, multicolored material. Hanging next to the bed was a cloth baby hammock. On a shelf, there were a few traditional nappies, blankets, towels, and a preloved little bodysuit. All were off-white, gray. You could tell at some point they were white.

In the corner, a wee stand stood with a steel washbowl and jug of water, towel, and washcloth. Above it was an old square mirror, tarnished black around the sides.

The smell was an overpowering mixture of spices, dust, sweat, and bodily fluids, all reacting with the intense heat. I was wearing a salwar kameez without the trousers. I remember thinking that's convenient, being comfortable in the unbearable heat. Sweat was dripping from my forehead, stinging my eyes.

Instinctively, I knew I was in labor. I was in intense pain but not in labor like I experienced previously. This time it was an intense, all-over body pain; my chest unbearably heavy, every breath harder than the one before.

The whole labor process I was alone, helpless, and scared for my baby. Inevitably, my body was doing what it needed to do. I wasn't in control any more. I remember scanning the unhygienic carriage. Next, I look down. I have a tiny, pink baby in my arms. I grab a towel and swaddle him, drying him.

I lie on the bed feeling so overwhelmed by the rush of emotions, of amazement, love, connection, fulfillment filling my whole body. Tears rolling down my face while taking in all his tiny features. The smell of my newborn son, you never forget. Time stood still. The pain stopped. In those moments nothing else mattered, a true moment of blissful happiness, love, and contentment.

As I held this beautiful bundle in my arms, he opened his eyes. My breath was taken away by the lightest of eyes, ice-blue like the sea. They were not black like his brother's. I was shocked at how different he was to his brother. This would later haunt me.

I believe it's natural when you have other babies, you compare them to your first. He was so different, darker complexion, some dark hair, chunkier, longer, his own unique person.

Feeling tired, I fed him and took him carefully over to the steel bowl, holding the wall to steady myself as the train rocked and rolled. I washed his soft hair and tiny body, dried him and attempted to do a real cloth nappy. I knew it was a feeble attempt, but I was so tired.

I needed rest. I swaddled him again and I laid him, peacefully asleep, in the hammock.

I lay down next to him and went to sleep. I was awoken by tiny squawking. As I put my hand down to get him out to settle him, I looked down. My hand and he were covered in poo! I can still remember the putrid smell.

I rewashed him again, attempting to do another nappy, worried the same would happen. I began shouting for help, but no one came. I left the carriage with him in my arms, searching and searching the crowded train, asking, pleading for help. No one would help. They only bowed their heads to me.

As if by magic, the train stopped. I walked down the wee steps, and I was met by a very stern, stereotypical, traditional matron from the 1960s. She met me with a half smile, took my baby, and directed me to the wheelchair. While she held him, her body language softened and she spoke in a soft calming voice, "Let me look at you, prince." Readjusting his blanket and looking directly at him, she gasped: "What beautiful and magical eyes, little man!"

Then, just like a blink of an eye, I was in a normal maternity unit, presumably in Scotland, familiar and modern. Once I was settled in a clean, white, bright maternity ward, all the nurses would come to see his magical eyes. On his cot, there was the little blue bear name tag displaying "Baby Mason." All the nurses would visit Baby Mason purely to see his eyes that bored deep into your soul.

The next part is where I have many mixed emotions. A few years later, this coma dream would become reality. While in the process of waking and regaining consciousness, I was extremely distressed and confused, as my family would show me picture and videos of my son Mackenzie but none of Baby Mason. The pain and confusion were heartbreaking and frustrating.

Weeks and months passed with me unable to speak due to the tracheostomy and ventilator damage and being physically paralyzed. As I got strength back, and I was improving, and after months of therapy, I began to communicate. First, I would just rock my arms like

I had a baby in them. But I was given more pictures of Mackenzie. I would become angry, frustrated, and distressed, but my family and nurses didn't know why.

Later, when I was able to talk again, I explained the whole story to my husband. But how to explain reality and coma dreams? This was the hardest thing of this whole event. I can remember Mason's smell, touch, every part of him—including his magical eyes and the whole birth story—but it didn't happen. Yet I'm left with all these emotions, like my heart was ripped out. I lost my baby.

Coming to terms with the fact that Mason didn't physically exist is extremely difficult. I feel the loss of a child after experiencing the overpowering love for him. It's no different from my "real" sons. Mason still follows me around daily in my thoughts. Some days I have happy thoughts of the short time I spent with him; other days I feel his loss immensely and it breaks my heart.

It wasn't until two years later that I went to get professional psychological counseling. My feelings were ripping me apart, inside and out. I was grieving for a baby that never existed, plus all the consequences of having a near-death experience. It was just too much for one person to cope with.

With the help I was given, it allowed me to open up about my experiences. But also, in a weird way, it gave me permission to feel what I felt and experienced. And I started to grieve for Mason, as he was real and very much part of me. Then, the twist in fate when I was given the gift of my baby Ruaridh [Red King in Old Scottish].

Leaving hospital [after the coma], I was told I wouldn't be able to carry another child. While this was sad, to be honest, it wasn't something I was thinking about. My thoughts, and all my strength, were to get stronger and better for Mackenzie and my husband.

Fast forward nine months, and I started to get sick. Pregnancy was far from anyone's mind, including mine, and especially the doctors'. I wouldn't have planned this, but my pregnancy saved me and my family. I have never been so grateful for anything. It made me push myself and become a better version of the new me. My relationship with Mackenzie slowly got where it was before. We, as a family, were so happy, truly happy. I felt amazing. The pregnancy went amazing and, in all honestly, I didn't think of Mason at all.

The memory of the day we met our new son will forever be bittersweet. The labor and delivery went well, and I had a healthy, happy baby in my arms again. As the midwife was doing the health check, she let out a gasp. "Wow!" she said. "His eyes! His magical eyes! They're a blue I've never seen before."

My husband and I both stared at each other, and all the memories of Baby Mason came flooding back.

Our new baby was named Ruaridh, and it's taken me years of counseling to come to terms with it and process the similarities between Mason and Ruaridh. But they are two very different babies.

People would always comment on his very special eyes. It would reduce me to tears. I felt confused and guilty for my feelings. It was hard to process and, well, it's hard for anyone to understand my reality.

I'm thankful for the support of my husband. He knows and accepts Baby Mason as part of our family. He is included in subtle little ways that only my husband and I know, but it means the world to me.

I should add that I was pregnant when I went into the coma, and I was given a medical abortion, as they thought I could have internal bleeding. Sadly, I don't remember being pregnant, but my husband knew, and he was totally freaked out when he saw me rocking a baby while not being able to talk.

6

Apaches and Poets
A Reality Greater than a Mind Could Possibly Bear

At the height of the Great Depression, American anthropologist Morris E. Opler set out on a mystical quest. Early Spanish writings had told of a plant "which the native people call peyote and which they venerate as though it were a deity." He was on the trail of *Anhalonium lewinii,* a tiny gray-green cactus that was rumored to sing and talk and to guide its devotees to the ultimate reality. We now know that it is rich in the psychoactive ingredients tyramine, hordenine, pellotine, anhalonidine, and, primarily, mescaline.

In the summer of 1935, Opler gained access to the Mescalero Indian Reservation in New Mexico, where he found Antonio, the oldest surviving member of the Lipan Apaches and one of the few people to retain knowledge of this magical plant.[1] The Lipan Apaches had once held a vast territory stretching from the Mexican state of Chihuahua right up to Colorado. The Spanish conquistadors could never subdue these warlike people, and it was not until 1880 that a combined force of Mexican and U.S. troops finally wiped them off the map. A handful of survivors were dumped on the reservation of their archenemies, the Mescaleros.

According to the writings, this strange, button-like cactus was an entity as fully conscious and aware as any living being. It could open the doors of perception and irreparably alter a person's views on life, the universe, and just about everything. But it was also a tricky character that could turn viciously nasty against those who refused to take it seriously.

"I don't recommend anyone to imbibe this cacti lightly!" Larry Shroyer told us via Quora.com, recounting a number of peyote experiences. "This is not something you want to eat and go to the laundromat or Walmart."

He cautions that the setting and those around you are of vital importance. "I would have an experienced person or two," he says. "Don't imbibe around people that are evil or dishonest or have bad agendas because about the time you start looking at the trees as 'tall people' you don't want jerks around. It's really hard to explain the peyote road to anyone who hasn't been there. Your spiritual eyes will be opened like never before. Trust me on this. You will probably never look at life the same again. You will be communing with God. My first time was eighteen hours of intense vision and absorption of the natural realm. People that think plants can't talk have never eaten peyote. Plants do speak very loudly and they don't lie—like people—so be prepared."

One explanation for the apparent ability of plants to communicate with humans is that we share similar chemistry. Botanists now know that plants communicate among themselves and with other species by using messenger molecules called amines. In humans, amines moderate emotion, meaning, and awareness. In both cases, these amines share the same molecular antecedents.

Preparation for the journey and the correct mindset are also essential. "Don't play games with Mr. Peyote or he'll kick your butt like it was never kicked before. It will open your eyes to so much that you will need time to process all of these new life lessons.

"Above all, be humble and not cocky. Peyote has a way of being the great leveler and cocky people will get their inflated egos busted like a pin pricking a balloon. Think of it like looking at yourself in a mirror, through a magnifying glass. Handle with care and respect. I can't say anything more," Shroyer says.

The writer Robert Anton Wilson, in his 1977 autobiographical book *Cosmic Trigger*, recalls various encounters with a little green man during and after his peyote journeys. This "spirit of the plant" was well known to the Lipan Apaches, who called him Mescalito.

> I was weeding in the garden and a movement in the adjoining cornfield caught my eye. I looked that way and saw a man with warty green skin and pointy ears, dancing.
>
> This experience had all the qualities of waking reality and differed only in intensity. The entity in the cornfield had been more beautiful, more charismatic, more divine than anything I could consciously imagine when using my literary talents to portray a deity. As the mystics of all traditions say so aggravatingly, Those who have seen, know.[2]

Opler found that Antonio was only too happy to open up on the mysteries of this curious cactus. His people had acquired the knowledge from the Carrizo people in happier days and had since passed it on to their new companions, the Mescaleros. Peyote grew like weeds in Lipan country in both Mexico and in Texas, growing especially well around the Rio Grande near the border. "If you are having a hard time finding them," Antonio explained, "when you find just one by itself you eat it. When it takes effect, when you get a little dizzy, you will hear a noise like the wind from a certain direction. Go over there. You will find many of them. When you see one, another appears and so on, till they all come out just like stars."

The key for any peyote ceremony, Antonio told the anthropologist, is to find a chief peyote and then lots of little ones. The buttons must be carefully sliced away from the roots and the fuzzy coating scrapped off. The chief peyote must be brushed until perfectly round.

Whenever the Lipan's shaman felt like holding a peyote party—a male-only event—he would beat his drums, and, one by one, those of

the tribe who wanted to take part would stroll over to the specially prepared tepee, which was decked out in sage—virtually the only other
plant the peyote could abide. But first they had to scrub themselves
clean, smear mint all over, and brush their hair with an agave leaf.

"The Peyote Leader [shaman] is the one in charge there," Opler
recorded. "But the Chief Peyote is the main one to look to. This Chief
Peyote is pretty tough. It watches what's going on. It keeps everything
straight. It is a plant, but it can see and understand better than a man.
If someone has wrong thoughts, he had better look out or he will go
crazy."

The ceremony begins with chanting, singing, and the beating of
drums. The smaller peyote, now dried, are laid out in front of the shaman. The chief peyote sits alone on a bed of sage. Antonio explained:

> When they are singing at the meeting, they often hear a woman's
> voice singing. Then they listen. It sounds to some as if it's a woman's
> voice far away. They hear it come right from the chief peyote. Then
> they know that the chief peyote is a woman. It may be man or a
> woman. You cannot tell which it is till it sings. Sometimes a gruff voice
> is heard, a man's voice. . . .
>
> All peyotes are good to eat whether they are big or small. They do
> not like to take the very large ones for eating. They want them just big
> enough so that a whole one can be eaten at once. . . .
>
> Some people, if they eat four, or just a few, or even as many as
> twenty buttons, do not feel good. It just makes them dizzy. But when
> they eat fifty or more, the good time is right there, if they are not
> afraid of it. . . . Once, way back, peyote made me cry, gave me a bad
> dream. Sometimes it makes you dream something pleasant; sometimes
> it makes you dream something dangerous.

Generally, it takes around thirty minutes for the effects to kick in.
The first signs are an increase in heart rate, blood pressure, and body
temperature. Sometimes people experience nausea, a bloated stomach,
sweating, or chills. This can last for up to two hours. Visual effects are

common, with brighter colors, greater visual depth, and intricate animated patterns. When laboratory rats have been given large doses of mescaline, their EEG readings have been known to go haywire. From there on, what are termed "subjective, psychological effects" take hold and gradually decline after ten or twelve hours, although the aftereffects can last days.

These include mystical feelings of transcendence with clear consciousness and rational thought, together with a oneness and unity, self-realization, and an end to ego. Many experience empathy or a collective conscious with those around them and a deep euphoria.

For those that take a heavy dose of one hundred or more buttons in a single sitting, a prolonged, death-like sleep may come over them. Antonio noted: "Tell your people not to bother you, not to wake you, that you will come back. Tell them not to bother you after the ceremony even if you sleep four days. That is the way you will travel somewhere."

Today, peyote ceremonies have been revived and are a cornerstone of the Native American Church (NAC), where they help guide people through psychological, spiritual, and physiological issues. Devotees say the peyote journey offers deep insight into the self and the universe, giving one a greater sense of connection and spirituality. It is also known for fostering compassion and alleviating psychological disorders such as anxiety, depression, PTSD, and addiction.

One of the few outsiders to attend an NAC ceremony was James S. Slotkin, associate professor of social sciences at the University of Chicago, during the 1960s. "They certainly were not stupefied or drunk," he recalled. "They never get out of rhythm or fumbled their words as a drunken or stupefied man would do. They are all quiet, courteous and considerate of one another. I have never been in any white man's house of worship where there is either so much religious feeling or decorum," he wrote.[3]

Some thirty years before Opler set out on his quest, a small circle of British intellectuals, artists, and poets had by chance stumbled upon an article in the *British Medical Journal* written by the American neurologist Silas Weir Mitchell, who described the brilliant visions experienced by those partaking of the peyote cactus.[4] What Mitchell did not mention in his article was the ease with which he had acquired his peyote, available in powdered form as an over-the-counter "cardiac tonic" from the drug company Parke-Davis, today a subsidiary of the pharmaceutical giant Pfizer.

Always on the lookout for inspiration, the London creatives were determined to give it a try and finally managed to track down dried peyote buttons from a mail-order catalog by the London pharmacists Potter & Clarke, whose patented Potter's Asthma Cure had long been known to bring on its own brilliant visions due to its high composition of datura, a South American plant of the nightshade family.

In the cozy, red-brick, London mansion flat of decadent poet and art critic Arthur Symons, fellow critic and qualified doctor Havelock Ellis ground up three dried buttons and brewed a rather distasteful tea. "The first symptom observed during the afternoon was a certain consciousness of energy and intellectual power," Ellis recalled in his subsequent article "Mescal: A New Artificial Paradise." He continued: "This passed off, and about an hour after the final dose I felt faint and unsteady; the pulse was low, and I found it pleasanter to lie down."[5]

As the afternoon wore on, both men found themselves captivated by the beauty of the most mundane objects. "I was surprised, not only by the enormous profusion of the imagery presented to my gaze, but still more by its variety," wrote Ellis. "I would see thick glorious fields of jewels, solitary or clustered, sometimes brilliant and sparkling, sometimes with a dull rich glow. Then they would spring up into flower-like shapes beneath my gaze, and then seem to turn into gorgeous butterfly forms and endless folds of glistening, iridescent, fibrous wings of wonderful insects."

Although both men had taken what would seem to be a ridiculously small dose by Lipan standards, they both experienced the most sublime, magical moment of their lives. "It seemed as if a series of dissolving views were carried swiftly before me, all going from right to left, none corresponding with any seen reality," recalled Symons. "For instance, I saw the most delightful dragons, puffing out their breath straight in front of them like rigid lines of steam, and balancing white balls at the end of their breath."

As dawn approached, and Symons felt a wave of nausea, his friend handed him a dry biscuit. "For an instant, I held the biscuit close to my leg," he said. "Immediately, my trouser caught alight, and then the whole of the right side of my body, from the foot to the shoulder, was enveloped in waving blue flame. It was a sight of wonderful beauty. But this was not all. As I placed the biscuit in my mouth it burst out again into the same colored fire and illuminated the interior of my mouth, casting a blue reflection on the ceiling."

Around this time, German chemist Arthur Heffter succeeded in identifying and isolating mescaline, the main active ingredient in peyote, making it the first psychedelic compound to be extracted and isolated. But it was not until 1919 that mescaline was first synthesized in the laboratory by Austrian chemist Ernst Späth. It soon became a highly valued but misunderstood street drug, trading under the names of mescal, big chief, and buttons.

One of the first to give the drug a full philosophical appraisal was Aldous Huxley (1894–1963), author, philosopher, and early psychedelic adventurer. "Thus it came about that, one bright May morning, I swallowed four-tenths of a gram of mescaline dissolved in half a glass of water and sat down to wait for the results," wrote Huxley in his 1954 book *The Doors of Perception*. "But I had not reckoned, it was evident, with the idiosyncrasies of my mental make-up, the facts of my temperament, training and habits."[6]

At first, Huxley watches a slow dance of golden lights and bright nodes of energy that vibrate with a continuously changing, patterned life. Soon his eyes turn to examine a nearby vase of flowers. Now he was seeing them with entirely different eyes. "I was seeing what Adam had seen on the morning of his creation—the miracle, moment by moment, of naked existence. And along with indifference to space there went an even more complete indifference to time."

Wanting to see more of this newly revealed nature, Huxley steps out into the garden and finds himself thunderstruck. "It was

inexpressibly wonderful, wonderful to the point, almost, of being terrifying. And suddenly I had an inkling of what it must feel like to be
mad. Schizophrenia has its heavens as well as its hells and purgato-
ries," he wrote. "The fear, as I analyze it in retrospect, was of being
overwhelmed, of disintegrating under a pressure of reality greater
than a mind, accustomed to living most of the time in a cosy world of
symbols, could possibly bear."

Huxley's epiphany led him to come up with the concept of Mind at
Large. The human brain, he believed, filters the ultimate reality of the
world around us—the perfect, unimpeded celestial awareness—by limiting our incoming data to allow us to function on a daily basis, otherwise we might never cease to wonder at it all, and we might easily starve
or freeze to death. Almost fifty years before the DMN was discovered,
Huxley concluded that mescaline and other compounds—by switching
off certain parts of the brain and thereby removing the filter—exposed
the user to Mind at Large.

"To make biological survival possible, Mind at Large has to be fun-
neled through the reducing valve of the brain and nervous system," he
maintained. "What comes out at the other end is a measly trickle of the
kind of consciousness which will help us to stay alive on the surface of
this particular planet."

Huxley believed that certain individuals may be born with a bypass
to the reducing valve. "In some cases there may be extra-sensory perceptions. Other persons discover a world of visionary beauty. To others again is revealed the glory, the infinite value and meaningfulness of
naked existence."

Schizophrenia, he realized, might be akin to a permanent state of
mescaline influence. The sufferer is "unable to shut off the experience
of a reality which he is not holy enough to live with, which he cannot
explain away [and which] scares him into interpreting its unremitting
strangeness, its burning intensity of significance, as the manifestations
of human or even cosmic malevolence, calling for the most desperate
countermeasures, from murderous violence at one end of the scale to
catatonia, or psychological suicide, at the other."

In summing up his mescaline journey, Huxley concluded his book by saying, "To be shaken out of the ruts of ordinary perception, to be shown for a few timeless hours the outer and the inner world, not as they appear to an animal obsessed with survival or to a human being obsessed with words and notions, but as they are apprehended, directly and unconditionally, by Mind at Large—this is an experience of inestimable value to everyone and especially to the intellectual."

While Huxley may be considered one of the finest writers in the English language, he admittedly struggled to find the words for what he had witnessed. How could he ever describe such an experience to those who had not an ounce of understanding? It would be like trying to explain the color yellow to a blind person.

"It is impossible to describe what the mystical experience really is, as the mystical experience lies beyond words," says François Pontvianne of the Swiss École Polytechnique Fédérale de Lausanne in his research essay "Psychedelics and Buddhism: Inter-Relationship and Ethical Considerations." He continues:

> The mystical experience is a unifying experience in which the organism feels itself to be as one with the rest of the fabric of existence. In this kind of state, consciousness doesn't see life in words, it doesn't process it with thought. Words are just small mouth noises which don't have a meaning apart from the one we decide to ascribe to them. They have no ground in physical reality in the sense that the word 'water' will never quench one's thirst, or the word 'money' won't help you buy anything. The mystical experience is then an experience of ultimate truth, in which the web of inter-relationships is revealed to the experiencer. . . . There is only—as Buddhists call it—the Mind. . . .
>
> One of the most fundamental Buddhist insights revealed by the mystical experience is that there is no self, only the illusion of one.[7]

In his paper, Pontvianne quotes Alan Watts (1915–1973), the English writer and theologian who experimented extensively with psychedelic substances from peyote to LSD and psilocybin magic mushrooms. Watts tried to explain the experience by breaking down the mystic journey into four main characteristics. In 1968, he wrote:

> The first characteristic is a slowing down of time, a concentration in the present. One's normally compulsive concern for the future decreases, and one becomes aware of the enormous importance and interest of what is happening at the moment. . . . Other people, going about their business on the streets, seem to be slightly crazy, failing to realize that the whole point of life is to be fully aware of it as it happens. One therefore relaxes almost luxuriously into studying the colors in a glass of water, or in listening to the now highly articulate vibration of every note played on an oboe or sung by a voice.
>
> The second characteristic is the vivid realization that states, things and events that we ordinarily call opposite are interdependent, like back and front, or the poles of a magnet. By [this] 'polar awareness' one sees that things which are explicitly different are implicitly one.

The third characteristic, he maintained, is awareness of relativity:

> I see that I am a link in an infinite hierarchy of processes and beings, ranging from molecules through bacteria and insects to human beings, and, maybe, to angels and gods—a hierarchy in which every level is in effect the same situation. . . . I realize that fruit flies must think of themselves as people, because, like ourselves, they find themselves in the middle of their own world with immeasurably greater things above and smaller things below. To us, they all look alike and seem to have no personality. Yet fruit flies must see just as many subtle distinctions among themselves as we among ourselves.

The fourth characteristic is awareness of eternal energy:

Often in the form of intense white light, which seems to be both the current in your nerves and that mysterious e which equals mc^2. This may sound like megalomania or delusions of grandeur, but one sees quite clearly that all existence is a single energy, and that this energy is one's own being. Basically, therefore, there is simply nothing to worry about, because you yourself are the eternal energy of the universe playing hide-and-seek (off-and-on) with itself.[8]

Since the 1960s, when an early war on drugs began in the United States to stem the antiwar hippie movement—fueled prominently by the mind-altering drug LSD—any connection between mysticism, spirituality, and so-called drugs suddenly became a concept to be denied both morally and legally in the Western world.

According to Watts, "Western culture has, historically, a particular fascination with the value and virtue of man as an individual, self-determining, responsible ego, controlling himself and his world by the power of conscious effort and will. Nothing, then, could be more repugnant to this cultural tradition than the notion of spiritual or psychological growth through the use of drugs."

Such a "drugged" person, says Watts, is by definition "dimmed in consciousness, fogged in judgment and deprived of will. But not all psychotropic [consciousness-changing] chemicals are narcotic and soporific, as are alcohol, opiates, and barbiturates. There is really no analogy between being 'high' on LSD and 'drunk' on bourbon."

François Pontvianne of the Ecole Polytechnique Federale de Lausanne asks, "The mystical experience on drugs is said not to be genuine and to be illusory. But what does genuine and illusory mean?" He adds, "Neurologically speaking, the experience will be felt if the right neurotransmitters enter the brain. The body will not discriminate between the neurotransmitters coming from his glands or coming from the environment."[9]

The American research ethnopharmacologist Dennis McKenna maintains that every human experience is a drug experience. He explains that we're all on drugs all the time, largely because we are made of drugs.

William James (1842–1910), the "father of American psychology," believed that "Our normal waking consciousness, rational consciousness as we call it, is but one special type of consciousness, whilst all about it, parted from it by the filmiest of screens, there lie potential forms of consciousness entirely different. No account of the universe in its totality can be final which leaves these other forms of consciousness quite disregarded."[10]

"I AM GOD. THE UNIVERSE. EVERYTHING."

According to a writer for the *New Yorker* magazine, we are all living in the "Age of Kale," with an obsession for wellness, mindfulness, detoxification, and organic produce. People today, insists Ariel Levy, are willing to suffer for their soulfulness. But just how far are they willing to go, she wondered, and could she push herself to the outer limits?[11]

And then, right under her nose in Manhattan, she discovered that hundreds of people were gathering nightly in small, discreet circles in a quest for a postreligious kind of spiritualism that involved dressing almost entirely in white, abstaining from most delights, and sampling a mystical, psychoactive brew that only the bravest of souls could stomach.

Ariel was about to sample ayahuasca, an ancient medicine from the upper Amazon that, with the help of a shaman, shows you your true inner self, enabling a "vision quest" and imparting the secrets of the universe, while detouring to meet entities that prove impossible to describe and even alien-like creatures that both impart and extract knowledge from the partaker. Ariel, on the other hand, would come away both underwhelmed and somewhat sickened by a concoction that has driven others to the depths of insanity and killed a few more.

One of the first Westerners to sample the brew was English botanist Richard Spruce. Soon after drinking from a small wooden bowl in eastern Ecuador sometime in the 1850s, he felt his nervous system excited beyond measure. "All the senses liven up and all faculties awaken," he wrote. "Then a sensation of being lifted into the air and beginning an aerial journey [viewing] gorgeous lakes, forests covered with fruit, the prettiest birds who communicate the nicest and the most favorable things."[12]

The experience turned rather nasty on Spruce when he began to come down some hours later, describing "terrible horrors" out to devour him and "entities" alerting him to the misfortunes that lay ahead in life. Also having a bad ayahuasca trip some seventy years later, French anthropologist P. Reinberg feared that the natives in the Peruvian Amazon were out to poison him. He eventually managed to revive himself by sniffing from a handy bottle of ether that he happened to have about him and downing a lot of strong coffee. He likened the overall experience to strychnine poisoning.[13]

Those who overimbibe can experience serotonin syndrome. Symptoms include confusion, rapid heart rate and high blood pressure, diarrhea and vomiting, seizures, respiratory arrest, and coma. Ayahuasca is best avoided by those with serious medical conditions and mental disorders such as schizophrenia. Today, ayahuasca is the most studied of all traditional shamanic plant "hallucinogens," but still very few can lay claim to a full understanding.

In 1956, in *Heaven and Hell,* another of his essays, Huxley sampled the brew and reported: "Like the Earth of a hundred years ago, our mind still has its darkest Africas, its unmapped Borneos and Amazonian basins. Like the giraffe and the duck-billed platypus, the creatures inhabiting these remoter regions of the mind are exceedingly improbable. Nevertheless they exist, they are facts of observation; and as such, they cannot be ignored by anyone who is honestly trying to understand the world in which we live."[14]

The brew itself has been perfectly understood for millennia in the Amazon. Ayahuasca is a combination of two plants—the *Banisteriopsis caapi* vine and *Psychotria viridis*—which, when mixed into a tea together, allow the human stomach to absorb and process N,N-dimethyltryptamine (DMT), a hallucinogenic found in many plants and animals, including humans. However, even the term *hallucinogenic* is misleading, as hallucination is a conscious state. A more accurate term for these substances, many researchers say, is *mind manifesting* or *psychedelic,* meaning substances that affect all the senses, altering a person's thinking, sense of time, and emotions. Researchers have concluded that the effects obtained from ayahuasca are unlike any other naturally occurring psychedelic substance. The two plants taken individually, however, produce virtually no effect.

Perhaps the most baffling element of the ayahuasca journey is the consistency of the reports. Those who partake, and manage to get it right, all report near identical experiences, as if they had left our normal waking world and travelled to a distinct other dimension. Users consistently report a complete replacement of the normal subjective experience with a bizarre and complex alternate universe filled with strange and powerful sentient beings who actively interact with the individual.

"Invariably, the visions impress their viewers as marvelous," says cognitive psychologist Benny Shanon in his book *The Antipodes of the Mind—Charting the Phenomenology of the Ayahuasca Experience.* "They introduce drinkers to what seem to be enchanted realities that fill them with wonder and awe. . . . Often, people say that their exposure to Ayahuasca has radically changed their lives. They were no longer the same person."[15]

A common theme among those who imbibe, Shanon found, was that they had entered a realm of magic, governed by invisible forces, energies, or beings. "Often coupled with enchantment is the appreciation of powerful energy," he explained. "Over and over again, in different locales and contexts, I have heard people comment that this energy is the force that sustains all Creation. The powerful energy is also regarded as the source of all wisdom and knowledge, and the ultimate fountain of health and well-being."

In an attempt to get a scientific angle on ayahuasca, neuroscientist Draulio Barros de Araujo of Brazil's Brain Institute administered the brew in 2014 to ten participants and then measured their brain activity with an MRI scanner. He was surprised to find a significant decrease in the activity of the DMN and concluded that while the DMN was temporarily relieved of its duties, the thalamus—which is involved in awareness—became highly activated. These changes in the brain, he noted, were similar to those seen in long-term meditation.[16]

Various studies around the world have shown that ayahuasca can be used in the treatment of addiction and other lifestyle diseases. Trials in the Czech Republic have also shown that it can be highly beneficial in the treatment of diseases of the gastrointestinal tract, skin problems, depression, parasitic infections, allergies, and asthma, as well as in strengthening immunity.[17] It has also been used to prepare terminal patients for the afterlife, proving both enlightening and reassuring.[18]

Mother Ayahuasca, as this magical brew is often termed, is a fickle mistress that must first test the nerve of all who dare imbibe, never sure if they will see her nurturing nature or a nightmarish dark side.

Ariel landed somewhere between the two when she arrived at an overwarm, windowless yoga studio in a hip Brooklyn neighborhood, situated beside a thumping dance club with the sound of drunk people filtering through the walls. Here she would meet Little Owl and a dozen or so other white-clad women, all poised to take the plunge.

> *Little Owl had set up a perch for herself at the back wall, surrounded by bird feathers, crystals, flutes, drums and wooden rattles, bottles of potions, and a pack of baby wipes. . . . When she finished waving her smoking sage at me and said, I hope you have a beautiful journey, I was so moved by her radiant goodwill that I nearly burst into tears. When it was my turn to drink the little Dixie cup of muck she presented, I was stunned that divine consciousness—or really anything—could smell quite so foul: as if it had already been vomited up, by someone who'd been on a steady diet of tar, bile, and fermented wood pulp. But I forced it down. . . . I was going to visit the swampland of my soul, make peace with death, and become one with the universe.*

While Ariel's hands begin to tingle, women around her begin to moan, and some start to cry. And then comes the sound of retching. Ariel throws up into the bucket provided.

> *As I was wiping my mouth on a tissue, a girl across the room started hollering,* I love you! *Some of us giggled a little. She kept at it with*

growing intensity: I love you so much! It feels so good! *All of a sudden, she was on her feet, flailing.* I've eaten so many animals! *she screamed.* And I loved them all!

It was the flailing that got to me. . . . Any second now, I would be descending into the pit of my being, seeing serpents, experiencing my own death or birth—or something—and I did not necessarily want that to happen in a windowless vomitorium while a millennial in crazy pants had her first psychotic episode. Her yelling was getting weirder: I want to eat sex!

The intrepid journalist was finally forced to leave the room, where presumably the floor-to-ceiling mirrors were multiplying the horror.

It occurred to me that this wasn't working—that nothing was working, and now I would have to find another hippie to give me this disgusting drug all over again. And then maybe my Default Mode Network shut down for a second or maybe I had a surge of serotonin, but for whatever reason the whole thing abruptly seemed hilarious, fascinating, perfect.

Helen Cox is a France-based tech pioneer who has made a study of the psychedelic experience. She recounted a number of trips to the Amazon, after considerable due diligence. "I was feeling polarized," she told us. "I was looking for balance." Three things would be important: the right shaman to guide her; the perfect, natural Amazonian environment; and, she stressed, "The vital importance of doing it with the right people."

She spent a long time preparing for each experience, avoiding certain foods and alcohol. And then, just before things were due to get underway, the shaman told Helen that she must first clear her eyes for the journey.

"It's a bit like putting lemon juice in your eyes. It's a plant extract, it's very painful." Helen was being conditioned for the pain she would be seeing. Then she would need to have her pineal gland cleansed with shamanic snuff, delivered via nose pipe and composed of very finely ground plants mixed with tobacco and ashes. "It's really horrible, but it allows you to stay centered, to bring you back to the now," she explained.

After the first time, the vomiting ceased to be an issue. "You're purging something energetic," she says. "Sometimes it feels like purging a mushroom, a worm, or parasites. You achieve balance by getting something out of the system."

Helen knocks back the disgusting brew and reclines in the long-house. She says of her first time with ayahuasca that she was taken by the hand and given a tour, a common first-time experience. "It's difficult to explain because it's telepathic, there's no words. There's a communication happening with you and another entity. But you don't know quite how you're communicating. It's like the thoughts are just kind of happening and unfolding in your mind."

The entities that Helen encounters are also a common feature. John Heuser, in his paper "Ayahuasca Entity Visitations," a study of entities reported online by ayahuasca users, says they can be broken down into 144 different categories. Aliens, robots, "machine elves," insectoid creatures, clowns, deities, and mythic beings are regular entities for Western users, as are meetings with deceased loved ones or family members.

"Some Ayahuasca drinkers say that they communicate with entities to obtain clairvoyant knowledge, insights as to psychological well being, and instructions leading to physical health of themselves and others," says Heuser, adding that: "Ayahuasca entities raise questions about psychological universals, because they sometimes present features that some writers think are unprecedented in psychological literature, and unexplained by existing Western psychological models."[19]

Helen told us:

At one point there were lots of different entities. I was able to turn my head from left to right and just observe these different entities. Some of them were totally cool and peaceful. Some were a bit weird and some were kind of cheeky, and lots of different energies. There was one in particular that I was fascinated by. It wasn't looking at me but the more I looked at it, the more it turned and looked at me. And then eventually it stared at me. And I realized that I was putting my energy onto this entity.

On another occasion, Helen came face to face with herself.

It was just me; it was me at this present moment. I was just standing in front of myself. And, at that point, I knew that I was going to see myself die. And I was like, No, it's alright, I know I'm gonna die. I'm fine with it. I'm totally cool. But I was getting this message that you have to keep looking because there's nothing to worry about. And I just saw myself gradually die, to decompose in front of me. And eventually worms were coming out of my other body and I was okay with it. This is my body disappearing. It's not me. It's just my body.

And then, suddenly, I was gone. I wasn't there. And I was not in the room anymore. I wasn't aware that I was breathing. I wasn't aware of my body, I was completely gone. And I was in another dimension or a place I'd never gone to before. I'm totally unable to describe what they look like, what the place looked like, except very powerful. It felt angelic and alien all at the same time. But I wasn't able to recognize a human figure.

The classic alien abductions, with odd, otherworldly creatures prodding and poking the earthling, imparting information while sucking out a lifetime's memories, are also common features of the ayahuasca experience. Helen found herself in just such a situation.

It was like I was receiving a download. They gave me something, but they also took something from me. It felt like tentacles grabbing the top of my head. They were downloading lots of new information into me. It felt like energy. But I was getting a bit freaked out because I didn't know if I was breathing, and I felt that I had to go back and check. And so I came back and I opened my eyes and this [other] dimension, the colors, the energy were still in the room completely. But everyone in the room disappeared, and there was only me and Juan Carlos [Helen's guide].

Having the right shaman acting as a personal guide was utterly essential. She recalled with wonder:

He came and got me! And then I felt like I had a tornado running through my entire body. I didn't know how to deal with it. There was energy coming from the ground up through my entire body.

On a later trip, this time in the south of France, Helen found herself being given a universal tour.

It takes you through all the rounds of illusion and shows you that you're not just in this material world, you're everywhere. You can be anywhere and everywhere. I felt I was dissolved within everything. There was no me anymore. I was God. I wasn't seeing or experiencing a god outside of me. I was the God and my whole understanding of what love was completely shifted after that. But love is not a feeling, it's a state. It's the state of creation. The expression of expansion. The universe expanding and the universe contracting. You can feel it within your body. My whole understanding of love completely shifted after that. But I didn't have any visuals. I just felt I could have been inside a cell or nucleus or I could have been the universe itself.

"WE KNOW THIS PLACE"

The pineal gland is another of life's little mysteries. It lies nestled within the brain but is not part of the brain. It is about the size of a pea, resembling a tiny pine cone, sitting back a bit from the point between our eyes, but nobody can definitively explain why we have one, nor what its precise function may be. To the ancients, this was the seat of the soul or third eye, the Crystal Palace, the organ of spiritual vision, our personal means of communication with the universe. The little that we do know today would only appear to add to its mystery.

Divided into two fine hemispheres like a mini brain, the gland is activated by light and believed to control various biorhythms of the body as well as produce melatonin, which regulates sleep patterns. The pineal also maintains the biological clock in humans and hibernation in some animals. The deeper the state of unconsciousness, the more active the gland appears to be.

Another mystery is that the key ingredient in ayahuasca—N,N-dimethyltryptamine (DMT)—occurs naturally in the human body, yet nobody can definitively say where, how, or why. Some think DMT is produced in the lungs or the adrenal gland, or "somewhere in the brain" and throughout the cerebral cortex, or perhaps even within the eyes, but the most popular theory holds that DMT is produced by the pineal gland during moments of high stress but also within deep meditation. High concentrations can be found in the urine of schizophrenics. Deeper examination has proved tricky because it would be unethical to prod and probe the pineal gland of a healthy individual. However, a study in 2013 did find significant concentrations of DMT in the pineal glands of rats.[20]

Then, in 2019, Jimo Borjigin, PhD, associate professor of molecular and integrative physiology, was studying consciousness during waking and at near-death, as well as the mechanisms of sudden death. She removed the pineal gland from a number of laboratory rats and found no appreciable change in the levels of DMT within their brains. She believes the pineal too small to produce the levels of DMT necessary to have any affect. A typical dose when smoked or injected is around twenty milligrams, while a shaman might administer between fifty and one hundred milligrams. The pineal, she believes, is not up to the task. But we do know, she told us, that "DMT is produced in the brain, with or without the pineal gland."[21]

"I was drawn to DMT research because of its presence in all of our bodies," says Dr. Rick Strassman, MD, formerly associate professor of psychiatry at the University of New Mexico School of Medicine in Albuquerque. "I believed the source of this DMT was the mysterious pineal gland [because] Western and Eastern mystical traditions place our highest spiritual center within its confines."[22]

Strassman wondered if excessive pineal DMT production was involved in naturally occurring psychedelic states—such as visions and hallucinations—and if it played a part, too, in birth, death and near-death experiences, psychosis, and mystical experiences. To find out, he began a five-year study administering around four hundred doses to sixty human volunteers.

"It is important to remember that while we understand a great deal about the pharmacology of psychedelics, we know nearly nothing about how changes in brain chemistry directly relate to subjective, or inner, experience. This is as true for psychedelics as it is for Prozac," says Strassman in his landmark book *DMT—The Spirit Molecule.*

"The most general hypothesis is that the pineal gland produces psychedelic amounts of DMT at extraordinary times in our lives," says Strassman, who coined the term *spirit molecule,* believing that it plays a vital part in our life journey, first entering the fetal body forty-nine days after conception and again at birth. "It may be that the pineal is the most active organ in the body at the time of death," he says, and wondered himself if our life force eventually exits the body through the pineal.

"Blinding white light, encounters with demonic and angelic entities, ecstatic emotions, timelessness, heavenly sounds, feelings of having died and being reborn, contacting a powerful and loving presence underlying all of reality, these experiences cut across all denominations," he says. "They also are characteristic of a fully psychedelic DMT experience."

It is also possible, he believes, that the gland becomes active in those nearing death or that the recently dead produce DMT for a few hours—and perhaps longer—yielding a lingering consciousness. And he questions if a flatline on the EEG truly reflects a person's inner mental state at that time.

DMT was first synthesized in 1931 by German chemist Richard Helmuth Frederick Manske (1901–1977), but its psychedelic qualities were not noticed until 1953 when Hungarian chemist and psychiatrist Stephen Szara decided to inject himself and his Budapest laboratory colleagues with a small dose.

"Within three minutes the symptoms started," he recorded in his diary, describing tingling, trembling, nausea, increased blood pressure and pulse rate, and then, "brilliantly colored oriental motifs and, later, wonderful scenes altering very rapidly."[23]

Despite occurring naturally in the human body, DMT is outlawed over much of the globe following the 1971 United Nations Convention on Psychotropic Substances. In the United Kingdom, it is listed as a hallucinogen under the Misuse of Drugs Act and classified as a Class A drug, earning prison sentences of up to seven years or an unlimited fine, or both. As a street drug, it is generally smoked, and trades under the names elf spice, fantasia, businessman's trip, and 45-minute psychosis.

Those undergoing Strassman's trials described being literally blown away in the instant the DMT hit the bloodstream via an intravenous injection. *Like a freight train* or a *nuclear cannon* were common descriptions. "Nearly everyone remarked on the vibrations brought on by DMT," Strassman recorded in *DMT: The Spirit Molecule*. "The sense of powerful energy pulsing through them at a very rapid and high frequency. Typical comments were: *I was worried that the vibration would blow my head up. The colors and vibration were so intense, I thought I would pop. I didn't think I would stay in my skin.*"

Some volunteers said they thought they had actually died. They no longer had any sense of a body. *My body dissolved. I was pure awareness.* Next came all manner of unimaginable things, from kaleidoscopic geometric patterns to strange sentient beings, and all with an intensity never before experienced. Merry-go-rounds feature regularly.

One volunteer recounted watching life-sized dolls, men and women dressed for the late 1800s, riding a carousel. "The women were in corsets," he told Strassman. "They had big breasts and big butts and teeny, skinny waists. They were all whirling around me on tiptoes. The men had top hats, riding on two-seater bicycles. One merry-go-round after another after another. The women had red circles painted on their cheeks, and there was calliope music in the background. And there were some clowns, flitting in and out, not really the main characters but busier, somehow more aware of me than the mannequins."

Another test subject reported sitting with a Mexican family on the porch of their house. "I was playing with the kids. I was part of the family. I had a sense of an old man standing behind me. It seemed so natural and complete. It wasn't a dream at all. I thought, *It seems like a pretty common day.*"

After a few DMT trips, one recreational drug user attending the trials tried to explain the experience to Strassman. "DMT has shown me the reality that there is a real possibility of adjacent dimensions. It may not be so simple as alien planets with their own societies. This is too proximal. It's not like some kind of drug. It's more like an experience of a new technology than a drug. It's not a hallucination but an observation. When I'm there, I'm not intoxicated. I'm lucid and sober."

Strassman was confused by what he was hearing. "It was at this point that I began having to fight a tendency to regard these stories as dreams or figments of their DMT-amplified imaginations," he wrote. Or were they really somewhere else? he wanted to know. "What exactly were they witnessing?" The volunteers were even more baffled. How could their imagination generate a scenario that felt more real than waking consciousness? And if it were "real," how could they live knowing we coexist with invisible realms inhabited by intelligent life-forms?

One volunteer found himself looking down on a city of fabulous colors and hues. Odd entities floated above the city. "I noticed a middle-aged female with a pointed nose and light greenish skin sitting off to my right, watching this changing city with me," he recounted. "She had her right hand on a dial that seemed to control the panorama we were watching. She turned slightly toward me and asked, *What else would you like?* I answered telepathically, *Well, what else have you got? I have no idea what you can do.*

"Then she stood up, walked up to my right forehead, touched it and warmed it up, and then used a sharp object to open up a panel in my right temple, releasing a tremendous amount of pressure. This made me feel much better than I'd felt before, even though I realized I'd felt fine in the first place."

Within a short time, the volunteers formed a self-help group, desperate to share experiences that no one else would ever comprehend. *I can't talk with anyone about these things. No one would understand. It's just too strange. I want to remind myself that I'm not losing my mind.*

Strassman found that he had just as many questions once the five-year study came to an abrupt and premature end. "It is almost inconceivable that a chemical as simple as DMT could provide access to such an amazingly varied array of experiences, from the least dramatic to the most unimaginably earth-shattering. From psychological insights to encounters with aliens. Abject terror or nearly unbearable bliss. Near-death and rebirth. Enlightenment. All of these from a naturally occurring chemical cousin of serotonin, a widespread and essential brain neurotransmitter."

Strassman was left to marvel at the end of his book: "It's just as fascinating to ponder why nature or God made DMT?"

"In my view, these aliens and entities are the gods of our ancestors," says Anton Bilton, entrepreneur and founder of the Tyringham Initiative think tank for deeper understanding of the human experience. "Come what may and, given the vastness of the universe, it would seem churlish not to accept the possibility of other living entities and that their form may be as diverse from ours as we are to some of the living creatures on our own Earth."[24]

Bilton would like to see far more research in this field. "Today we are technologically advanced and can examine these visitations with a greater intensity than our ancestors," he insists. "We can create experiments to gather evidence, to ask the entities for answers, to access their realms and to act on their advice. Spending billions with NASA in a search for extraterrestrial life seems almost wasteful when we can spend fractions of that and experience alternate sentient presences via alternate consciousness-expanding practices as our ancestors did."

Instead of manned space missions, future explorers may travel in teams to these easily accessible dimensions, say some. There are numerous reports of people taking DMT and going on the same journeys together. "My partner and I have both experienced these 'machine elves' several times," Michele Boyer told us via an online forum. "Only we call them 'little tree people' or 'woodland elves.' There's no doubt they are real as we were seeing them and hearing them at the same time. If it were merely an illusion, how could two people be seeing and hearing the same thing at exactly the same moment?"

These DMT entities are regularly described as benevolent guiding forces, capable of imparting valuable insights, but occasionally they appear hostile and critical, imparting hard life lessons and analyzing past errors. In all instances, they appear instantly aware of the DMT travelers' arrival. "You burst into this space and they're saying, *How wonderful that you're here, you come so rarely! We're so delighted to see you!*" explained the ethnobotanist Terence Kemp McKenna, who made numerous DMT journeys.

McKenna was a major advocate of in-depth scientific research into DMT and other naturally occurring psychedelic plants. He travelled the world offering DMT to various spiritual and religious leaders.

"I gave it to Tibetans; they said *This is the lesser lights of the bardo. You cannot go further into the bardo and return. This takes you as far as you can go,*" McKenna told a workshop in 1990. "When I gave it to shamans in the Amazon, they said, *It's strong but these are the ancestors. These are the spirits that we work with. These are ancestor souls. We know this place.*"

"Debbie" (Continued): The Chain of Love

Does anybody else miss their coma? This is a question that "Debbie" posed on the ICUsteps forum and allowed us to share. She did not get many positive replies.

• • •

It was such a mind-blowing, amazing experience. I was surrounded by the purest of untainted love in my coma. I miss it so much. It was enlightening and awe-inspiring and not a love found anywhere on this earth. The love was flawless and completely pure and it filled me. It was all around me. I grieve for it like the loss of a very close, dearly loved one. I feel a part of me never fully came back from my coma.

I didn't have horrific or truly scary coma events. Some parts were eerie and weird, but I really don't like to call them "dreams." I was filled with the purest of love by beings that were not aliens but not human. Their arms linked around my bed, which was more like a platform for a stage than an actual bed.

They were levitating me with their minds while I was flat on my back, levitating or hovering above it. They spoke to me with their minds to reassure me and make me know I had to fight. As they linked arms or hands, they filled me with love, they repaired all my internal life-wounds and freed my mind and whole body of depression; of all the hurt and sadness. It was sucked out and pure love pumped in. It was overwhelmingly, beautifully, heavenly.

They were my protectors. They chanted and reminded each other with their minds not to break the chain. I was innately aware they could not hold their position forever to protect me from Death. They warned me not to catch the eye of this gigantic, hulking, gray, dark, smoke thing that was to the left. It was inactive or asleep but moving in its dark corner. It was Death. It was ominous but not evil. I was aware that if I caught its eye and it became aware of me, it would try to take me and that would be that end of me for good. No heaven, no hell, just gone. Dead.

I wasn't scared, I was just aware. It was just a matter-of-fact thing. It was ominously over there, and that thing was Death. Whereas, I guess, the others were life, love, healers and protectors. But they needed my cooperation, my inner determination to fight and to survive.

Part of me is still semisubmerged as if in quicksand. I'm in between worlds. Part of me is still on that bed, intubated. Am I really awake or is this part of a long, intubated coma dream because everything since then has been strange and glitchy, just off? Right, but not right. Differences that make me look more closely at people. They aren't who they were before but a pretty good imitation. I can see people for what they truly are. These are not the people or family I had before.

Stephen (Continued): The Setting Sun

Stephen the medical statistician wakes up to find himself back in the Cushioned Room. He feels "trapped under the dispassionate, baleful eye of the cyclops cushion—Ominous. Oppressive. Stifling. Silent. Still. Imprisoned."

But to his right he sees an open door, leading to another room. Early evening sunlight filters through the open French windows revealing a hotel room with period furnishings and the gold-trim glint of reflected light. Stephen begins to wander. He turns to the left and sees another room. Peering in through the open door, he sees the following scene.

. . .

Partying socialites; sequin-dress ladies, tweed-suit men; cut-glass sparkle, champagne fizz; chitter-chatter, chinking-glass laughter; glistening, glittering, sunny glow. Just then a middle-aged man, drink in hand and heavily flushed face, drifts into the sunlit room and ambles over to the windows to gaze outside. I ask him, Excuse me, please, can you help? There's someone trapped inside that room.

I am ignored, as if I did not exist. Lost in musing, the man turns from the windows and slowly gazes around the room. I try again, Excuse me, please, there's someone trapped. Please, can you help? *But the man just wanders away, back to the party.*

Stephen listens to the distant chitter-chatter, the rippling laughter, and then a lapping sound turning to lapping water, purple-dark, reflecting orange-gold. As the sun goes down, Stephen sees in silhouette small fishing boats gently bobbing in the distance; on deck, men are busy casting lines. He looks around and sees a harbor built of ancient stone. Seated on a bench at the far end of the stone-built pier's edge, he gazes, squinting into the bright red sunset.

A peeping, hiding, sinking sun behind dark trees beyond. Shaded, sleepy doors of the houses strung along the quayside prom. Calm repose, tranquil peace, relaxing rest.

From behind comes a drowsy, distant voice. I turn to see a *gray-brown dirt road, running arrow-straight to the horizon, across wide-open, sun-bathed fields, basking warm, glow-gold-green; a high hedge borders the road, the sun glinting gold on its leaves.*

And there, across the road, fresh, young, smiling in her blue nurse uniform, yellow apron and hat; holding school-crossing 'lollipop' sign; there before me, an image of Mum. Come on, everyone. This way. Come on! *she beckons.* Everyone, come on, this way . . .

The light changes. Beneath a dome of harsh, white artificial light, small, dirty, gray rabbits with bob-white tails hop quietly about the loam-dark soil, shyly scampering beneath green vegetable leaves; each carrying a message of healing and hope.

From amid the shadows, something stirs. Then, boldly moving in, slowly encroaching, determined to hold sway, a larger brown species drives the gray rabbits away. The oppressors prevail, the grays are all gone.

Enclosed now by dark brown, wood-paneled walls, trapped in a small claustrophobic room, prostrate in bed, unable to move; sturdy oak doors open to dim empty corridors. . . . Late now. Long, long night ahead, but soon care will come. Suddenly, colluding with fear, sly brown shapes slam the oak doors shut: locked, bolted. Alone. Ear stretches to far echoing voices. Call out, weakly, Help, thirsty, you're supposed to be here. *Vending machines whirr. Fading footsteps, distant door slams, TV sound, feet-up, drinking, laughter. Thirsty, thirsty, long, long night ahead.* You're supposed to be here, supposed to be here . . .

Mother Superior, at edge of sight, seated in wheelchair, lips moving in silence; harbinger of the dawn . . .

Kathy: The Raft of Autumn Leaves

Kathy Drown, a medical auditor from Minnesota, spent three weeks in a coma following a botched operation in 2016 when the surgeon mistakenly sliced into an artery. She was flatlining, bleeding out, and given the last rites twice. Nobody expected her to live.

. . .

Archangel Raphael came to see me every day. He was so cool. He had long, braided, gray-black Rasta hair and brilliant blue eyes. He was wearing a surgeon's outfit. He told me he'd been in Jamaica lately and that's why his hair looked as it did. He came and sat with me every day. I didn't ask any questions; he just answered me as if I asked a question.

I'm seeing my body on the bed, and I'm talking to Raphael, and he's sitting on a chair in my hospital room, but I'm not concerned with my body at all. We're just talking about me going to heaven.

He told me stories that I know were true, about life and the world and wars of religion. He built me a nest of autumn leaves on the ocean, like a raft. There was no concept of time; it was like forever. There was no morning, no afternoon. There was no clock. There was just the beauty of light and darkness. There was no sun or moon. They just weren't there.

I floated on the ocean with mountains in the background. Sometimes there were major waves, but it was all so peaceful and relaxing. On the bed of leaves, I could see the sky, the clouds, mountains, and just total beauty, just relaxing on my raft. The leaves were very soothing. It was a feeling of complete peace. Complete fulfillment. You can't imagine until you've been there. Pure bliss, pure calmness.

I love the mountains. The fall leaves are my absolute favorite. I love all four seasons. I love nature. Whenever I'm emotionally traumatized, I go to the mountains to heal.

As things got worse for me medically, or so I believe, Raphael was there for me. He kept me at complete peace. He not so much took me places but he let me see places, but I don't know where they were. They weren't earthly. He said, as long as you're on this bed of leaves and have at least one leaf left, you will come back to live your life!

My leaves were my safety and I floated forever on them until I had only one leaf left. There was no fear. I didn't want more leaves. I was calm. Anxiety, what's that? That's when I experienced standing at the threshold of heaven.

Way behind me was evil and, thankfully, it was well far back. I was looking forward, praying, and then my brother and relatives appeared. I knew instinctively that they were my family. I just knew. You don't hear voices like here. I was just aware of what they were saying.

The threshold was a small hump that was pearly white, but I could barely put my being on the threshold. I was trying so hard to get in. The gates were open. It wasn't a tunnel, but an open, beautiful, innocent, cloudy background all around me.

My brother and others relatives said, It's not your time yet, you have to go back. *They gave me the powerful feeling I had something imperative to do in the future. I think I did just that. It took me a long time to get back to here. When I came out of the coma, everything was sort of blurry, like I was still one foot in and one foot out. After this, it's like I'm free to go to heaven anytime.*

Father Whalen from my church told me, for sure, that he knew I was dead. He said my eyes were wide open. I believe that you were at heaven's door. I've seen death a lot of times, *he said.*

I wish I could have died then, but I know I will be going back.

7

Dark Brings Light
Touching the Void

I f NASA ever decides to launch a mission to other dimensions, they should first chat with the Dalai Lama, because Buddhists maintain they have been constant visitors to these other realms since soon after the days of King Solomon.

To most Buddhists, death is not final. It is part of a pattern of constant rebirth. But when we slip this mortal coil, they say we embark into the bardo, the six stages between this life and the next, the final stage being the lesser lights and no chance of return once beyond.

To experience these six states, death is not imperative. It is possible to step across the threshold after years of intense meditation or by literally jumping off the deep end into the most extreme state of grace imaginable, the dark retreat. Since the dawn of time, mystics have taken themselves off to the darkest recesses of caves, seeking a spiritual connection. Today, such ascetic delights can be booked online.

"The thought of doing a forty-day dark retreat came quite unexpectedly to me during meditation," explains Kalianey, a French software developer and self-confessed nirvana hunter. "If I could last six weeks in solitude in the dark, I was not a spiritual tourist any more. I was hoping to finally face myself fully. I would learn to sit, watch, and accept my mind and my emotions for a prolonged period of time and hopefully get some insights in the process."[1]

When a person is placed in a pitch-dark, soundless, featureless cell for lengthy durations, strange things will happen to the mind. Buddhist monks and others will tell you that the withdrawal from the physical world opens the doorway to the spiritual world, and by taking such a step one is entering a death-like existence, with the six stages of bardo to explore.

"Complete darkness profoundly changes the sensibilities of the body and brain," explains Taoist master Mantak Chia in his helpful guide to dark retreats, *Darkness Technology*. "Darkness shuts down major cortical centers in the brain, depressing mental and cognitive functions in the higher brain centers. Emotions and feelings are enhanced. Dreams become more lucid and the dream state manifests in our conscious awareness. Eventually, we awaken within ourselves the awareness of the source, the spirit, the soul," maintains Master Chia. "We descend into the void, into the darkness of deep, inner space."[2]

For those attempting to understand the mechanisms of the dark retreat, the belief that naturally occurring N,N-dimethyltryptamine (DMT) is released at key moments of life and death helps explain why the experiences of Kalianey and others appear to match those recorded by Dr. Strassman when he submitted volunteers to the first trials of intravenously introduced DMT.

Kalianey was on her way to meet Emma Carruthers, who runs the Hermitage, a solitary and dark retreat center on the shores of Lake Atitlan in the highlands of Guatemala. "I think that the release of DMT in dark retreats can be responsible for a lot of the visions," Emma told us. This intentional DMT experience has been likened to a form of conscious unconsciousness, with the ability to process the events from a clear, rational perspective.

When we shared some of the accounts from the coma survivors who have been helping us, Emma seemed far from surprised. "All of those sound like the experiences that I personally have had in dark retreats, and I've done over ten. I've heard the same from the people who have run through our dark retreats, and we've had close to five hundred now. We talk individually to every single one afterward."

Emma says the ultravivid nightmares experienced during coma are a common early feature once one begins a dark retreat and that alternate lives or even past lives tend to feature large in the accounts of those who visit her retreat. "People also have projections about the future. People see a lot of other people in the room. Depending on their belief, they may see the Virgin Mary or Buddha. Sometimes they see an angel, or they see other beings and even aliens."

DMT was literally spelled out to Emma, she says, during the early stage of her second voyage into the darkness. While lying in bed, she suddenly became aware of an entity standing beside her. He held out a hand and asked, *Who wants some DMT?* "So I sat in the prayer position like I was receiving communion, and they put it on my tongue."

Next thing, Emma is thrown backward.

And then, suddenly, I was swimming down to the bottom of the lake here. There was a big trapdoor where water was blowing gold. And I opened it and swam up into a swimming pool. And I was in a whole other world.

It was like this amazing 1950s society of really elite people. They were playing beautiful music and there was a whole different light. And they looked at me and they said, Come with me, you've arrived. *And I said,* Okay. *And they put me in a room and said,* You're going to stay in this room for ten days, it's going to be dark, and we're going to study you, but you won't notice us studying you.

At some point, I did feel that I had to come out. I'm going a bit crazy wondering if the spinning lights and the feeling that I'm the center of the universe would ever stop. And I couldn't really sleep much. There was also a sound that was going hmm, hmm *for the whole seven days. It was a pretty crazy time.*

At her retreat, Kalianey now faces forty days in solitary. It took her a short while to get accustomed to her surroundings: a comfortable bed, meditation bench, single shelf, composting toilet, and cold-water shower. The small room never gets above 15 degrees centigrade (59 degrees Fahrenheit). "I moved around with my fleece jacket and hoodie on 24/7. On the plus side, it was a bit like being in a Himalayan cave," laughed Kalianey. "It kept me very sharp during meditation and made me feel like a true mountain yogini!"

Food is passed through an airlock mechanism twice a day. "A lot of veggies and a bit of rice. That was my only contact with the outside world for the forty days." At first, Kalianey finds herself sleeping a lot, with highly lucid dreams. As the dark days wear on, she first sees highly detailed geometric patterns. She says:

> And then the vision of a beautiful, bright white moon and castle in the sky appeared, and very pictorial visions never stopped again until the end of my retreat, only growing stronger and brighter as time passed.
> The visions were quite varied, from cartoon-like Technicolor movies to a 360-degree immersion in a beautiful purple or turquoise landscape with characters moving around, interacting with me, from flying boats filled with kittens wearing hats to huge stone faces staring at me.

The first few days are known as the melatonin stage, when the body feels an urge to hibernate and the regulatory hormone melatonin quietens the mind. Soon after, the pinoline stage begins, with melatonin levels soaring and generating lights, sounds, and a sense of the self dissolving. Time ceases to have meaning.

"In the Darkness, our mind and soul begin to wander freely in the vast realms of psychic and spiritual experience," explains Master Chia. "When you enter this primordial state or force you are reunited with the true self and divinity within. You literally conduct the universal energy. You may see into the past and future, understand the true meaning of existence, and begin to understand the order of things. You return to the womb, the cocoon of our material structure and Nature's original darkness."

Throughout this time, Kalianey concentrates hard on her meditation, attempting to block out the dramatic events surrounding her by sheer willpower.

It was quite challenging sometimes, as the room was in one moment crowded and I had to pass through all these characters and animals, even walls, to go from one side of the room to the other.

I got scared a few times by very dark floating shadows or characters coming from horror movies, not so much from their presence—although my first reaction was fear, I decided very firmly from the beginning that I would not be scared by my own mind—but from their sudden movements. It's already a bit unsettling to be doing your yoga, trying not to watch the tortured woman from the Martyr movie crawling toward you. But I really jumped in shock when she suddenly extended her arm to touch me!

Kalianey laughs about it now but at the time the image proved deeply unsettling.

As the Tibetan Buddhists say, whatever is in your mind at the moment of death will face you during the bardo, so a dark retreat is also the opportunity to face these images and fears in a more conscious state than after death and integrate or release them. So the first week was mainly about mental purification, accepting and letting go of fears and attachment toward disturbing images.

Some believe that the human body is also capable of producing another form of DMT, in this instance 5-methoxy-N,N-dimethyltryptamine, or 5-MeO-DMT for short. So far, however, it has only been found in a few plants and animals, including the Sonoran Desert toad, which lives exclusively in peyote country around the Mexican and U.S. border. The psychedelic toxins in the toad's skin have been used for millennia in shamanic rituals. Today, a handful of practitioners offer the Toad to those seeking a high-speed spiritual awareness lasting no more than twenty-minutes.

According to "inner travel agent" Chad Charles, the effect is not unlike having the top of one's head blown off. "It's a process that brings memory—repressed memories, cellular memories—to the surface," he explained. "It's like shaking a bottle of fizzy water." And taking Toad, he says, "is like prizing the cap off!"[3] Some have likened the effect to clasping the warhead of an intercontinental ballistic missile at takeoff.

Kalianey, at around her second week, is said by some to be experiencing this 5-MeO-DMT stage, where an internal light emanating from the body illuminates the surroundings and a deeper, more profound meditative state is achieved. Kalianey is spending extended periods each day deep in meditation.

> I literally see myself being somehow inside my own heart, which became huge and is shining with an incredibly bright, blinding white light, exactly like a diamond. During this week, I see light shining extremely bright from my body, huge beams of white light shooting out of my heart or my head, bright red light coming from the navel, glistening gold or purple light filling the whole room.
>
> My whole body looks transparent and usually glistening with light, which can become quite tiring, as the bright lights shooting right in my eyes prevents me from sleeping, as if having cars coming toward me with headlights on full beam.

As Kalianey enters her third week, she is expected to pass through the DMT stage when production is at its highest, fueling intense visions and a sense of vast energy, together with transcendental feelings of universal love and compassion. "My body is shaking more and more from inside in meditation, and I really feel an inner tremor growing as I go deeper inside. Sometimes it feels like my whole body is vibrating and the whole room shaking with me. I do not see the darkness anymore, as everything is so colorful and bright most of the time."

Kalianey is fascinated by the variety of colors and textures, images and scenes, depending on the state of her mind.

> For example, after eating, I get visions of caves made of clay or stone, filling the whole space around me and full of people looking like medieval peasants or wooden figurines, transferring a feeling of

heaviness and constraint. When I am restless and my mind keeps thinking about what I could do outside, I get fast-moving landscapes with very bright lights. When I'm extremely happy, amazing blue sky, turquoise, pink, and purple glistening light.

In my extremely peaceful and blissful states, the quality of the light becomes even more subtle and beautiful, the space becoming huge, sometimes looking like the inside of a gigantic and beautiful cathedral. If I'm upset, though, everything shrinks, the walls become closer and closer and more dense. I get lines of characters surrounding me, shouting at each other and at me, upsetting scenes or landscapes spinning faster and faster, exhausting me. All these different images allow me to watch closely my state of mind and realize how truly important it is to be careful of the kind of thoughts and feelings I am allowing to settle inside myself.

Kalianey counts off the days in her head. By the time she reaches the midway point, it begins to rain inside her silent cell. She recalled:

I felt the rain purifying me from the past and allowing me to be reborn into the new. I am more and more feeling like being in a dream, witnessing worlds arising and falling in my mind's eye.

Some might argue that Kalianey is having a full-on psychotic incident, that the lack of all external stimulation has pushed her over the edge into outright madness. Others might feel that Kalianey is close to death, and perhaps even venturing beyond, and that she is tapping into the same world sought by the mystics with their magic carpets—the other dimensions and alternate realities, populated by helpful, sentient entities, that have been a recorded feature of human existence all along.

But what happens when we are at death's door? Those that have undergone a near-death experience all tell remarkably similar tales of tunnels of light, flying free of their bodies, visiting bucolic landscapes, meeting dead relatives, and gaining an understanding of what life really means. Ultimately, the experience has helped change the perspective of most, they say, with long-term improvements in psychological well-being and greater concern for others, together with a new appreciation for nature and a less materialistic outlook. Most say they now have no fear of death.

These, as it turns out, are also features reported by those who sample ayahuasca or take their DMT by other means. When Dr. Strassman conducted his trials in the late 1990s, he concluded that DMT is likely released in significant quantities at the time of death and that this release is responsible for the spiritual experiences that people report both in DMT trials and NDEs. In short, he thought they were one and the same thing, that the human body releases these compounds to help ease our passing from this life.[4]

But it was not until 2018 that a team at Imperial College London decided to find out if they could demonstrate a more direct connection.[5] They hit on the idea of getting thirteen healthy volunteers to take an intravenous dose of DMT, together with placebos, and then complete the Greyson NDE Scale—the definitive measure of the NDE, described by its inventor, Dr. Bruce Greyson, as the only "reliable, valid and easily administered scale for differentiating NDEs from organic brain syndromes and nonspecific stress responses."[6] Anyone scoring 7 and above is deemed to have had an NDE.

Those undergoing the trials were given sixteen questions ranging from *Did you suddenly seem to understand everything? Did you feel at one with the universe?* to *Were your senses more vivid than usual?*

"Results revealed that all thirteen participants scored above the standard threshold for an NDE," reported the paper's authors. "Taken together, these results reveal a striking similarity between the phenomenology of the near death experience and experiences induced by DMT."

Dr. Mitchell Liester is a psychiatrist who has made a study of NDEs and has also partaken of ayahuasca on a number of occasions in Ecuador. He sees a very clear connection between NDEs and the effects of DMT. "A feeling of peace is very common both with NDEs and with ayahuasca," he told the 2014 IANDS Conference in Newport Beach, California. "Out-of-body experiences are common to both. People on ayahuasca also will encounter spirits of the dead—relatives, family members, loved ones—that they talk with."

Other parallels, he says, are that people often communicate in both cases via thought transfer, rather than with words and speech, and they often find themselves rapidly rising skyward and experience a cosmic consciousness and a very bright light. Nightmarish events—a prominent coma experience—are also features of ayahuasca and NDEs. "People experience tremendous fear. They see things that are unpleasant, uncomfortable, frightening. At other times it can be ecstatic."[7]

At the same time, there are also numerous differences, according to John Chavez, founder of the nonprofit research and educational organization DMT Quest, which aims to unveil the mysteries of human perception as well as their potential.

"While there appears to be overlap between NDEs and DMT experiences," he said in an interview, "they do appear to have some differences in terms of the type of beings they interact with—life review for NDE but not for DMT, geometry-centric visuals for DMT but not for NDEs." His organization believes that naturally produced DMT in humans holds much deeper significance than simply inducing strange, meaningless hallucinations.

"DMT plays a role in modulating our everyday waking perception as well as a heightened state of mysticism and trauma," he says, adding that he does not believe DMT is necessarily acting alone because "neurochemistry operates on dozens of chemicals acting together."

He points to recent research indicating that human-produced DMT is significantly increased, or upregulated, during times of stress. In a 2019 study by Jon Dean, a postdoctoral research fellow in Fadel Zeidan's laboratory at the University of California San Diego, it was discovered that DMT levels in the visual cortex increased 600 percent following cardiac arrest in animal models.[8]

Such activity is best monitored by studying gamma rays in the brain. A 2017 human study also found a surge of gamma waves following cardiac arrest. "The gamma wave increases seem to be a somewhat reliable indicator of altered states of consciousness and potentially endogenous

DMT upregulation," maintains Chavez, who authored the book series *Questions for the Lion Tamer: Delving into the Mystery That Is DMT*.[9]

"When ayahuasca, DMT, and 5-MeO-DMT are administered, they all exude a reliable EEG signature of increased gamma wave strength," he told us, adding that the same effects have been monitored in long-term meditators undergoing transcendental states. He would like to see similar trials carried out on volunteers undergoing dark retreats.

The latest DMT research in mammals indicates that DMT is produced not just in the pineal gland but throughout the choroid plexus—the site of cerebrospinal fluid production and the blood brain barrier—and the cerebral cortex.

Recent studies have also shown that DMT is produced naturally during normal waking hours at similar levels to serotonin—a close cousin of DMT and a key hormone that stabilizes mood, feelings of well-being, and happiness together with the chemical messenger, dopamine. This, they conclude, means DMT is also a likely modulator of our regular waking reality, as well as transcendental and mystic states, making it a key element that defines who we are and an essential part of our makeup.

When we asked coma survivors to complete the Greyson NDE Scale, the majority achieved scores above 7, ranging from 0 up to 19 out of a possible 32. Many struggled with the questionnaire, as it appeared to have no relevance to their own experience—that what they underwent has no parallel in any annals, medical or spiritual. There is, however, considerable overlap between all three—coma, NDE, and DMT—together with considerable differences.

Nightmarish episodes are a predominant feature reported within coma, as they are in DMT, together with death and rebirth, meetings with dead relatives and friends, telepathic communication, and visits to alternate yet everyday realities—from Belgian hospitals to Mexican verandas—together with the curious medical examinations, although those in coma tend to feature torture rather than the exchange of information.

In the case of all three experiences—near-death, DMT-induced, or coma—one common theme runs through all: the absolute clarity of vision, the sense that what they were experiencing was more real than real. The majority of doctors and psychiatrists today dismiss such accounts from within coma as false memories, which is something that rankles many survivors: to be told that such an experience, which was equally as real as any other—and even more so—has no value because it is somehow deemed false by people who have a limited conception of the experience.

This has been likened to returning from a voyage of discovery to distant lands, only to be told by those who believe the world ends at the horizon that your accounts are no more than false memories or hallucinations.

Despite widely varying effects from deep sedation in the ICU, almost every patient who experienced some form of altered reality is diagnosed as delirious. With the NDE being so widely reported across time and place—and so consistently in its different elements—coma survivors are left even more confused when these same events are diagnosed as false memories, delusions, or hallucinations. Those who return from their comas having experienced alternate lives—encompassing incredibly detailed events with all the sights, sounds, and feelings of regular reality—are unable to process the clinical explanations that dismiss them outright. It is even more baffling for those who return with newly acquired skills, such as Nick's sudden handyman abilities.

"We're really fascinated with these alternate lives," says Emma of the Hermitage Retreat. "People [in dark retreat] tend to see it as visiting their past lives. Often within comas, people are having alternate lives, but they're set in the past, sometimes not so far back."

The major difference from those who enter dark retreats or undergo DMT trials, compared to those who experience coma, is that they spend time preparing themselves for the experience and they have others with whom to discuss the strange happenings, removing the feeling not just that they are alone but that their minds may actually be permanently damaged. In the case of coma patients, if they are undergoing a DMT release, no one has prepared them for the experience and few ever get the opportunity to analyze the events later with knowledgeable counselors, leaving so many to question their sanity.

"If people were exposed to DMT without their knowledge," says Helen, who underwent a number of ayahuasca journeys, "they will end up seeing themselves without all the normal filters. And, if they're not prepared for that, I think it can be very seriously damaging. It could drive people insane."

"Even with preparation," Chavez tells us, "the processing and integration following a transcendental experience can be challenging for some people." Those whose experience mirrors that of an NDE may discover positive aspects. "A coma survivor's psyche has the possibility of having positive effects from their experience due to the potential shedding of the fear of death," he believes. "At the same time, they can also feel disoriented in society as people will not be able to relate to them or their experience."

Coma, as we have learned, is not a one-size-fits-all affair. It is different things to different people. The varying sedatives employed, and the degree to which patients are medicated, mean that some on the lightest levels are left to hover just below the surface, absorbing the environment into their dream world in the true sense of delirium, while others go much deeper, allowing them to experience the depths more common to DMT or those recorded by the mystics of old or even the teachings of the bardo. Those pushed too far may simply be touching death's door and sharing similar experiences to those who find themselves briefly clinically dead with a cardiac arrest. Meanwhile, doctors are happy to use the off-the-peg diagnosis of delirium or hallucination for each and every case, which leaves many coma survivors feeling both belittled and insulted.

It is also safe to say that when doctors prescribe such a debilitating cocktail of sedatives and analgesics to patients—from morphine and propofol to ketamine and benzos—they can never be certain just what effect is taking place in the brain. They have just two concerns: to limit the supposed trauma of ICU and to keep the patient in a quiet, manageable state, enabling rest and recuperation. In recent years, some ICUs have introduced a range of antipsychotic drugs that supposedly limit the delirium and hallucinations during coma, without any clear understanding—or even knowledge—of the visions and realities taking place behind closed eyes.

It is highly contentious to say so, but coma-level sedation can oftentimes be avoided because there are safer, kinder ways and means that do not entail rendering patients senseless and that result in significantly lower instances of long-term debility, psychological damage, and alarming and ultimately unnecessary loss of life. And while there is a wealth of scientific data to back up this proposition, there is scant, if any, evidence to support deep sedation. When we asked editors at *The Lancet* how many papers they had published recommending coma-levels of sedation, they could not name a single one.

As Kalianey reaches her fortieth day in the dark, she increasingly sees the world in which we live as yet another projection of her mind.

It showed me that what I consider the "real world" outside of the retreat could as well be a projection of my mind and I would have no way to know. There was this constant distance showing me that everything experienced in the mind is very much like a movie projected on a screen: distant, unreal, and unrelated to me. In the dark retreat, I could see that my mind was constantly creating some sort of universe, projecting people, landscapes, or even bliss experiences into the so-called outside world.

The question, says Kalianey, is:

How to make somebody who has not experienced it conceive that everything existing in the world are just concepts in the mind, that without thought there can be no world, that everything is dreamlike and without substance? So my take on this is that the waking world is as unreal as the dream world, that coma experiences, psychedelic experiences, and real-world experiences are the same, unreal product of the mind.

She believes that all the experiences of near-death, psychedelics, and coma are closer to the experiences that long-term meditators undergo through their practice.

> *It gives us a glimpse into other level of consciousness, and this may be valuable, as it makes us question our assumptions on what reality and life are.*

"It really depends on the way we process the experience," maintains Helen. "With any psychedelic trip, as long as it's done in a conscious way, it will be about integration and how one can bring all these lessons back into our lives. It's all about awareness, it always comes down to that. We don't even need psychedelics to achieve this, it's just a bit of a shortcut."

Helen sees all of these attainable levels of consciousness as being equally real, of holding the same value and lessons. "All these other realms and dimensions that we experience on psychedelics are just as real as this reality. They are all illusions, I believe, but they are still real, they are entirely real in this subjective world."

Kalianey maintains:

> *Spiritual, DMT, or coma experiences can be very difficult to integrate for everyone. It's why, traditionally, long dark retreats and intense spiritual practices were always done under the direction of a master who could guide the disciple, reassure him when needed, and dismiss fanciful interpretations of these experiences. For an uninitiated person, these intense experiences can be very unsettling without guidance.*
>
> *The best-case scenario for the unprepared would be that the DMT experience is seen as a beautiful journey, which then fades in memory but gives a sense of interconnectedness and meaning to life.*
>
> *On the other end of the spectrum, there can be a lot of grief associated with the knowledge of the unreality of the world, or when cherished beliefs are shattered and the world doesn't make sense anymore.*

I guess it's important to remember that no matter how powerful or real these experiences seem, there is no way for us to know what is imagination and what is real, so we should always be circumspect of what the mind presents us.

We do know that the human body produces its own psychedelic DMT, and it has been demonstrated that DMT is released at the point of death, prompting a remarkably consistent glimpse of whatever it is that may lie beyond. When a person is placed into a coma, it is fair to say that they are so seriously unwell that they are already close to death and that the heavy sedation pushes them even further. Might this then bring about a DMT release, rather than the accepted medical view that the scrambled brain simply invents memories—highly detailed and remarkably consistent memories—after the event?

No one can definitively say why we produce DMT in our system nor what its precise role may be, while, equally, no one can safely say what happens at the point of death or beyond. But it does seem certain that the brain is capable of producing a cocktail of chemicals that may be nature's way of either taking the sting out of death to ease our passing or, perhaps, to open a doorway to what lies ahead.

Asked if the wondrous effects of DMT release might be a common experience among both humans and animals at the point of death—or at the perceived threat of death—Chavez gives a resounding yes. "I do believe DMT is involved in the near-death process, and it seems that for whatever reason humans and possibly all mammals are capable of having these events."

Naturally occurring DMT in humans might also go some way toward explaining the more common forms of hallucination experienced by those at the end of their endurance or by others undergoing spontaneous mystical experiences or religious apparitions.

Again, John Chavez believes DMT is a contributing factor. He said in an interview, "Yes, it seems that extremis and spontaneously induced altered states of consciousness induce distinct changes to one's neurology. Electrophysiological changes via EEG measurement have shown distinct changes to the brain," he points out. "Hopefully, in the future, noninvasive technology can be developed to synchronously measure biochemical fluctuations that take place in the brain during these moments of altered perception."

"We know that DMT is produced in the brain, with or without the pineal gland," confirms Jimo Borjigin in an interview. "But we have not worked with human subjects, healthy or otherwise, thus far and are not in the position to comment on that area."

For the time being, the medical world remains as deeply in the dark as the patients they sedate to coma levels. And while many doctors appear content to dismiss the coma experience as a form of confusion, many ICU nurses—with greater hands-on experience—are beginning to question the practice.

In the course of writing this book, we have spoken with many who felt that they died within their comas and yet returned. They tell of something that lies beyond, of other levels of consciousness yet to be explored, and of other dimensions previously recounted by others across time, continents, and cultures. When all appear to offer remarkably similar accounts, it becomes harder to dismiss their accounts out of hand as fantasies or delusional mumbo jumbo or the consequence of addled minds.

Numerous scientific papers demonstrate that certain sedatives switch off the default mode network, much as psychedelic drugs and deep meditation do, and that as a result the mind is seemingly set free, which allows an expansion of consciousness.[10] As further research is undertaken, it will become ever more apparent that the human body is capable, in extremis, of producing some remarkable drugs of its own that also set the mind free and expand consciousness.

Whichever is the case, artificially induced comas are clearly opening the door to other levels of consciousness. They may even lay a path to other dimensions and realities, but until serious research is undertaken in this area, Borjigin, one of the world's leading neurologists, tells us: "Nothing can be ruled out."

"I think science will never accept those experiences and other levels of consciousness," Kalianey tells us. "It's so beyond anything conceivable, and it's not something that can be measured. Looking at brains of advanced meditators or at brains during the psychedelic experiences is the closest it can get, but without experiencing those states no one can truly believe in them or comprehend what they mean."

If the scientific world continues to cling to its limited materialistic views, dismissing the firsthand accounts of mystics, philosophers, psychedelic explorers, near-death experiencers, and coma survivors, we may never fully understand consciousness nor grasp what the mind is ultimately capable of. These are subjects that have exercised some of the greatest thinkers from antiquity to the modern world, from King Solomon and Plato to Carl Jung, Aldous Huxley, Albert Einstein, and Alan Turin. If we continue to ignore their compelling evidence, we may never be able to answer the ultimate question—the meaning of life and our role within it—and we may never advance beyond being the "moist robots" the materialists would have us believe we are.

Stephen (Continued): The Kiss of Warm, Soft Rain

Stephen the medical statistician wakes up to find himself lying in bed in a small, windowless room. The light is yellow. He sees pale wood panels and brass fittings.

. . .

Easing into awareness, a sense of motion, soft swaying, gentle rocking, faint vibrations: distant, rhythmic throb of huge engines, waves washing: a ship's cabin. A sense of nighttime passing; long, slow.

The rhythmic note of the engine changes, the bed vibrates. Morning is approaching, and the ship is coming in to land. He makes his way on deck and looks to the shore. He spots the quayside and then a hospital.

Drawing closer, closer; ablaze with light, alive with life; tiny, dark figures move about with intent; queuing along quay. Hurrying to prepare, awaiting the ship's docking.

Stephen takes a last look out to sea and sucks in the breeze.

Silver morning promise on the horizon; entrapment of night coming to a close; dawn is here. Washing waves of the sea, washing the ship, washing, ripples, rippling, rippling . . . waking . . . dawn, no more feeling alone.

It's time to celebrate. Stephen is suddenly surrounded by nurses and their excited chatter. But now they wear their glad rags, all dressed up for a disco night out. They all pour out onto the dark, rain-wet streets, racing down steps, pulling him along. He falls through a dark tunnel with disco strobes, music, and neon lights flashing by. Arms reach out to grab him, and he find himself strapped in tight, unable to move.

Punitive phantoms brandish punish-sticks. Anguished faces peering, desperate helping hands stretch from neon dark corridors. Then, from one side, a flood of bright daylight . . .

Time appears to slow, grinding to a halt. It stops. Dead. Back in the Cushioned Room amid a quivering, gloom-gold lamplight.

. The cushion sits there on its wall, huge, silent, still, close, a looming, shadowed threat.

The room is smaller now and daylight is darker.

Yellow wall lamps, period pictures, floral furnishings, cushioned armchairs; silent waiting, watching windows. And cushions, cushions, strewn about, placed on chairs, on seating along wall. Lying amid lamplit, deaf-deadness. Stifling. Suffocating. Muffled silence.

Except the ticking. Tick, tick, tick. Interminable hours. Tick, tick, tick. And the Cushion glowers over, in yellow shadow-light, flickering, shimmering. Tick, tick, tick. Darkness enveloping, cloaking blackness.

Now a gentle, white glow. It grows brighter as it comes closer, slowly taking form, now a floodlight of bright, icy, white light. Skaters glide and slide by, small dark figures gracefully tracing patterns in the ice. Stephen stands on the ice, and ahead of him he sees a great, gray wall, a vast building stretching into the sky— blank, windowless, featureless, lifeless; disappearing into inky dark above.

He finds himself slowly rising into blackness, as the great building slides by.

Now alone, in silent blackness; the solemn building, ghostly glow-lit, slowly, silently, glides by. But a consoling comfort, an embracing warmth: gentle quiet from above, a soft mist of warm rain. I lift my face, close my eyes, feel blessed kiss of warm, soft, soft rain. I find restful peace, consoling comfort, soothing solace.

I'm not alone, there's a presence here; but it's not for now: a white noise hiss pervades the hushed air; emerging around me, misty-soft, the atrium, the splashing fountain; enveloping, enfolding, healing fountain mist. Then rising into light, the light of birth of a new day.

And there before me, on its green wooded hillside, firm-standing pink granite in the warm morning sun. Shining metal and glass, arcing around the hill contours with magnificent grace: the hospital, its green lawn sitting quiet, flags rolling lazily in the morning breeze.

But the spell is broken. Suddenly, urgently, a new scene comes.

Racing from the hospital down the winding road, two gleaming, powerful sports cars: one gold, one white . . .

Ted's Dad (Continued): Hell and Heaven

Ted's Dad, the composer Stephen Watkins, found his coma experiences rather nice overall. Some were baffling and others vague, one was especially heavenly, another the stuff of his personal nightmares—chairing a board meeting of Ipswich Town Football Club.

• • •

Yeah. Where did that come from? I've no interest whatsoever in football. Ipswich is a gritty little town. I don't know the names of any players. I don't know anything about them. I can just about work out if one person puts the ball in the net. And that's about it. I was a rugby player at school, not football. I've got absolutely no interest in football at all.

But there I was. I was in bed, attending a board meeting. And I was in bed after having had the [heart] operation, having quite some trouble. And this was my idea of hell—football!

The community involvement that decent clubs have, that's okay, I admire that. But me, chairing the board or whatever, I wouldn't know where to start. I just couldn't work out why I was there. And having the thought, Well, if you want some normal person with a different perspective on things, I'm quite happy to lie here and have that different perspective. But you better keep a nurse handy.

And then there were other scenarios as well, which were really nice, although some of them were very, very puzzling to me. I was in Germany, standing next to a church. And I had played in the church before. I had choral music by me performed in the church.

And I was lying there in bed, and they weren't sure how ill I was or whether I was going to live or not. But they wanted me to hear my music being performed. And it was Christmas, a very German version of a Charles Dickens Christmas, with the Christmas market and stuff between the church and the schloss [chateau]. I knew this place.

Then the doors opened, and there were senior military people and minor royals coming to see how I was. They made sure the doors were left open so I could hear the concert, my music. You can't ask any more than that, can you?

Zara: Balancing on a Feather

For Zara the artist, the flesh-eating bug is spreading fast, putting her life at risk. Doctors tell her they need to operate on her leg, that she may be left with a limp. But things go awry. They amputate the leg right up to the spine. "There was a stage toward the end when I wanted to die," she says. But the drugs kept her just below the surface. "I was hovering."

• • •

I was on the edge of dying. I was bleeding out, losing so much blood. And that's when I had an out-of-body experience. I was above my body, and it was just slumped and drenched in blood. But it wasn't me in the bed. It was me as somebody else. I was looking at somebody else who I had killed. And there was blood everywhere. I was shocked at the reaction of everybody in the room, the panic in the room.

I could see things. I definitely could see things. I told the nurses that I could remember the surgery. I remember going in and I remember this pole being put through my back, drilling this hole in my back. They said, Well, you wouldn't remember that. But I did remember it.

And I was the cause of all of this panic. I was guilty. I hadn't connected that the person I was looking at was me. I was just taking in everything in the room. And I was the cause of it. That was my mental state. I had to bear witness to all the grief that was in the room, of which I was the cause.

My levels of consciousness were going up and down. There was a point where I was put into a box, and it was a bit like a coffin, but it was probably another scanning machine. But I was in this box, and then flames came, and I knew that there was fire all around me.

It was really, really hot, and I was frightened that it was going to penetrate the box because it wasn't just me in there. There was my husband and my kids, and all I could think was that they were going to be burnt alive and they shouldn't be there. But then I realized that the flames weren't penetrating the box. And it was okay.

The only point where I actually, physically, found myself completely somewhere else was when I ended up on a dockside in China. And there were these old men sitting off to the side. They were very old and wore ancient clothes with long, gray beards. And I knew they were deciding my fate. I knew they were talking about me.

It was a beautiful spring day, and the breeze was just beautiful. And I found myself on the edge of a feather, and I was balancing on this very fine edge and the water was there beneath me. It was just absolutely crystal clear and the sky was really blue. And it was then that I found out that I was going to live. And I heard their whispers, saying that I was going to make it. I was going to live.

Corey: Everything's Gonna Be Okay

Corey the Alabama hospital chaplain finds himself in a totally pitch-black world. He is in a heightened spiritual state and is expecting to come face to face with his God. He sees a mountain of light.

. . .

And then, in gold writing, scripture verses would come across in my mind, like the 23rd Psalm, The Lord is my Shepherd, *and it would come up and then fade out and disappear. And then* I shall not be in want *came up word for word, and then it would fade out and disappear.*

But there were verses that I hadn't ever studied before. And when I was finally out of my coma, I was able to look up those verses, and they were exactly the verses in the Bible that were across in my mind but I hadn't ever studied them before.

But I remember having such peace, that if I had died in that moment, it would have been okay. It would have been okay. And, you know, I heard hymns from my church, back when I was a kid. Just hearing the choir sing, I was right there in that moment.

The way I see it, God is telling me it's going to be okay. You know, to trust Me. But I didn't see an image of God, I didn't see a vision of Jesus, or anything like that. I just saw a mountain of light.

My wife said that when I was comatose, I was quoting scriptures. And I saw scripture verses that were real. Versus that I didn't know. And to me, the experience proved my faith was real. That everything I read in scripture is one hundred percent real. It's not some clever story invented by talented writers. This is a very real thing. And it put a definitive stamp on everything that I believed from my childhood to now.

I don't have a fear of dying. I'm not afraid of it. I don't have the uncertainty of it that I had before the experience. And I learned that God gives us exceedingly more grace as we near the end of life. In those moments of the dying process, we truly are with Him. This just confirms it. You don't have to fear, you don't have to be worried. You don't have to be anxious, it's okay. It's okay.

Nick the Rainbow (Continued)

So I was free falling and I was free falling into complete nothingness. I mean, there was nothing around. Then, all of a sudden, I would be encapsulated in a color. First, it was an orange color that was just the most beautiful, sunny, delightful orange you've ever seen, so vivid, so intense. I've never seen a color that beautiful. But I wasn't in the color. I was the color.

The color was everywhere around me. It was all I could see. It was me. And then I was falling through that color and I was completely soaking wet. And then, next thing you know, I'm in another different color—blue, the most beautiful, gorgeous, blue-baby-blue you've ever seen. You can't even describe it, incredible, unbelievable.

Then I fell through that color and was soaking wet again, and next thing I'm in the most bright, beautiful yellow you've ever seen. I fall through that one, get soaking wet, fall through a pink color that I can't even describe, and so on. And I don't know for how long, but those four colors I vividly remember. While I was in those colors, while I was in that moment, I was God. I was everything, everything was me. I can't even explain it further than that.

It was so intense, it was so pure, it was so worry-free, it was so without thought, it was so meaningful, it was so powerful. It was an incredible feeling that I've been searching for ever since and don't think I ever will find, not until death.

Just the pure feeling I had of ecstasy was incredible. It was like nothing I'd ever felt before. It was just incredibly pure. I don't know how else to put it. I didn't have a single worry or problem. I was completely present. I was completely enthralled in that moment. I was one hundred percent, completely happy and didn't wanna leave it.

This whole time, I didn't know if I was in a coma or dying, if I was living or my consciousness was. I'm not religious. I don't believe I was in heaven. I don't believe I was in hell. I don't believe I was in limbo. I believe I was in the universe, like on another dimension that we can't see or fathom.

But I'm gonna leave it on that note for now. My adrenaline is pumping just from getting this out!

PART 3

The Reality of Life after Coma

8

The ICU Death Trap
How Did We Ever Get It So Wrong?

By the time the World Health Organization declared a global coronavirus pandemic in March 2020, intensive care units around the world were already finding themselves stretched to the limit and beyond. Many of the best practices learned over the years were thrown out of the window in the rush to help as many patients as possible. Within the first year, 750,000 patients with COVID-19 worldwide required mechanical ventilation, many of whom were sedated to coma levels, says the COVID-19 Intensive Care International Study Group[1]—defying just about all current medical recommendations.

The commonly held belief that comas are benign affairs that allow patients to rest and recuperate—as regularly portrayed in media and film and echoed by many doctors—flies in the face of long-established procedures and numerous studies that prove the precise opposite.[2] It has been known for years that prolonged deep sedation leads to brain damage and substantially increases the chance of death.

"COVID had everyone panicked," says Washington State nurse practitioner Kali Dayton, DNP, AGACNP-BC. "A lot of new nurses and doctors were thrown into the field with limited idea of the best practices that had been developed." Dayton talks from considerable experience. She is a renowned critical care consultant working with teams across the United States and around the world, with years spent working on various ICUs.[3]

"COVID was such an unbelievable challenge for nurses because it was lethal," says a seven-year veteran of close ICU care, Jill Larkin Storer, BSN, RN, CCRN.

I mean, once you got to the point of ARDS [Acute Respiratory Distress Syndrome], there was really not a whole lot we could do. It's basically game over. . . . And the standard practice with ARDS has long been to render patients so deeply unconscious that the respiratory drive comes to a halt, allowing the ventilator to take over and set the pace.

I think we all did the same thing with our sedation practices during COVID. . . . We just decided, *Oh my god, I have no idea how to oxygenate this person unless I sedate and paralyze them.* . . . COVID-19 . . . was a new frontier where nobody had a map.

I've never seen a respiratory disease like that in my seventeen years of nursing. It was so unforgiving, so uncompromising, and we didn't have the tools. But the silver lining for COVID for me is that you could clearly see what ICU-acquired weakness does to your patients.

ICU delirium was running rampant. And this sudden realization was her lightbulb moment. *Why are we sedating these people?* she asked herself.

In most cases, it's because of the historical, cultural belief that it's more humane. [Few nurses ever get to see the full effects of deep sedation and the lasting aftereffects of delirium.] Because there was never that follow-up. That does not exist in the American health care system. It's one of my life goals to close that gap.

"Throughout the pandemic, it's become increasingly obvious that the lack of evidence-based practices are having a devastating effect on

ICU patient care," insists Dayton, who also hosts the popular podcast *Walking Home from the ICU,* where she advocates an entirely different, more compassionate, form of treatment.[4] "Over the last two years, I've seen countless examples of this, and it breaks my heart because most of these tragedies are totally preventable. We are unnecessarily harming patients and increasing the workload for staff."

Rendering patients senseless just makes them sicker, she says. It has been repeatedly shown that by doing so, patients spend longer on the ventilator, adding to the length of their hospital stay, causing more suffering for patients and families, and burdening health systems while overloading long-term care facilities. "This is a product of a culture, habits, and an overall health care system that has created the ICU death trap," Dayton maintains.

Back in the 1990s, most nurses and doctors believed deep sedation to be a fairly harmless procedure, says Professor Michele Balas, PhD, RN, CCRN-K, FCCM, FAAN, associate dean for research at the University of Nebraska Medical Center. But, she says, "We knew for years that patients in intensive care units get really confused. Delirium was just starting to get the attention that it deserves. Back then, we knew it was common, but people weren't using the right language at the time. We used to call it 'sundowning' or 'just ain't right syndrome.' I remember telling family members myself that everyone gets confused [but] they'll definitely get better by the time they get home. *Oh, boy!* Was I wrong! Now we know [the procedure] actually hurts our patients."

In 2016, Professor Balas told the American Association of Critical-Care Nurses' convention in Orlando that many nurses continued to persist in the belief that patients on mechanical ventilators need to be deeply sedated. "As nurses, we would talk to each other and say, *If I'm ever in the ICU, make sure I'm on the vent and make sure you keep me sedated. I don't want to be awake. I don't want to remember anything.*"[5]

"Nurses' attitudes toward sedating patients receiving mechanical ventilation have shifted in the past decade, with fewer nurses now believing that all patients should be sedated," concluded the 2019 U.S. national survey "Nurses' Attitudes and Practices Related to Sedation."[6]

"However, more than half of nurses [66 percent, down from 81 percent in 2010] still agree that sedation is needed for patients' comfort—highlighting the need to consider nurses' attitudes when seeking to optimize sedation practices during mechanical ventilation."

To this day, nurses new to the ICU are generally told that patients requiring ventilation should be sedated as a matter of course. Not doing so can be dangerous, causing the patient to gag or vomit, which may clog the airways and cause damage to vocal cords. According to the *American Journal of Critical Care*, "The need for sedative therapy in critical care adults receiving mechanical ventilation is well established," noting in 2012 that 85 percent of ICU patients "are given intravenous sedatives to help attenuate the anxiety, pain, and agitation associated with mechanical ventilation."[7]

Many doctors will explain that the natural tendency to gag when a tube is inserted into the throat can be distressing to the patient. "So we place people in deep sedation," says Dr. Esther Choo, an associate professor of emergency medicine at Oregon Health & Science University speaking to Vox.com in April 2020. The article explains, "After the tube is placed in the trachea, patients have to stay sedated—in the case of some COVID-19 patients that can last for several weeks." Without the right medications, "That experience can be agonizing," Choo says.[8]

Such commonplace views are often difficult to change once firmly planted in the minds of many long-serving doctors and old-school nursing staff. Yet such attitudes need to be urgently reevaluated, says Dayton. "Most nurses don't believe patients can or should be awake on the ventilator," she tells us. "It's in our minds that every patient on a ventilator has to be sedated, but I have scoured the research and there's nothing to prove that. But the problem is that we're not questioning enough because we're not aware of the risks."

There are obviously cases when patients do need to be deeply sedated, for example those experiencing continuous seizures such as status epilepticus and intracranial hypertension, a buildup of pressure around the brain. In such cases, brain activity needs to be suppressed to prevent lasting damage. With complications following cardiac surgery, where the heart is not pumping sufficient oxygenated blood around the system, the patient needs to be kept as still as possible to prevent hypoxia. Often, in such cases, the patient is connected to a bypass machine, known as an ECMO (extracorporeal membrane oxygenation), that takes the place of the heart, and all physical activity needs to be halted to conserve the oxygen in the system. Additionally, patients with particular types of wounds, such as abdominal, also need to be kept as still as possible. But deep sedation is all too often applied when it is not strictly necessary due to a lack of understanding of the damage it will cause.

"We know that a lot of the things that we did in the ICU—that we really thought were the best things for our patients, that we did for very good reasons—are actually causing more problems than what we were initially trying to treat the patient for," maintains Professor Balas.

"We kept them very heavily sedated with the thoughts that we're helping them forget this terrible experience, but we now know that practice of deep sedation is very harmful to the patient," she warned. "It hurts their brains, it hurts their body, [causing] physical and functional disability."

Slowly, at first, this understanding began to creep into a modest number of ICUs around the world. More and more papers were published decrying deep sedation, and greater care was given to preventing delirium and muscle wastage—then COVID-19 struck. The levels of stress that ICU staff underwent during the pandemic had never been seen in peacetime before. Drastic measures were called for. It was time to go back to square one.

In early 2022, a study in Spain concluded that almost half of ICU staff were at high risk of mental breakdown, with many exhibiting signs of anxiety, panic attacks, insomnia, depression, substance abuse, post-traumatic stress, and suicidal notions. Those worst affected were staff drafted in from other departments and those obliged to work in the hastily constructed emergency ICU units.[9] For all concerned, increased workloads led to both burnout and difficult ethical dilemmas.

Late into the second year of the pandemic, the French health minister conceded that thirteen hundred new nursing students had handed in their notice because of the stress of working on COVID-19 wards. A flash survey at the time found that French hospitals were experiencing shortages of staff in most departments, from nurses through to anesthesiologists, as were hospitals across Europe.[10]

That same year, the head of the Australian College of Nursing, Kylie Ward, told ABC's evening news that more than twenty thousand frontline nurses had quit the profession due to the workload caused by the pandemic.[11] Across the United States, many smaller hospitals feared they might have to file for bankruptcy with the additional cost of hiring agency workers to fill the nursing gaps.

In Britain, medics working across all branches of the National Health Service quit in record numbers. In a three-month period halfway through 2021, more than twenty-seven thousand workers resigned, citing burnout and emotional trauma.[12]

"I was diagnosed with PTSD in February 2021," ICU nurse Joan Pons Laplana recounts in his book, *Destiny and Hope: My Life as a Nurse in Great Britain—Brexit, Covid-19 and Vaccines*. "I couldn't face going back to work. It cost me my mental health and my marriage. My life fell to pieces after the second wave. I realized I didn't want the stress and the pressure."

As such, only a tiny minority of ICUs could maintain the accepted two-to-one patient-nurse ratios. Seemingly, the only way to cope was to revert to practices of old, to deeply sedate the patients, put them into a more manageable state, and lighten the workload. This, it was believed, would also spare them from the unnecessary trauma of a hectic hospital environment. As a result, almost every intubated COVID-19 patient in almost every ICU around the world was heavily sedated. As a practice, deeper sedation has been gradually making its way back over the years, and many now fear it—together with limited or no mobility and a continuing halt to the family visits as established throughout the pandemic—is becoming the norm for other critically ill patients in cash-strapped facilities with fewer staff.

For the health care professionals trapped in a system that now appeared to be harming patients—with the shocking effects of deep sedation slowly becoming apparent—nurses often found themselves facing painful moral dilemmas, obliged to carry out procedures that a growing number were finding deeply questionable.

"Sedation is given by nurses with intentions rooted in compassion. Nurses are some of the most sympathetic, ethical, and humane people among us," Dayton stresses passionately. "Nurses take their role in patient safety, comfort, and success as sacred. If there's something they believe will relieve and prevent suffering, that will be just as important as any other medical treatment to them. So when sixty-six percent of nurses still believe sedation is for patient comfort, they give sedation with the intent and understanding that it's sparing patients the struggles and stress of critical illness."

And while it might appear expedient to sedate most ICU patients to coma levels in the time of COVID-19, remarkably little is understood about the long-term effects of the procedure. It is worth noting how often doctors refer to deep sedation as sleep. But in reality, the heavy sedatives prevent proper sleep, leaving patients sleep-deprived and leading to overwhelming cases of brain-damaging ICU delirium, where brains are left exhausted and broken, stuck on a hamster wheel of terrifying, nightmare-like events. "The sedation we use to make patients comatose disrupts the brain so severely that it prevents them having restorative sleep," Dayton tells us.

Back in 2018, the *BMC Journal* published the report "A Hospital-Wide Evaluation of Delirium Prevalence and Outcomes in Acute Care Patients: A Cohort Study." They concluded that of those patients receiving lengthy deep sedation, around 80 percent developed ICU delirium.[13] By playing down the true severity of this hospital-acquired condition—generally not covered by medical insurance—its significance goes unreported. ICU delirium has been proven to have lethal consequences, both in the ICU and soon after discharge. Few, if any, patients or their families are ever told of the risks associated with deep sedation. Many are discharged without being warned of the immense problems that lay ahead.

The *BMC Journal* confirmed that those with the condition stayed much longer in ICUs and hospital generally, requiring significantly more nursing hours, which raised costs considerably. They also warned that such practices led to a statistically higher death rate among patients.

"Early deep sedation is associated with adverse outcomes and constitutes an independent predictor of hospital mortality in mechanically ventilated patients," say the authors of the 2014 report "Early Sedation and Clinical Outcomes of Mechanically Ventilated Patients."[14] Although they pointed out that oversedation has not been fully studied, nor is it really understood, they did concede that "deep sedation was associated with increased disease severity, longer duration of ventilatory support and higher need for tracheostomy" and that it has been demonstrated to lead to higher mortality.

In 2021, the journal *Critical Care Research and Practice* confirmed multiple earlier findings that delirium added to the length of stay for the majority of ICU patients. "Patients with delirium often require prolonged mechanical ventilation and take longer to reach a cognitive and physical state that enables discharge from acute care," said the authors.[15]

Due to the vast ethical issues, no proper research has been conducted by the medical world into sleep deprivation in humans over dangerously lengthy periods. However, the military world has far fewer scruples. Many special forces regularly undergo several days at a time of being REM sleep-deprived as part of their training, and it is used extensively as a form of torture prior to interrogation.

Former U.S. Navy SEAL Stew Smith recounted surviving just three days on no sleep but said it played havoc with his cognitive functions. He mistook one military aircraft for a flying horse and saw most things in cartoon-like terms. "I would never wish this kind of treatment on anyone," he said.

In U.S. military prisons like Guantanamo and Abu Ghraib, detainees were regularly submitted to the "frequent flyer program" where they were moved from location to location every three hours, denying them uninterrupted sleep for up to three weeks at a time. Such treatment was regularly followed by three-week periods of total isolation, often in pitch darkness. Plaintiffs have repeatedly argued that such practices have left them with brain damage and deep psychological issues. Courts have subsequently ruled that when inflicted intentionally, both should be classified as torture.

The physical effects on the brain during lengthy periods without REM sleep are also poorly understood. Dr. Charles Czeisler is an American physician and sleep researcher. He says that during normal sleep, cells in the brain shrink temporarily, allowing "drainage tubes" in the lymphatic system to expand and remove toxins from the body. When denied sleep, "brain cells remain tight and the brain can't get rid of these toxins efficiently," he told ABC News.

This can result in short- and long-term memory impairment, reduced concentration, headaches and back pain, hyperarousal, severe depression with vegetative symptoms, nightmares, feelings of shame and humiliation, incoherent speech, disorientation, irritability, anger, paranoia, hallucination, and delusions, together with PTSD.

Nevertheless, that sedation equals sleep is just one of a number of myths current in the medical world despite years of research demonstrating the opposite. In one trial in 1998, "Temporal Disorganization of Circadian Rhythmicity and Sleep-Wake Regulation in Mechanically Ventilated Patients Receiving Continuous Intravenous Sedation," it was shown that restorative REM sleep could be identified in just two out of twenty-one coma patients. And the authors had to admit they had great difficulty determining if any patient was really sleeping.[16] "We were unable to identify in our ICU patients any of the elements of normal sleep-wake regulation," maintain the paper's authors. "This suggests that critically ill patients receiving mechanical ventilation and intravenous sedation exist not only in an altered state of consciousness but may be continuously sleep-deprived, a condition that could exacerbate their condition and compromise their recovery."

In 2008, another study, "Sleep and Delirium in the Intensive Care Unit," by Dr. Giovanni Mistraletti of the University of Milan and others concluded that sleep disturbances in the ICU are not only poorly understood but that they are the single greatest contributing factor for delirium. "ICU patients almost uniformly suffer from sleep disruption," reported the paper's authors. "A harsh ICU environment, underlying disease, mechanical ventilation, pain and drugs are the main reasons that underlie sleep disruption in the critically ill."[17]

In common with other findings, they concluded that hypnotic agents like benzodiazepines, which are routinely administered in coma care, severely disrupt sleep patterns. Trading under the street name of benzos, these psychoactive drugs lower brain activity but are also known to produce muscle weakness and memory problems. They are addictive, prompting withdrawal symptoms, and they impair cognitive function. Street users are strictly warned never to combine them with opioids, which are widely combined in the coma cocktail.

"Sleep disruption and the development of delirium are frequently related, both because of sleep scarcity and inappropriate dosing with sedatives," Dr. Mistraletti found, adding that delirium exacerbates existing problems and increases the likelihood of death within the ICU and soon after discharge. "The intensive care provider must recognize that although patients may appear to be sleeping, benzodiazepines and opioids significantly alter the normal sleep pattern."

In 2021, a major study examined COVID-19 patients in the ICU, covering sixty-nine hospitals across fourteen countries. They found that some 80 percent of COVID-19 patients were placed into comas—the majority soon after arrival—and that a good half or more contracted delirium. The major contributing factors to delirium they found were benzodiazepine infusion, which added a 60 percent higher risk, and the lack of family visits, which added another 30 percent. The report produced by the COVID-19 Intensive Care International Study Group concluded that clinicians had reverted to outdated and potentially harmful treatment strategies of deep sedation with widespread use of benzodiazepine, immobilization, and isolation from families due to the pandemic. "These changes in clinical practice are associated with significantly higher prevalence and duration of delirium and coma . . . leading to a major risk for ICU-related dementia and survivorship," they maintained.[18]

Their study, they insist, provides clear evidence that clinicians should revert to proven therapies that avoid deep sedation and that they should also allow safe in-person or virtual visitation for patients with COVID-19. The human factor, they concluded, was a vital part of the recovery process. They also found that COVID patients were receiving higher doses of sedatives and analgesics than patients prior to the pandemic. Other contributing factors to delirium were the shortage of certain sedatives and the use of non-ICU trained staff.

"Although the true prevalence of delirium in critically ill patients with COVID-19 is unknown," the group says, patients with COVID-19 are at high risk of delirium due to systemic inflammation and neuro-inflammation, other organ system failures, increased risk of thrombosis, and the effects of deep sedative strategies and prolonged mechanical ventilation.

"When possible, health-care providers should adhere to current sedation guidelines for mechanically ventilated patients, even those with COVID-19, which recommend . . . avoidance of continuous infusions of benzodiazepines, light levels of sedation, frequent awakening and breathing trials, and mobilization." The group noted that of the 2,088 COVID patients studied, 28 percent—more than six hundred people—died within just twenty-eight days of admission to the hospital.

Such practices, it says, have been proven to improve short-term outcomes and "might also reduce the risk of PICS, which affects a high proportion of acute respiratory failure survivors." It is crucial, underlined the group, that ICU practitioners avoid deep sedation.

Although the report's authors do not say so directly, it is hard to ignore the obvious conclusion that such procedures have led to an increase in the number of deaths from COVID-19, deaths that may have been entirely avoidable if earlier protocols limiting sedation had been followed, together with early mobilization and more human contact.

Many medical professionals, however, believe such heavy sedation spares the patient from the harrowing effects of a lengthy ICU stay, preventing instances of PTSD, which can affect anywhere from 5 percent to 63 percent of patients, depending which research papers you read.[19]

And while a majority of ICU patients have limited recall of their hospital stay, most coma survivors frequently report that the horrors experienced under sedation felt more real than reality itself, and it is this that leads to traumatic stress and not the hospital environment.

"I've had clinicians tell me that they sedate patients on ventilators for the purpose of preventing PTSD," says Dayton. "What they don't understand is they have caused them that trauma with the sedation. I can understand how we would develop that sense of logic, as our patients seem so peaceful and cozy when they're comatose. But this reasoning does not harmonize with what survivors and research has been telling us."

Another common myth among medical professionals is that comas are relatively harmless and even more humane. However, most coma survivors will say that the effects of the coma itself were infinitely more harrowing and damaging than the condition that led them to being placed in a coma initially.[20] Research has also shown a greater chance of hospital-induced infections,[21] pressure sores,[22] blood clots,[23] muscle wastage and ICU-acquired weakness,[24] depression, an increased likelihood of pneumonia, and, again, a proven increase in death rates.[25]

Other research in recent years has shown that the longer a patient spends on a mechanical ventilator, the greater their chance of developing significant muscular atrophy. Propofol, marketed as Diprivan, is commonly administered in efforts to produce deep sedation, yet is known to cause myalgia—muscle aches and pains affecting much of the body—when administered just briefly during surgery. Prolonged use of propofol causes diaphragm dysfunction, disrupts neuromuscular connection, causes insulin resistance, and is likely myotoxic, leading to severe muscle necrosis. It is also known to cause slow-wave-sleep suppression, reducing restorative REM sleep.[26] This is the drug that is believed to have killed the "king of pop," Michael Jackson.

For those patients spending in excess of three weeks on a mechanical ventilator, the risks increase significantly, and they require extensive rehabilitation and outpatient care. The Society of Critical Care

Medicine (SCCM) found that the majority of ICU patients with COVID-19 had returned to work six months after discharge, but that most of them reported reduced work effectiveness with prolonged sick leave. Subsequent unemployment was found to be common among survivors.[27]

The risks of kidney failure increase with the duration of sedation, according to a study undertaken by Dr. Thomas Strøm, PhD, a clinical associate professor in anesthesiology at the University of Southern Denmark.[28] "A patient with renal failure—when the kidneys stop working—is in a really bad situation," he explained to the medical website sciencenordic.com in 2012.

With the kidneys out of action or functioning poorly, red blood cell production is reduced, blood pressure increases, and waste materials, toxins, and medications—both sedative and analgesic—are not flushed out of the body, leading to a potentially fatal buildup. "We can see that an induced coma can give a patient a poorer physical condition than he or she would have otherwise had. And, just by turning off sedation, renal function returns. The use of induced comas as a standard treatment must be changed."

Another apparent misconception is that ventilated patients need to be kept as still as possible, although research has demonstrated that mobility is a key factor in swift recovery. "Bedrest during critical illness can no longer be considered a benign intervention, as it is associated with atrophy and ICU-acquired weakness," maintain the authors of the 2013 report "Acquired Neuromuscular Weakness and Early Mobilization in the Intensive Care Unit."[29] It has also been shown that just one week of bed rest can result in the loss of up to 40 percent of lean muscle.[30] Other studies have shown that skeletal muscle strength declines more than one percentage point for every day of bed rest.[31]

Such muscle wastage is not always apparent, as the body retains the additional fluids pumped in to maintain blood pressure and keep the heart pumping. Often, an average sized patient can take on an extra fifty pounds in weight of excess fluid, swelling to such an extent that damaged muscles go unnoticed.

"Neuromuscular weakness is commonplace in the ICU and can persist for years after discharge," warn the authors of the 2013 report. "Early mobilization is a safe and feasible intervention for many critically ill patients, and is associated with improved outcomes." But, they say, such early mobilization programs require a culture change.[32]

To grasp the scale of the problem, consider that there are around thirty-three million hospital admissions each year in the United States, which works out at around 10 percent of the population.[33] This means the equivalent of the entire population of 333 million people is admitted to hospital every decade. And more than 5.7 million patients are admitted annually to an intensive care unit. It is fair to assume that between 20 and 30 percent of these admissions include an ICU stay with the resulting deep sedation and lack of mobility.[34]

"Every citizen in the US and likewise throughout most of the world will probably experience two or three ICU admissions in their lifetime," says Dr. Peter J. Murphy, clinical professor of pulmonary medicine at California Northstate University College of Medicine. "That's a horrific number of people being admitted and discharged with the potential risks of PICS syndrome," he maintains.

"Few nurses and doctors outside the ICU world have even heard of PICS, much less the public at large," explains Dr. Ely of Vanderbilt University Medical Center in his compassionate book *Every Deep-Drawn Breath,* in which he attempts to track down the causes of ICU delirium and PICS to bring about change.[35]

"The most striking point about PICS is that patients are not experiencing the residual effects of the original health problems that necessitated their admission to an ICU in the first place; instead, these are new conditions brought on by the lifesaving treatment they received," maintains Dr. Ely.

"Most patients and their families—and many doctors, too—consider discharge from an ICU as the victorious end to a struggle against critical illness, but often the hardest part of a patient's experience is just beginning," he insists.

"A big problem with the current program is that the ICU providers, both physicians and nurses, have almost zero awareness of what happens to their patients once they leave the ICU," says Dr. Murphy. "Our criteria for success at the present time is that the patient leaves the ICU in a relatively stable condition with no concerns for postdischarge anxiety, depression, PTSD, cognitive, or physical impairment," he told us. "We simply have no mechanism to get any feedback on our patients."

This is especially troubling in the developed world, he says, because most people don't die suddenly or in accidents, and most of us will, in the end, wind up in an ICU where we will receive "this dangerous, substandard form of treatment."

Having become especially worried about one patient, a mathematical whiz who, after discharge, struggled to add up her checking account, Dr. Ely decided to analyze the brains of ICU survivors using an MRI scanner. The study, termed "Visions," showed that one in three patients developed dementia as a result of their ICU stay, with symptoms resembling Alzheimer's and traumatic brain injury.[36]

"When I looked at the scans of the ICU survivors, the results were chilling. The brain dysfunction was writ large," he recalls in his book. Prior to the scans, the math genius took a standard IQ test and was seen to have a catastrophic drop from an impressive 140 down to a low average of 100. Such a drop for a person of average intelligence would likely render them mentally subnormal. This fifty-two-year-old woman now had the brain of an eighty-five-year-old with dementia. In effect, her brain had shriveled.

"The survivors' extreme cognitive impairment and memory loss showed up as a reduction in the size of the hippocampus and the frontal cortex, regions of the brain that control neuropsychological tasks of memory and executive function," he says, underlining that both the brain problems and the physical disabilities must be considered ICU-acquired conditions.

Such practices are lethal, insists Dayton. "And yet there are only a few of us really speaking out about it. The public is vastly unaware that patients are being sedated in many situations in which they can and should be awake and walking and having totally different outcomes. The public has a right to know what's really going on," she says.

For most ICU staff, there is a missing chapter in the care of their patients and little reward in not knowing how the survivors fared. Meanwhile, those rendered effectively brain-dead during their coma are left to deal with the problems alone. To be told that their experiences from within coma, from NDEs through to alternate lives, are simply delirium—an obvious form of confusion to anyone with a dictionary— leaves them baffled by their experience. The physical damage all too often comes as an utter shock, leaving coma survivors to live half-lives of limited mobility, the zest for life often lost. With no exceptions, the survivors who have been helping us with this book received no warning of the damage that may have been done to them. They have had no satisfactory explanation for the more-real-than-real experiences from deep within coma, and almost all have been left to question their sanity.

"Before we automatically sedate every patient, let's stop and ask ourselves each time—does this patient really need to be sedated?" suggests Dayton. "Is it in their best interest? Do the potential benefits outweigh the psychological and physical costs? Step into the patient's hospital socks and see it from their eyes. Let us strive to truly prevent and treat pain, anxiety, and trauma for our patients—not cause it."

Deborah (Continued): You're Never Asleep

Deborah spent eighty years while in her coma as a living mannequin in a serial-killer-themed bar.

. . .

So, out of the eight beds in our ICU, half of us in that room are trying to get our heads around what just happened to us. I was in hospital for three weeks. I was then bedridden for another eight or so weeks at home.

It's weird, my dreams are so much more vivid now and I remember them in greater quantity than before my illness. They're so realistic that I can't distinguish what's true. I honestly thought I'd gone to Corfu for four days!

You're not actually sleeping [in a coma]. You never get the luxury of going through your circadian rhythm or whatever it is. You're in a constant state of not being able to fully sleep. You end up being somewhere between two worlds. And people assume that you're asleep but you're not. I'm telling you, you're not.

I've been getting and providing a lot of comfort to other people on chat forums like HealthUnlocked and ICUsteps. There's loads of people there who support me with advice and emotional comfort, help with losing my hair, not sleeping for fear of nightmares, not believing if this world is real, and worrying if I'm really dead.

What I guess really worries me the most is the time it will take for me to fully recover. It will be at least two years for my stamina and strength to return, but I read posts from people saying five years postcoma and they're still suffering with horrific depression and anxiety. But we all end up experiencing broadly the same traumas or issues, just different paths. And, you know, the great thing is that you're welcomed; you realize that you're not crazy. What you're going through is perfectly normal.

But, because nobody gives you a pamphlet or a leaflet, you just think you've lost the plot. The hardest thing is when physically you look fine and mentally you come across as fine, but emotionally you're all over the place.

I went from being one of the most confident people in my own abilities to just the most crippling self-doubt; feeling like I couldn't do my job. I'm really struggling with numbers, and I work in account management, working sales, and numbers are everything. But I was also conveying that I couldn't do my job. And then the company where I worked started believing that I couldn't do my job. So I ended up leaving that firm after six years.

It got to a point when I realized this is as good as it's going to get. I've had to accept that I am improved, but nowhere near what it used to be. And it's massively noticeable to me. It's not as noticeable to *other people. You really do wonder if you're still capable of doing the job you've been doing for god knows how long? But my brain has changed. I've gone from a female kind of brain—multitasking, plate-spinning— to a mind like a man, only able to concentrate on one thing at a time.*

Isobel (Continued): Death Was Beautiful

When I woke up, I couldn't even move my index finger. I could roll my head slightly, and I could make facial expressions. I couldn't talk for three weeks. You just lie there and suffer. I remember the first time I managed to lift my hand thinking Wow! I can lift my hand! *It's extremely traumatic being paralyzed. But I would rather that than being put in the coma where I knew I was trapped. I remember begging my kidnapper to kill me, to inject me with heroin. They were heroin addicts. I remember saying,* Please, just kill me. *And a nurse told me later that I was begging her to kill me.*

I sat there for hours looking at my toes, willing them to wiggle. At some stage, a nurse got hold of my phone and called my parents, so they could see me. This was when they briefly brought me out of sedation. But I thought I'd been kidnapped again for more organ harvesting and if my parents paid a ransom, I'd go free. I remember looking into my parents' eyes, and I was trying to tell them, Pay the ransom, pay the ransom. *And they were just crying and crying, saying it's just going to take time. So I'm telling them to sell my house, I don't care about my house, I just want to come home. And they just kept saying it's just gonna take time and crying and crying and crying. Then the call ended, and that's when I tried to rip the tracheotomy out of my throat, thinking help's not coming and even if it kills me I have to rip out this chain and try and run. And, apparently, that did happen, I ripped out the tracheotomy, and then I got chained to the bed for real.*

All of my hair fell out. I was told I was never going to be able to have a child again. Someone told me that I'd be able to go home soon.

But I knew that I'd never get home. I'd been gone eighteen years in my mind by that point. My husband had remarried, my life had gone. My mother was dead. But people say to me there's nothing worse than dying. That's a stupid comment! Only people who haven't suffered to such an extreme level can actually say that.

For me, death was a beautiful experience. I was in a big, green field and the grass was blowing in the wind, long, lush grass. There was a horse. And I carried on walking and there was a big lake with beautiful trees hanging over it and there were wooden, gnarly, nobbled steps going into the sky. And I knew that the bottom was life and at the top was death. And I started walking up the stairs.

At first, I'd been fighting to live, but I'd suffered so much in the coma that I chose to die, and I walked up those stairs and I was four steps from the top. It was like night but without stars, pure, expansive, and just calm. And that was the happiest I've ever been in my entire life. I've never experienced DMT on any synthetic level, but I can imagine that my dying experience being so beautiful was like DMT on steroids. And I was four steps from the top and I heard my name being called. Isobel, you can't leave. You have to come back. I was so pissed off! I turned around and stomped back down the stairs.

I don't come from a Christian family, but I don't want to say I'm agnostic. We were raised to be open, to be free to choose what you believe. My mother had been dying for so long, and there was always the question of where was she going? But dying myself has completely altered my perspective on life. And I know that it's a beautiful thing. I know that anybody who goes there is in for the best time.

So, later, I went to see my mother. They took me in a wheelchair. She was on morphine. She wasn't conscious, and they left me alone with her. And they said to me, She can't hear you and she doesn't know you're here, but she's not suffering. So they left me with her and I thought that's just what they said about me. I held my mum's hand, and I said, We'll be alright now. You can go. She died ten seconds later.

Kathy (Continued): I'll Never Be Who I Was

Kathy Drown, who had found herself floating on a raft of autumn leaves, says she didn't recognize humans when she came out of the coma.

. . .

I just keep looking around, following my mum around the room at the time because I didn't know who she was. I didn't know who anyone was. It took me nine months to remember my kids' names. I was scared. I wanted to go back to where I was. It was so peaceful, so beautiful. It was a feeling of complete peace. Complete fulfillment. You can't imagine until you've been there.

The doctors wouldn't discuss anything except for my wounds. One of my best friends is a psychiatric nurse. I was talking to her about it because I trust her implicitly. You know, *she said,* doctors say there's a medical explanation for all this, but that's just bullshit. *At the end of the day, no one can come up with a scientific explanation for what happens.*

I realized about nine months after the coma that my entire life, world, friends, family, and my livelihood had changed on a dime, and I didn't know me nor the world. So I went to therapy to get help, to get through this devastating cloud I was in.

I've been going to therapy for six months once a week. I still have a long way to go. I'll never be who I was. I changed. I'm focusing on trying to get more of my memory back.

Megan: This Was Never Delirium

Megan Johnson developed COVID-19 in March 2020, one of the first in Wisconsin. Initially worried by a tight chest, she decided to go to the hospital for a test but did not feel too bad. They decided to keep her in, and she spent several days on the COVID-19 ward while they waited for a result. Inside her coma, she experienced an equally vivid, altered reality where, instead of the caring nurses she knew in real life, callous and sadistic amateurs left her in torment. Of the eight people in her ICU, she says she was one of the very few to survive the experience.

. . .

I felt well enough. I was up and walking around, taking showers when they weren't looking. I felt fine for the most part. And then one morning they came and said they wanted to intubate me, and I was like, Oh, really? I don't think I need that. *I wanted to speak to a doctor I know. He really explains what's going on and doesn't talk to you like an idiot. But he wasn't there. My mum used to be a nurse, but not that kind of nurse. I asked her what she thought.* You have to do what they tell you, *she said.* If they say you need it, then you need it. *I reluctantly consented.*

It would have been my birthday in a week so I asked them if they thought I'd be off it by then and they were like, We've no way of knowing. *So, I said, what about all these other COVID patients on the vent? When are they going to come off? And they said,* To be honest, we don't know. *So there were eight of us in that hospital. I was on for seventeen days. During that time, one of my kidneys failed, so I was on dialysis for the last couple of weeks of it. They had to put me on some kind of special ventilator that only breathed every ten seconds. This type of ventilation is more uncomfortable, so it requires more sedation.*

When I woke up, they thought I might need a kidney transplant, but I just bounced back. I did really well. You don't often hear that, not after seventeen days. I don't have long-term effects, aside from mild PTSD, but I do think I'm a little less. I also have less lung capacity than before. I don't think I have brain damage; that's something I'm paranoid about. I asked my family, Am I normal? Would you tell me if I weren't? But, maybe, you guys are just humoring me?

But a lot of the memories [from inside the coma] transfer over now into my waking world. I was so drugged. I probably wasn't asleep, just knocked out. I wanted to go home because I didn't think they were taking care of me. But the whole time I didn't know I was in hospital. I thought I was in the Ridgewood Nursing Home and that I'd been admitted without my consent and that my family had abandoned me there. For a while, I was dumped outside.

At night, the nurses weren't real nurses, but were almost like babysitters. They just didn't care. They just wanted to go out and party. They put an old guy named Willie into the bed beside mine, divided by a curtain. He was tied to his bed but we could talk and he had COVID, and this worried me. I didn't want to be in a room with someone with COVID. I thought I was in for brain surgery.

I didn't have to be tied up because I was paralyzed. At some point Willie died, and they wouldn't take his body out of the room for three days. And there was this little boy that came in. But he died, too. And there was endless grieving down the hall. Really excessive grieving about the boy. And there were endless, excruciating TV infomercials for different products. I know that when I did wake up, there was a TV on, so that explains that.

But these events didn't happen, they tell me. They just seemed like they happened. When I was awake, I was really confused. I thought it was 2024, and I'm thinking I've lost four years. What about my dog, the car lease, my mortgage? I probably don't have a house anymore. But others in there with me, they died. I got lucky and they didn't. I felt guilty a lot at the beginning. It's kind of subsided now.

I understand the need to sedate, but you have to find a balance between people being agitated and potentially causing harm and people being completely unconscious. There has to be a happy medium.

Sure, I heard about delirium and I read about it, but I don't really think that's what it is. That's not what this is—like I had some kind of nap and got confused. You can't know unless you experience it. People think it's like a long, restful sleep. But this wasn't sleeping.

Thinking about all these experiences that I had and the memories that I had—and to be told they're not real! It seems to be a thing, *normal for people on the vent, but they keep calling it ICU delirium. But, the thing is, it doesn't seem like that. The term doesn't make sense. I don't have real memories. Everything is fake memories. But it's not the same as being awake and having delirium, in any conventional sense, that's different. When they call it delirium, it makes you feel crazy.*

Jo: I Thought I'd Gone Insane

Jo Nelson's coma experience was a never-ending succession of seeing her friends and family die and of attending their funerals.

• • •

The original reason I had the coma was the easy part; getting myself physically better is harder still, but the mental effects of the coma live with me every hour of every day.

Physically, I had to learn everything again—writing, eating, walking—but that to me was the easy part. I've been left with memory problems and exhaustion, which I never had before. Severe anxiety, which I didn't have before, constant flashbacks, a feeling of being useless, of questioning myself.

I am still trying to make sense of it, if I'm honest. I know now I had out-of-body experiences. I had awful nightmares and dreams like nothing I ever had before, just so vivid and in so much detail. I'm not the same person. I'm short-tempered and irritable, which I hate about myself.

I was never given a proper diagnosis, and it was only when I got my medical notes and read about it that I heard about delirium. I had to do my own research. Then everything started clicking into place. For a good while afterward, I honestly thought I'd gone insane. I had all these vivid memories and none of it made any sense at all!

Seeing the psychologist, to be honest, hasn't done me any good. They put it all down to delirium, but to me, it's not delirium. They just fobbed me off, saying everyone gets it, like it's something every person goes through. I think it would help speaking to someone who's gone through the same, but the medical people aren't interested.

I have such vivid memories, which I'm told aren't real. I could never explain just how terrifying the whole experience was. It left me so vulnerable. It must have been hard on my family, too. It's hard, as I lived through this nightmare. I think at the time, if I'd been told about delirium, I would have accepted it more than actually finding out months later. I got to the point after my coma where I wanted to end my life, as I honestly thought I'd lost my mind.

"Debbie" (Continued): Nothing Seems Real Now

"They tell me there's no brain damage, no cognitive impairment, but I feel there is. I have brain damage," says "Debbie," who earlier asked if anyone missed their coma.

• • •

I forget things and start forgetting and sometimes catch myself forgetting. Tablets go untaken, or I have no memory if I took them or not. Lost memories, lost hours during the day, not being able to do things the same as I could before. Everything's slower, more difficult, things don't look right. Part of me is still submerged in coma. I am never far from feeling I'm going to be completely submerged back into it.

Nothing seems real. Things seemed staged, people look like actors. It has a sinister feel. In the ICU, I did have delirium but it wasn't all scary, so I kept my mouth shut. I knew they'd keep me in longer if they knew what I could really see and feel.

My hell started after my coma and hasn't stopped since. I long to return to that pure, untainted, protective love I felt. I've not found that anywhere on Earth, as it isn't earthly. Everything now is more difficult, and nothing makes sense. It's a different world I returned to, not the one I left, and I don't like it. The people, my family, they're glitchy, not as they were, hostile, unloving, detached, removed, uncaring. They're not the people or family I had before. I certainly came back from my coma with insight and ability to truly see people. Maybe that's why? I don't know.

There was something in and under the floor of the ICU once I was awake that wanted to get me. It was evil and had a vibration I could feel, like an earth tremor. I still feel it now, watching and waiting. It's the underworld, where there's heat and steam, vibration, and everything is bathed in an orangey, red-amber glow.

It was horrendous and very scary. A nurse with blood stains on her uniform, who looked like she belonged in an asylum porn film, wanted to inject me in my stomach, while an old, demented hag peered around the door, cackling. Two nurses ranted on about the devil and redemption. I kept quiet about most of it.

Chrissy: I Am Angry!

"There are things that keep coming back to me," says Chrissy Statham who recalls being raped while in her coma, amid a cycle of death and dying.

. . .

I was on a plane and looked up to see bodies looking down on me. My doctor's surgery has the same square plastic ceiling tiles with lighting in them, and if I have to sit in the waiting room I start to feel panic and anxiety. I'm absolutely terrified of square Perspex panels now.

I'm affected by trigger sounds around me. My PTSD stems from sounds I obviously heard while in the coma. There was a disposal chute that would start up, and helicopter sounds because the emergency pad was near the ICU, and the constant beeping of the machines.

I had a ten-week course of counseling for PTSD, trying to make sense of it all. Some helped me control my feelings, but sometimes I just lose it. It took about a year to be diagnosed, and nobody has explained why I got it.

I'm told the rape was probably down to bed baths. I recall them touching my face to wake me up and that still freaks me out, seeing long fingers on TV or my face being touched. I guess the war or people trying to kill me could have come from the TV news and crossed over into my world.

When I woke up, I was unable to move. Before, I was very active, walking four miles every day. I had to build up my core muscles, then I had to learn to walk again. I was so weak. My mobility has never fully recovered. My joint pain can be off the scale! My memory is so bad now and my balance is awful.

I've been left with breathing issues, COPD—chronic obstructive pulmonary disease—chronic ligament weakness. I have fibromyalgia, a condition that causes pain all over the body. In some way, I appreciate each day, every one is precious, but I'm also angry because I'm unable to live life the way I did. My life stopped as I knew it. I'm now on full disability. My six-year-old son became my carer, bless him!

The events within coma I've kept to myself, as people would think I'm nuts. Some things I still carry with me. I want to draw images, but only people who've gone through it would understand. I live day to day. I was under intensive care for over a year, and in rehab and physio for longer than their record at the hospital.

I don't like crowds of people. In fact, I don't like being around people. I can't walk far, as I fall regularly and struggle with breathing and tiredness. But people don't understand because physically I look fine. I think families feel the professionals know best and, so long as they believe the treatment being given is the best for the person, they don't question it. Personally, I know the coma and the drugs are to blame. I thought of writing a book myself, but people would think me crazy.

The Awake and Walking ICU

And How Some People Never Learned Their ABCs

It's not often that intensive care nurses have the time or the inclination to become good friends with patients or their families. For one thing, it can lead to additional heartache. But sometimes it does happen, and it happened to one shock-trauma nurse working at the LDS Hospital in Salt Lake City in July 1994.

For Polly Bailey, RN, APRN, automatic deep sedation and paralyzing drugs were the norm for patients on a ventilator. When young mother Joy was admitted to the ward suffering from acute respiratory distress syndrome (ARDS), Bailey was assigned as her bedside nurse. "I didn't know her," Bailey recalls. "But she was from my home town. I felt bonded. I became close to her and her family. And so, for the first time in my career, I watched what happened to a patient that left the ICU."

But Bailey was not prepared for the shock and pain that lay ahead, nor did she have any idea just how she would help change the course of critical care medicine for the better, resulting in dramatically improved patient outcomes and an unknown number of lives saved.

After being revived from several weeks of deep sedation in the ICU, Joy was transferred to a rehab unit, and, when Bailey swung by to pay her a visit, she was alarmed by what she saw. "I still think about it now," she says. "She was just lying in that bed. No motor control. She couldn't even use the call light. She had no voice. She couldn't call for help." Joy was in such a desperate state that she was swiftly readmitted back to the ICU and back on the ventilator once more. It took a long time before she was finally allowed home.

When Bailey paid her first home visit she was equally stunned. "I couldn't believe what we'd done to her," she recalled. It was taking Joy nearly two hours just to shower each day. She barely slept at night and was too weak to use the bathroom. Climbing the stairs and even the most basic activities left her drained and distraught. She struggled to string together simple sentences and had no hope of playing with her children. How, wondered Bailey, could she ever slip back into her role as a mother?

"So every day I would go there," she recalls. "And I would watch what was happening. And I would come back and say to my boss [Dr. Terry Clemmer, an early pioneer in critical care medicine], *We can't do this anymore. We've got to stop what we're doing.*" The next two years of Joy's gradual and partial recovery would prove a learning curve for Dr. Clemmer and his team.

He recalls the first time Bailey told him of the damage they had done to a patient. For Dr. Clemmer, everything changed "when one of my nurses actually followed a patient longitudinally out of the ICU into rehab, actually to her home, and discovered what terrible harm we had done to her—the pain of all the rehabilitation, the psychological problems, flashbacks and PTSD."

"Dr. Clemmer told me to go and do a literature search," Bailey says. "And figure out what to do. Well, I spent days trying to do that, trying to figure out how to care for these patients differently. And I came back and I put this stack of articles on his desk, and I said, *Okay, here's what I can find. But there's nothing there. We have to make this up.* There wasn't literature about delirium, there wasn't literature about weaning sedation. There wasn't literature about mobility, there wasn't literature about anything."

Bailey got the go-ahead to trust her instincts and try something different, something so radical that many of her colleagues were deeply reluctant to get involved. "We tried to think outside the box," she recalls. "We used early mobility, music therapy, pet therapy. We got families involved. We started showering patients in the ICU for the first time." Bailey introduced physical therapists to build back patients' muscle strength and worked with staff to dramatically wean patients off the deep sedatives and get them up and about. This would not be an end to sedation but rather careful consideration before it was ever administered. "We just don't use sedation to make them unreasonably unresponsive. We want a patient to be calm. We want them to be comfortable, but we want them to be cooperative," she says.

Dr. Clemmer was skeptical at first. "But then I thought, *Why not?* Polly is a good nurse and she protects her patients. So let her try it, and we quickly discovered what a wonderful idea it was to actually have patients communicate, have them walking and helping in their own care."

In a very short time they saw a significant difference in patient outcomes. Patients were getting off the ventilator far sooner and, with aided mobility, they were swiftly up and about, walking several hundred feet each day around the ICU, all while connected to a portable ventilator. "We had some patients running their businesses on their laptops, in their hospital bed," says Dr. Clemmer. "We learnt that mobility is very therapeutic. If your patient starts to have delirium, we learned to actually walk them around the unit and we saw the delirium clear."

"We just tried to do as much as we could to make the patient experience as human as possible," explained Bailey. "We just learned so much about how to take care of patients in the right way. And when we would tell people what we were doing, they would say, *Oh, you can't do that! Your patients aren't sick. We could never do that. Our patients are too sick.*

"They would ask how do we control anxiety if we don't use Ativan? Well, we get them up. We move them around and walk them around, then they go back to bed. They're restful, it's a restorative rest. That's how we treat anxiety."

"We used to send all our patients to rehab. They were so deconditioned," remembers Dr. Clemmer. "And then, all of a sudden, she [Polly] says, *We're not doing that anymore. Our patients aren't going to rehab. They're going home.*"

"I came from that initial age in the late eighties, early nineties, where we were doing really heavy, deep sedation," recalls Bailey. "I can remember being at the bedside when nurses would give paralytics so that they can give a quick bath. We had no idea that we were harming people. Of course, we look back now and Dr. Clemmer and I wonder how many people we harmed."

By 2007, Bailey had gathered sufficient data to publish her first paper, "Early Activity Is Feasible and Safe in Respiratory Failure Patients," suddenly adding a wealth of knowledge in just five thousand words and calling for a lighter and briefer sedation regime with added emphasis on early physical therapy for patients during their ICU stay, rather than waiting until they entered a care facility down the line.

"We conclude that early activity is feasible and safe in respiratory failure patients," she wrote, adding that, "A majority of patients treated using the early activity protocol were able to ambulate one hundred feet at the time of ICU discharge."[1] This when almost all those leaving ICU did so in a wheelchair. The paper hit nerves around the world and provided inspiration for others to emulate the success of the "Bailey Method."

When another trauma nurse, Louise Bezdjian, ACNP, joined the team, she was already well versed in the practice of deep sedation. "I thought it must be a terrible experience to be intubated," she says. "We wanted to shut off our patients' brains." At the Utah ICU she was introduced to the practice of early mobility. "But, I admit," she says. "I was terrified. I absolutely did not want to harm our patients. But the more I did it, the more comfortable I became with it."

It was not long before Louise also began to notice a swift and considerable improvement, beyond anything she had ever witnessed before. "Those patients that were mobilized initially and maintained their strength, they got to go home. They didn't have to go to a nursing home!"

Patients would receive a mild sedative when initially placed on the ventilator. "And we would talk to them," says Louise. "We could explain to them that this tube in your throat is helping you breath. It's keeping you alive. Sometimes it takes an hour, and then the patient understands what the tube is there for, rather than clouding their brains with all these medications that distort reality. We prevent delirium from happening. We don't create the problem."

The true horror of deep sedation and lack of mobility struck home for Louise when her sister's seventy-four-year-old husband contracted COVID-19 and began to sink fast. "We've seen with COVID that they get the disease, and then they begin to decompensate and the inflammatory response starts, and then they get really sick." This, she says, is what happened to her brother-in-law. He was eventually rushed to a small community hospital. "At three in the morning, he gets intubated, goes on mechanical ventilation, and is sedated because he's extremely agitated. He was like that for two and a half weeks! Even if he recovered, he'd never walk again!

"And I'm here in Salt Lake City and they're down in California," Louise told us. "I didn't have the heart to tell them this isn't the right treatment. This is just not the right kind of care. I asked if they could move him somewhere else, but they said he was too sick. I asked if they could Zoom him. *Maybe if he hears your voice, maybe things will turn round?* But the nurses said they didn't know how to Zoom! Seriously? I flew down there. They wouldn't even let us in to see him unless we took over his care. I've done this for twenty-eight years, fourteen of those years as a nurse practitioner, and I've never heard any of my colleagues say to someone you can't see them unless you provide care. That's not how we treat our COVID patients," says an exasperated Louise.

"Eventually they said, *Okay, you can come in and see him now.* And I take one look at him and say to my sister, *He's gone.* So, while we were in the waiting room, he passed away! I am convinced, based on what we do in my facility, that his care at this facility is what killed him, and I understand. I understand that people are overwhelmed with a huge population of COVID patients."

The tragedy led Louise on a path to educate other nurses and ICU staff and becoming a firm champion for early mobility and limited sedation. "I like to think of myself as a person that goes in and dispels the nurses' fears, that this is the right thing to do. But there's so much pushback, so much fear." The greatest difficulty is in trying to change the views of nursing staff who have been in the job for a long time. "They don't think it's the right thing to do. They say they don't have the time. They think we're being cruel, but the cruelty lies in sedating them."

When the time came to open a new respiratory ICU at the LDS Hospital, Bailey was put in charge. It was also decided to recruit staff with no prior ICU experience and no qualms about radically changing the protocols. Soon after that, a young Kali Dayton joined the team.

"I started my career in an awake and walking ICU, which I know sounds crazy," Dayton told a small online group of fascinated medical professionals in 2022. "That was my first job as a nurse, straight into this ICU. Patients were allowed to wake up after intubation. And we would just reorient them and say, *Hey, remember what we talked about twenty minutes ago? Here you are, you're in the ICU.* And it became normal to have patients texting us. We would have them up and walking within hours of intubation."

By keeping the patient alert and mobile and fully aware of the efforts being taken to care for them, Bailey's ICU found that they rarely slipped into delirium, and their chances of getting back to fully functional lives substantially improved. They discovered that patients rarely, if ever, needed to be placed deep into coma. "Some ninety-eight percent of survivors from my awake and walking ICU go straight home after discharge," Dayton tells us. "They're successfully taken off the ventilator without tracheostomies, they walk themselves out the doors, and get home.

"So I was never trained to just knock them out. That was never my expectation. So it was really abnormal for me to go to a different ICU later and have everyone comatose. And these were similar diagnoses that I was used to taking care of, but they were completely different patients because they were just sacks of potatoes in the bed," she says.

"And it was really confusing to me at first, wanting to stick to my own routine and do what was normal to me. I'd asked the teams, *Hey, can I wake them up and get them up?* And, of course, their jaws would drop and they look at me like I was crazy or speaking French, and say, *No, they're intubated.* And that didn't make sense to me because intubation wasn't an indicator for sedation or bedrest, let alone immobility."

Also adding to the fear factor for many nurses, panic often swiftly sets in when patients are brought out of deep sedation, fresh from nightmarish episodes of torture and chase. "The patients come out wild," stresses Dayton. "They're agitated, thrashing, breathing fast and erratic, biting the tube, trying to pull the tubes and lines out. Worst of all, you can see the terror in their eyes. It breaks your heart. No one wants to see a patient like that. So, to keep the patient 'safe and comfortable', they rush to turn the sedation back on."

Dayton is keen to stress that every nurse she ever met set out to help patients. But, she says, they have always been taught that we have to sedate anytime anyone's on a ventilator. And nurses deeply believe that's going to spare them PTSD. "But what we don't understand is what you actually are experiencing when you're delirious," she maintains.

"It is continually clear to me that we, as an ICU community, are very disconnected with what delirium is truly like." Those patients undergoing relatively mild sedation, she says, "are usually very aware of their surroundings, but the problem is that the sedation causing delirium disrupts their ability to appropriately interpret and process the experience. And this usually gets twisted into grotesque, violent, and morbid realities that they didn't even know their imaginations could conjure up."

The coma events that resemble the near-death experience are even harder to comprehend, adds Dayton, preferring not to use the word *hallucination* but rather *experience,* especially when they appear more real than our waking reality. "The peaceful, spiritual, and other experiences that seem to be more like NDE, I'm not sure how to fit these in, unless they were nearly or actually dead, or had arrests and were revived. I am a spiritual person. I am confident that we cross a veil when we die. I also believe we can cross and come back."

But the lack of comprehension of the patients' ICU experiences, she says, "is where the medical community is engrossed in a lot of its own misinformation. And when they are agitated and anxious, we just sedate them more. We shut them up. We think we fix it when, in reality, we just send them back for more."

Christiane Perme, PT, CCS, FCCM, is a physical therapist running ICU rehabilitation seminars around the world,[2] but when she first emigrated from Brazil to the United States, her English was not so good, and the only job she could get was draining the lungs of comatose patients in the ICU. "I just couldn't stand that job," she recalled for us. "But I did realize that I really enjoyed the complexity of the intensive care environment."

This was back in the early 1990s, and soon she had a good grasp of the language, and it was then, while working at Houston Methodist Hospital in Texas, that she met two surgical ICU physicians with a vision. "And the vision was that if I could get their patients out of bed and walk them around, they would get better," she laughs. "But I wasn't trained to do that. As a physical therapist, I was never trained to care for somebody in critical care. I was trained to take care of patients with a stroke or with knee operations. When I saw these doctors coming, I'd head for the nearest door because they were putting just too much responsibility on me."

But she began to hunt for any evidence-based practices or articles and always drew a blank. "I told them, I didn't want to do that. I could kill somebody. *Well, don't worry about it,* they told me. *Just sit them on the side of the bed, they're not gonna die.* There was no such thing as early mobility or early physical therapy, she says, but they told me that if they just lie in bed, they're gonna die. Period! So I started sitting them on the side of the bed, and I'm sweating. Next, they say, *You've got to start moving them around.*"

Many of the patients had emphysema, an invariably fatal lung condition, and the hospital began revolutionary surgery to remove the damaged parts of the lungs. "After the surgery, they would be ventilator-dependent, but these were not patients who were critically ill. They weren't dying from septic shock or organ failure. They were awake, and it was very easy to walk them around. And the more I did, the more I could see the results, and I became fascinated, but I was still scared because I didn't know how far they could walk."

Soon after, her hospital began to undertake organ transplants, and these patients were far sicker. "When I told the doctor that I can't move these ones around, I just can't, they're far too sick, he looked at me and said, *Let's make this very simple. I can cut their chest open, take their heart out and put in another one, and it works. And you're telling me you can't get somebody to walk around?* And I said, *Well, maybe you have a point.* There wasn't anyone to teach me, so he said, *Well, go figure it out.* So I did."

Within a couple of years, Christiane had all the patients up and about, walking around the surgical ICU, and the results, particularly the lack of delirium, were difficult to ignore. "One patient, I will never forget," she says. "As soon as he was able to talk, he said, *Thank you so much because the first time I walked and you helped me, that was the first time I felt like there was a slim chance I would be able to live and go home.* After that," she says, "I realized that I didn't want to do anything else in my life other than that, so that's what I've done for the past thirty years."

This was a surgical ICU where it became fairly common practice to mobilize patients as soon as possible. "But in medical ICUs, the physicians didn't do that," says Christiane. "The nurses didn't do that. And that was the case all over the country, all over the world. But our protocol was that the patient would have heart surgery and the next day the nurses would get the patient to sit on the side of the bed and stand them up and sit them in a chair. However, when I went to a medical ICU, I was the only one trying to get patients out of bed. They just didn't understand. It was like pulling teeth."

Christiane felt an overwhelming responsibility to share her knowledge with her new colleagues. Beginning with short ten-minute presentations, she soon branched out and spent virtually every free day traveling the country, talking to anybody who would listen. After being invited to speak at various conferences, people began to reach out to her. *"Oh my god*, they would ask. *How do you do that?* So I started teaching courses for physical therapists, and in two days I teach them the fundamentals of ICU rehab, everything they need to know to care for a patient in intensive care."

Then, in 2007, Bailey published her landmark article in *Critical Care Medicine*. "When I saw that article, I was jumping with joy!" Christiane recalls. "I just couldn't believe that somebody had written that, finally proving that ventilated patients didn't need deep sedation." Two years later, Christiane published her own article in the *American Journal of Clinical Care,* titled "Early Mobility and Walking Program for Patients in Intensive Care Units: Creating a Standard of Care," and another six thousand words had been added to the slim medical annals.[3]

Even when you can get colleagues to read the evidence-based research, there is still a major gap in their understanding, says Christiane. "The problem with professionals that practice in intensive care, not only in this country, but throughout the entire world," she says, "is we don't know the result of our work." On surgical ICUs, patients are routinely followed up. "If they have a broken leg, and they still can't walk long after discharge, you'd know something was wrong. But in this case, no one's even looking, and this is ultimately the root of the problem."

Occasionally, she says, patients are so sick that they return to the ICU, and only then does she ever see the shocking aftereffects. But, she says, "I don't know what happened to the majority of the patients that I cared for throughout the thirty years of my life, because once they leave, they don't come back. So we don't know what happens, we forget about them, because hundreds more patients are then admitted."

Even the term *post-intensive care syndrome* (PICS) is largely unknown to those who most need to know about it. Christiane was part of a group that, in 2010, made a study of the aftereffects of ICU care and coined the term. But she only found out about the condition herself by sheer chance.

"I decided to start writing my physical therapy notes," she says. "But my office was so very busy, I decided to take my laptop and go sit down in the hospital lobby, a beautiful place. So I tuck myself into a corner and start writing. And guess what? Patients and families would recognize me and they would stop and talk. So I learned what happened to my patients after they left, just by sitting in the lobby of my hospital. That's when I learned of the horrors! Oh, I could write a book about it!"

THE CANARY IN THE COAL MINE

Today, Dr. Ely is professor of medicine at Vanderbilt University Medical Center in Nashville, rated one of the finest medical schools in the country. When he began his career in 1989, he was immediately drawn to critical care for the challenge of bringing patients back from the brink of death. But during his training he had been taught to keep a professional sense of reserve and mental distance from the patients under his care. Getting to know them, he was repeatedly told, will only lead to problems down the line.

While training as a medical student in 1985 in New Orleans, a young woman who had attempted suicide was placed in his care, his first-ever patient but one already deeply sedated, restrained to the bed and breathing with the help of a mechanical ventilator. She was dead to the world, and there was no opportunity to think of her as an actual human being. She was simply the suicide in bed nine. It would be many weeks of close care before she could eventually be brought back to consciousness and discharged.

But this young woman had been left with a nasty chest wound that needing following up and so, six weeks after discharge, she was back again, and the young Wesley was looking forward to finally meeting his first success story. "She rolled slowly into the room in a wheelchair, pushed by an aide, her mother at her side," he recalls in his book *Every Deep-Drawn Breath*. "She gazed ahead, heavy bags under her eyes, a shell of a young woman. No greeting, no smile. She turned to me with a blank stare."

The young woman was effectively mute so her mother spoke for her. *She's a completely different person now. Why can't she bend her arms at the elbows or move her shoulders?* Many of her joints were locked, having calcified. But the problems did not stop there. The mother rattled off a litany of disastrous changes to her daughter's life. She could not swallow properly nor go to the bathroom. Sleep was virtually impossible because of the recurring nightmares from deep within her coma. She was reduced to a broken woman in a wheelchair with nothing left to live for.

"What if she never walked again? What if her brain was permanently injured?" he wondered. "In my gut I knew that something about the care she had received in the ICU had damaged her. She had come in with failing organs, and we had fixed them, but somehow she had acquired completely different ailments—new trauma to her body and her brain. I thought I'd found my calling, pulling patients back from the maw of death, but now I wasn't so sure. I started to wonder if saving lives was also causing harm."

Every day that followed, another five to eight patients were placed under his care. By turns, they were each deeply sedated via a benzodiazepine drip and topped up with morphine before being placed on the ventilator. "I'd started to feel unsettled seeing them lying there, tethered to their machines, stuck in suspended animation. It seemed that the sense of urgency we all felt when a patient was admitted, that shot of adrenaline that flared as we actively sought to save a life, dissipated once the ventilator was in place. It was as if we handed over care of our patients to the machines while we went off and admitted, intubated, sedated, and paralyzed the next one. My noble mission of saving lives had turned into a conveyor belt of care."

By 1992, Dr. Ely began training as a lung specialist, and the thing about lung transplants is that the medical team really need to get to know their patients. They need to know if the family support is there, and they need to know if the patient has the right outlook to overcome the stresses and strains as the body struggles to accept another person's organs.

Suddenly, Dr. Ely found that he needed to know everything he could about the person under his care. He made copious notes and got to know the family and friends—and even the name of the patient's dog. It was a world of change from the medical ICU and one that would also help set a new path for critical care medicine because the now more-learned Dr. Ely would return to the ICU with an entirely different outlook. "My transplant patients awoke something in me—a need for more humanity in doctoring—and I wanted to bring it to my ventilated patients in the ICU." But how, he wondered, when they were all rendered senseless by the drugs? The answer, he realized, was to follow up his ICU patients in the same way as he did the transplant recipients.

"I listened to story after story with a sense of growing comprehension and alarm. We had thought our ventilated patients were sleeping, protected by sedatives, paralytics, and pain medication from the intense discomfort caused by life-support machines. But, clearly, they were not serenely dreaming. They were delirious, afraid, and confused."

And what could he possibly say when the families asked about the distressing events from deep within coma? "Should they dismiss the stories and say that they weren't real, or should they acknowledge them?" he wondered. And how was he to account for the alarming mental and physical deterioration?

As he listened to the families, the same lines seemed to be repeating themselves. *She's just not right. She's not making any sense. She's just not the person she was.* "They didn't know it, but they were alerting me to a quiet type of delirium that was easy to overlook."

And delirium, Dr. Ely began to realize, was the canary in the coal mine, "alerting me to damage going on inside her brain." But in all his training, not one single lecture had touched on the subject. The textbooks were no help and nor were his colleagues in the ICU who were quick to dismiss delirium as nothing more than a minor blip that would wear off soon enough.

It was time to undertake some research of his own, except nobody was really interested and all attempts at funding met dead ends. Delirium, he was told by one leading neurologist after another, doesn't belong in the field of critical care. He was rebuffed by multiple journals and funding agencies. His study would have to be small, limited to just the patients passing through his ICU.

He had a lot of questions that needed answers. Just how long should patients be sedated and to what depth of consciousness? Need their minds be subjected to endless delirium dreams in the hope of curing the body? "We knew they were unconscious but had no idea exactly how far into the caverns they had descended," he recalls. "Where were they exactly, and what was happening to their brains?" What happens at a physiological level when someone goes from conscious to unconscious? And here we are, he thought, at the beginning of the twenty-first century, and we know next to nothing.

By the spring of 2003 he had enough data to work on and the results were unequivocal and alarming. Delirium in his ICU substantially increased the risk of death within six months of discharge. It also forecast longer hospital stays, higher costs, and a nearly ten times greater risk of cognitive impairment on discharge.

"I stared at the figures: eighty-two percent of the patients—my patients—had developed delirium while in the ICU under my care and of those, thirty-four percent had died within six months, a tripling of the risk of dying compared to those who did not develop delirium. It dawned on me that we were saving people's lives in the ICU only to have them die later from something we might have created ourselves."

Over the coming years, Dr. Ely and his growing team would carry out more studies and publish more papers on the subject of ICU delirium than anyone else, setting up the renowned ICU Delirium and Cognitive Impairment Study Group at Vanderbilt in 2001. They would also devise the definitive guide for critical care, now known as the ABCDEF bundle—or A2F for short—incorporating the work of Polly Bailey and Christiane Perme and offering the future gold standard protocol to align and coordinate care by focusing on avoidance of delirium through limited sedation and pain medications, reduced time on the ventilator, and early mobilization, together with the often forgotten role that families can play.[4] Critical care would advance light-years and a new humanity would enter the ICU.

But, true to form, very few were listening.

THE VEGETABLE GARDEN

"Let me tell you," says Dr. Murphy, an ICU director for over forty years. "I had a guy about two weeks ago. He's in room sixteen in my ICU, it was a Saturday. He's getting a little violent, totally agitated, delirious. The nurses are shouting at me to help out, and I'm shouting back at them to get him outside on the patio."

Dr. Murphy is head of his ICU and an early proponent of limited sedation with swift mobility, and yet he struggles to keep his nurses away from the sedatives. Almost every nurse he has ever met firmly believes that all ventilated patients must be deeply sedated, their concern always being to ease suffering. He struggles to get them to change. "It's an impossible hill to climb because people will look at you and say, *Are you crazy?*"

The patient in question became agitated around ten in the morning. "By about 11:30 he was actually walking around the ICU," he tells us. "And by 12:30 I'm writing a transfer order for him to go to the floor. Had I given him a whole bunch of sedatives, he'd have had three days of pharmaceutical oblivion, and not even real oblivion because he'd have all that bad stuff that we know about—significant postdischarge problems with delirium, anxiety, depression, PTSD, cognitive impairment, and muscular and skeletal deconditioning."

And it is this lack of awareness that lies at the root of the issue. "As doctors, we have no idea and no capacity to see the stream of debris that we leave behind us," he tells us. "Both physicians and nurses have almost zero awareness of what happens to their patients once they leave the ICU. We have no mechanism to get any feedback on our patients."

The first problem with bringing about change, he says, is this: "It defies our natural intuition that people can have a tube down their throat and not require massive amounts of medication. They all believe intubated patients require deep sedation even though there is no evidence for this. The second problem is there is essentially no education in medical schools to address this issue, and the biggest problem is that it has become the standard of care for the past fifty years, and that's hard to change. This would require a major culture change for physicians and an even larger change for nursing."

Nurse Jill Larkin Storer works today as a clinical educator in critical care with Meritus Health in Maryland, having spent seven years of her career as a bedside ICU nurse. As early as 2008, she was introduced to the concept of limited sedation and swift mobility. She sees it as her life's mission to change nurses' attitudes away from deep sedation and to embrace the A2F bundle. We wanted to know how successful she's been.

"Well, it's funny you should ask because just this morning I saw a group of night shift nurses in the cafeteria when I went to get my coffee. They are highly resistant to the idea, so I kind of felt a little nervous sitting in, just chatting with them casually," she admitted.

"I can't get people to stop giving baths and oversedating, and I tried to talk to them about it, but it just keeps happening," she says. She describes the night shift nurses as old-school veterans, "salty and tired, uninspired and burnt out and, quite honestly, uneducated. I hate to say it but it's true. And so how did it go? I failed, quite honestly," she admits.

"There's a certain breed of nurse that I came up through the ranks with, certain types of American nurse that are not nice. And I have some PTSD about that," she tell us. "So, you know, I failed today, but I just keep pushing forward with the people that are supportive and hoping that if you get one half of the staff, it's the early adopter bell curve. When you have your early adopters, you get to a critical mass and then everyone has to kind of follow along. I don't know what framework is gonna work. I'm on this journey right now."

She wonders why so many are apparently blind to the risks of sedation, when evidence is everywhere. "When I think about people who have had any level of sedation and critical illness, including my parents, who had routine open-heart surgery, they were never the same after that," she stresses. "But nobody will talk about that. Nobody will talk about the increase in dementia, the sort of mild executive functioning decline that happens after going on a bypass machine. I was an open-heart surgery nurse, so I know the clinical ins and outs of what they went through intraoperatively and postoperatively."

Coronary artery bypass grafts (CABG)—used to treat coronary artery disease—are one of the most common surgical procedures in the U.S. and much of the developed world. Patients require general anesthesia for between three and six hours. Research in 2006 demonstrated significant cognitive decline in around 80 to 90 percent of patients, including "symptoms of confusion, diminished concentration, and loss of short-term memory, and of word and face recognition," say the authors of the report "Differentiating Cognitive Impairment from Symptoms of Anxiety in Postcoronary Artery Bypass Grafting Encephalopathy." "These symptoms," they say, "may persist for up to five years post-CABG."[5]

"And even that's not as bad as what a typical sepsis survivor or ARDS survivor goes through; it's much messier," Jill tells us. For those patients, she says, this just leads to the recurring cycle of more and yet more sedation in an effort to ease suffering during their extended recovery. "But we don't have enough research or experience keeping people awake. This is a revolution. We know the A2F bundle has definitely proven itself, but the culture just can't grasp it," she maintains.

"There's this joke among nurses," she tells us. "*I want them sedated and ventilated. And I don't want any families.* But that's changing. It's changing. People are realizing that's not a sustainable emotional model for patients." Another hospital joke has it that those who work in the ICU are really just gardeners because all they ever do is just tend and water the vegetables.

"And that hurts my heart," says Jill. "There're a lot of people that get into critical care because they just want to turn patients every two hours and have them deeply sedated and not have to deal with it. But I like to talk to my patients, not treat them like a blob in the bed." Getting to know the patient is an integral part of the job, she insists, and a key element in their recovery.

"Let me tell you about the human aspect of it," says physical therapist Christiane Perme. "In my hospital, we have lots of transplant patients, often multiple organs. So these are very sick patients and they stay in the ICU for the longest time." One day, a patient told her something that would change her career forever, and it has helped her educate colleagues ever since.

"Here was this particular patient, a liver transplant, a very, very sick guy. He was an inspiration for me. He was waiting to have a tracheostomy, but he could talk with difficulty. I walk in to do his physical therapy and he was in tears. I asked, *What's wrong?* And he said, *No, it's nothing.* But if something is bothering one of my patients, then it's bothering me."

He went on to tell her and said, *"Well, I don't feel very well. I'm having this horrible diarrhea. And a nurse and nursing assistant came here to clean me up. They never looked at me. They talked to each other about their weekend, then they walked away without looking at my face. And I felt like I was a piece of meat."* As Perme recounts the story she has tears in her eyes.

"He said he felt he wasn't a human being. *I felt like a piece of meat that they were determined to clean. I am so grateful that they're taking care of me. I'm so grateful that I got this liver. I'm so grateful for everything, so I shouldn't be complaining.* But, he said, *Chris, I am more than a piece of meat."*

Perme continues, "That tore me apart. I was crying with him. And while I hate what happened to him, that was a gift to me because, from that day on, I would never allow that to happen again. Not for a moment should my patients think that they're a piece of meat. That was one of the most powerful moments I had in my career as a therapist."

While such incidents are rare, the sheer pressure, especially during the pandemic, has brought about a break in the traditional nurse-patient relationship, an essential part of the recovery process. And, by deeply sedating so many patients, such voids have become chasms. The return to more humane nursing has never been so imperative. "I think it would improve nurse burnout, too," says clinical educator Jill Larkin Storer.

"I think nurses would love to take care of patients through the whole spectrum of critical illness even though they say they don't want to." But ultimately, she says, many nurses have got stuck in the belief that deep sedation is the humane thing to do, and due to the almost universal failure to follow ICU patients after discharge, few have any idea of the damage being done. They need to hear the human stories to bring the reality home, she maintains. Only then can we move forward, because "change lies with the nurses at the bedside making autonomous decisions. They have a lot of power to make a different decision."

Ultimately, she believes the answer lies in recruiting a new breed of nurse. "That's why I'm putting my effort in the new people," Jill tells us. "We have new graduate RNs that everyone used to say, *Well, they aren't equipped to work in the ICU.* So we educate them. I teach the A2F bundle. I do simulations on making sedation choices based on validated scales, based on the exchange of communication between the physician and them. And they go through these series of classes and they have become my champions."

Nora Raher, BSN, RN, CCRN, is one such nurse. She experienced a baptism of fire in her second year when COVID-19 struck. Today, she works at an ICU in Virginia. She was not one who ever dreamt of becoming a nurse as a child. In college, her big thing was track and field, and this led her to take a course in anatomy in her senior year. "We had the opportunity to go to one of the local hospitals to watch an open-heart surgery, and I was fascinated with the dynamic of the operating room. I was amazed at the role given to nurses. I never thought that a nurse could be working so closely with a surgeon. I was hooked," she told us.

Within her first year as a nurse, Nora found herself attending a conference by the SCCM. The subject was Dr. Ely's A2F bundle and a new humanity in critical care. "And it changed everything for me," she says. "I realized that I wanted to be an ICU nurse." But what she was hearing on stage ran counter to the practices around her. "The patient is taken out of the equation when they're placed on a breathing machine. That was the culture everywhere, but it doesn't come from a bad place. We're taking care of so many problems with ICU patients—we prioritize the cardiovascular system, the respiratory system—so they get placed on the ventilator and sedated because everybody just wants to have one less thing to worry about.

"But when I went to this conference I learned that you don't have to do that. And you can treat these complex illnesses while still having the patient awake and involved in their care. And not only that, it's the most important thing for them to preserve their brain, to keep their muscles and skeletal system intact. And to ultimately get them better and out of there in a much more timely fashion than with the traditional culture of oversedation and immobility."

Back in Virginia, Nora suddenly found herself nominated the resident expert on the A2F bundle. Soon after, she was heading a project designed to bring change to her entire hospital system. "We created a new practice guideline that would really focus on having a patient awake and participating in their care. This was a big accomplishment and we were very proud of ourselves. But the biggest challenge was getting the word out to everyone about what we had done."

Her team met stiff resistance, despite seeing a profound improvement in patient outcomes and far fewer transfers to care facilities. "I don't think it's because people want to hurt patients," she says, shaking her head. "I think that it's just so hard to shift gears and change someone's mindset about how they take care of a critically ill patient, especially when someone's been in the field for thirty years."

Her colleagues appear blind to data, she says, so she tried to humanize the experience by giving them examples of success from the bundle. "And then I found Kali [Dayton] and her podcast, and we use that as education, and that seemed to strike a chord with people in the strongest way because it wasn't just data points that she talks about or studies. It's the patient telling a story about how they have PTSD now from the effects of deep sedation, or it can be the other end of the spectrum where a patient wasn't deeply sedated and they're back doing their job and they didn't have cognitive decline. And when people heard those stories, they were like, *Oh my goodness! This is amazing! How can we do this on our own unit?*"

THE UNKNOWN TRUTHS

The lack of evidence-based medicine in Japan prompted young Dr. Mikita Fuchita to finish his studies in the United States in 2015. "I had a mentor in Tokyo," he tells us, "who inspired me that patient care can be much better if you study the literature and learn what's harmful and what's helpful to the patient." In Japan, he says, they mostly practice experience-based medicine. "If your superior has been doing the same thing for twenty years, and they haven't noticed any issues, then they just keep on doing it, and you just say *Yes* to your supervisor."

But as a resident trainee in anesthesiology in Denver, he soon found that there was little difference between the two systems. While every research paper he could find called for limited sedation and early mobility, the patients he was assigned to care for in the cardiac ICU were just as deeply sedated as they were back home.

"It's like we're marinating these patients with continuous sedation medication," he says. "And the tendency for human bias is to stick with what's done because that's what other people think collectively is right." And it's very difficult, he says, to question an existing practice, "let alone think it's bad when everyone else, including your supervisor, believes that this is what's necessary."

As such, he says, once their patients have stabilized they are swiftly moved on to long-term acute care hospitals, known as LTACs, and nobody has the chance to see what damage might have been done. "We're done with the fun part [of] treating sick patients. We don't want to deal with it anymore and we just send them to LTAC. We don't follow these patients and see what happens to them. And who knows what happens then, the mess that we've created? And that's the dark side of ICU," he says.

And then, one day, he found Kali Dayton's podcasts, and everything changed when he discovered what he terms the "unknown truths." He recalls: "She talked about the LDS Hospital where they assembled a completely new ICU, gathering nurses with no prior exposure to critical care, and taught them that no sedation was the standard. They didn't tell them that all the other ICUs around the world were deeply sedating."

He continues, "And it made sense because I knew the literature and I knew what seemed right for the patient. And I finally found an ICU that worked differently, and they were able to execute it with perfection. This was a profound experience for me. We don't know we're creating misery. We think we're doing good."

He listened to every single episode, and "soon realized that the way I practice, even as a trainee, was causing harm to the patient. I was harming patients because of my ignorance." It was the personal stories of the damage that had been done to ICU survivors that brought it all home with a sudden shock, he says. "And I just couldn't stop crying."

This was not why the young Mikita had wanted to become a doctor. "I've always wanted to be close to the patient, to understand from their perspective, their struggles, and not to just treat the diagnosis in front of you but look at the patient as a whole person," he explains. "And Kali's podcasts just enlightened me to a whole new paradigm, one that changes the core tenet of ICU management, because sedation right now is at the core of managing patients on the ventilator. Without it, everything changes," he says.

"Everyone's workflow changes. Now we give patients a whiteboard to write on to communicate and have them do mobility exercises. Those are not part of the traditional routines. So there's lots of cultural barriers to overcome." This, he says, will prove a lengthy, uphill battle, pointing out that only 14 percent of groundbreaking therapy treatments ever get converted into practice and that generally it takes seventeen years to actually implement any new procedure. "But I suspect [ending sedation] will take longer to get there because it's such a culturally ingrained component of ICU management," he sighs.

"But I wanted to see with my own eyes, so I visited the LDS Hospital to learn about it, and, after I came back, I implemented that no-sedation approach in five of my patients. One thing that Kali talks about is that it's much easier to not start sedation than it is to wean and decrease the sedation. So I selected five patients who needed to be intubated and I gave them the option not to be sedated.

"I explained that we typically sedate patients on the ventilator. But I told them that it's proven in the literature that if you can stay away from sedation and keep awake, that will decrease the risks of depression, anxiety, PTSD, and death. You'll get off the ventilator faster and have a much better quality of life after ICU.

"Talking to them beforehand made a huge difference because, often-times, people are not told what's going to happen to them, they're just automatically sedated. And, by the time they have some semblance of consciousness, they're too drugged up to think clearly, let alone make any informed decisions." But, he says, "If we let them understand what to antic-ipate, they have some preparation in their mind that might allow them to cope with this new, disturbing condition of having the breathing tube in and not being able to talk. I reassured them that we still use medications to keep them comfortable and everyone said, *Yeah, sure. Let's try it.*"

His patients receive just sufficient sedation to knock them out for an hour or two while he connects them to the ventilator. "And I wait at the bedside and let them wake up and reorient. I tell them, *You're just coming out of anesthesia, and you now have the breathing tube. How are you feeling?* And one of them just smiled at me, right off the bat!" he laughs.

He says that of these patients—three females and two males—the men appeared to suffer the most anxiety when they awoke and were breathing much faster than usual and that they needed to be coached into a more relaxed state. For unconscious patients on the ventilator, the natural breathing drive is suppressed and the machine takes care of the rate of breath. "But modern ventilators allow the patient to initiate breathing," he explains.

Generally, he says, when patients wake up in an anxious state, the natural tendency is to give more sedation. "But I didn't want to do that," he explained. "One patient had his wife at the bedside and I asked her to try and help control his breathing, to calm his mind. So the wife held his hand and gently stroked his head. And it was remarkable. His breath rate dropped dramatically in a short while. By just talking calmly and relaxing the patient, this is more effective than giving medications, which have so many detrimental effects."

In our conscious state, we rarely give any thought to our breathing; it happens automatically. But patients waking up on the ventilator need help adjusting, and small quantities of sedation can be administered for a day or so just to relieve the anxiety and allow the brain to resume its automatic breathing pattern. "We don't want to make them too sleepy. We try to find a fine balance, and eventually the patient gets used to it and is off sedation," he tells us.

Dr. Fuchita shared with us some of the photos and videos he had taken of these five patients. In one instance, the husband and wife are seen kissing and cuddling, while the husband—who is sitting partially reclined in a chair—makes a joke with his bedside nurse by writing on a whiteboard. Another patient watches a Nicholas Cage movie. Beside his bed he has all the apparatus to administer sedatives, but there are no drips in place. Even more extraordinary, he has his own receptacle to urinate into and has no need for a Foley catheter to be inserted into his bladder. The most remarkable thing about these images are the clear eyes and the look of keen attention on each of their faces as they interact with visitors and staff.

"And something that I learned over time is that nurses just want the best for the patients," he insists. "So I focus on why I'm doing this. But I always need to be a pain in the butt, just staying at the bedside, not letting them use sedation. And, in time, they realize that it's okay. Patients have started using their iPhone three hours after getting the breathing tube. And in the early afternoon they realize, *Okay, maybe this patient doesn't need sedation.*

"So that's been my process. I was able to convince myself through those five experiments. I was like, *Okay, this is feasible. This isn't just the LDS that can do this.* If we can ingrain a new culture, it might be possible to change the entire hospital system just like Terry [Clemmer] and Louise and Polly did."

Deborah (Continued): Minutes from Death

One big myth is that people think the longer you're in a coma, the greater the side effects. This isn't true, apart from muscle wastage and the physical stuff involved in learning to walk again. Here's a list of some of the side effects people suffer and those which I feel too:

Hair loss—Yep, nice and short now.

Finger and toenail loss—Fingernails have ridges, but they often fall out two years post trauma.

Short-term memory loss—Oh yes! I was already a forgetful person, but this is taking the piss.

Depression—Yep, although I sometimes can confuse this with exhaustion.

Nightmares—Not had many since I awoke, although I didn't sleep for three nights postcoma in case they came back.

Personality changes—My short fuse is now "petrol fumes" according to hubby. I like to think I value him more, but I did notice in the first few months that I would scream at anyone and anything that upset me.

Anxiety—I get anxious in stressful situations. I've always been high on the anxiety scale, though. I commit myself to too much, then have to recant my commitment, such as visiting friends when I've spread myself too thin.

Guilt—This, everyone has. The pain we put everyone through when we can't remember a thing about it. Watching my family and friends cry when they saw me awake for the first time still seems weird in a nice way, because they love me. But I didn't then, and still can't now, comprehend exactly how poorly I was. I said to Mum the other day, "It's weird to think I was hours from death." She said, "You were minutes, not hours."

Muscle wastage—I was walking the other day to meet my bosses, and Dad said, "Why are you limping?" I couldn't answer him at the time but I guess I was limping because my muscles were aching from driving to Leicester, changing gear, and braking. I put the sprinkler on in the garden this week, and Dad said, "Run!" as I was being soaked. I said, "I can't, I've been in a coma!" If I were being chased by a mugger or knife-wielding monster, I'd just stand there. I really can't be arsed to run, it's too much!!

Bowel and urination frequency—Apparently, I had a tube up my arse in my coma and had a catheter for two and a half weeks. Now I pee nonstop. This is hilarious, especially given I couldn't pee for weeks *and had to have dialysis. I think I panic about this subconsciously. Now I'm up every twenty minutes. This means I'm now exhausted. I'm also farting. In company! Something I'd never have done before. I just don't realize I have done it sometimes. My husband, Adam, finds it hilarious as I was such a prude precoma.*

Pain—Both real and phantom. I have chest pains of a night still. I sleep cuddling a pillow so I keep my rib cage open. I also get the shudders, feeling that spikes are being removed from my neck—a horrid, horrid sensation which still makes me feel sick.

Recovery time—It will be two years, no matter what length of time you were in a coma, if not three. In my support group, both online and in the flesh, everyone takes this time to recover as best as possible, and sometimes never getting back to how they were precoma but good enough. I'd settle for good enough any day.

Janine: Don't Give In

No one mentioned ICU delirium or PICS to Janine Sarah Withers, who had found herself within coma confronting a withered hag in an abandoned theater. Soon after, she found herself teetering on the edge of death but had been told that she must return, to be with her family.

• • •

No one mentioned these things. I didn't know or understand what was happening to me. No one at the hospital spoke to me about it, but my partner Tracy and my daughter Ieasha tried their best to answer the multitude of questions I was left with. They listened to everything I was trying to explain, everything that I'd seen. I had no control over what I was saying, seeing, or feeling, no concept. I had no filter. I was totally overwhelmed with a mixture of fear, confusion, and panic, but relieved and happy to still be here.

My memory is neither short nor long term. I have black holes where memories used to be. I have to ask the same questions over and over again and then try and remember the answers to fill in the blanks, past and present.

I couldn't understand how ill I'd been nor the extent of what I'd been through. I couldn't comprehend it. Both the mental and physical pain took some time to process afterward. It's left me with massive panic attacks, nightmares, anxiety attacks that physically affect me at times, pains in my head, in my chest, and down my arm. A tightness around my throat. I have to have faith that they will pass, and eventually they do.

Now I just try to live in the moment and concentrate on getting well. I have mild PTSD but, because COVID was happening, I didn't get any aftercare. I was unable to walk, to talk, I couldn't swallow food or drink properly. I was left feeling sad that I had scared my family so, although I knew I wasn't to blame. But I did feel embarrassed.

Staff on the ward had no understanding. They didn't know why I was behaving the way I was. I had one good friend there [on the ward]—a patient who got me through the times when my family wasn't able to. She meant the world to me and still does. We are best friends made in times of adversity.

I never found it difficult to talk with Tracy and Ieasha, but the rest of my family don't want to understand or listen. They have too many problems of their own, so they can't comprehend. I understand, though. But just talking about it all brings up painful memories. But Tracy and Ieasha, they listen. I guess it's like therapy for all of us.

When I think back, I just feel overwhelmed. I've experienced things that were amazing to have gone through. But I realize now that I'm stronger than I ever thought and that there's so much more that we just don't know or can't understand. But I was presented with the choice to fight or give in. These things have shown me that I have previously unimaginable strength. That you don't just have to give in.

I believe life revolves and that we never really leave. I'm not scared of dying anymore, just worried how my loved ones would cope if I had to go. I know I've been through the most traumatic experience, and

I'm very much still here, still fighting, loving and holding on to those who mean the world to me. And just being the best person I can be.

I make the most of each day, good or bad. I leave nothing unsaid. I don't take anything for granted anymore. I see this as a blessing in disguise.

Simon: I've Lost My Memory

Simon Newton-Smith is a retired police officer from the British West Midlands who was hospitalized on two occasions in 2019, initially for pneumonia and sepsis and eventually with multiple infections and for an aortic valve replacement. On his first admission, they took one look at him and swiftly admitted him to the ICU, where he was placed on a ventilator and sedated to coma levels for the next eight weeks. When he subsequently got to read his hospital notes, he saw that he was marked down with ICU delirium within a day of deep sedation. His coma events were as real as any other in his life. But now his memory—which was never a problem before—is a serious cause for concern. He was finally allowed to go home just after his seventieth birthday.

• • •

The order of my reality doesn't follow any logic. There's the real reality, and there's my reality. And when you're in that reality it's extremely real. I was the same person through the decades but doing things appropriate to the respective time I was in—the eighteenth and nineteenth centuries mostly—but with technology that exists now. I travelled the world under the control of a company intent on raising civil war. I looked quite good in a Georgian wig!

The wig featured in two episodes, and there were four different locations. Mostly, there was the Dorset coast with high cliffs and a small port, more of a smuggler's cove, but that didn't come into play until World Wars One or Two, where I was an injured officer in a hospital train in a siding above the cove.

At one point, I returned to the port with gold bullion and I was taken to a secret Bank of England vault within the cliff that was fitted with the latest electronic equipment. It was ventilated, and there were other people and, judging from their dress, they were from all walks of life. We were stuck in there a long time and I tried to use my knowledge of electronics—which I don't actually have—to get us out. Inside the vault was a curious statuette of the Pied Piper, holding a balance, like in yoga.

When I was out of hospital and trying to get better, I took up yoga for a while. I would have liked physio but that's not available in our area. We were doing this pose, and suddenly I had a flashback to the statuette. I had to stop yoga. I had to stop because of the flashbacks.

Trying to make sense of this is very difficult. This is one of the problems I have. I've lost my memory. I'm the president of a caravan club. I went to the AGM, but I've got absolutely no memory of it. I can recall just one or two events. When I first came out, for the first four or five months, I'd be talking to my wife and I'd ask her five or six times in a day the same question. Now it's not so bad. It might be just a couple of times a day.

I've looked in my diary to try and work out what I've missed. And I've definitely got no memory of most things. People tell me things that have happened, but I only know they've happened because people have told me. I went to my wife's birthday party. I don't remember. I can't tell you what I had to eat. We went to see one of the grandchildren and I couldn't recall his name. Yeah. It's really, really difficult.

Stephen (Continued): Nothing Like Dreams

Stephen Taylor, the medical statistician, spent much of his coma either in the Cushioned Room or within the confines of a creepy Belgian hospital. His chances of surviving the burst colon and subsequent sepsis were put at 1 percent. On admission, he was swiftly sedated and placed on a ventilator. He spent ten days in a coma.

• • •

The ICUsteps intensive care guide for patients and relatives says that it's common for patients to have vivid dreams, nightmares, and hallucinations while receiving the powerful drugs used in their treatment—dreams of being tortured, trapped in bed, or being held captive—known as ICU psychosis or ICU delirium.[6] My "dreams" were a substantial and important part of my stay in the ICU, and I wanted to write them down while I still remembered them.

I place the word "dreams" in quotation marks because the word doesn't adequately express the nature of an experience that was more than an ordinary dream. Usually, I don't remember dreams or, if I do, forget them quite quickly. But these dreams have remained long after my stay in hospital; their impact and memorability is so strong that they transcend the ordinary type of dream. They were like real experiences taking place in real time. Later in my recovery in the ICU, as I was becoming more conscious of the "real" world, I couldn't distinguish it from the dreams, so the two merged imperceptibly into one complete reality. I can still go into my mind, back to these dreams, and relive parts of them.

I must mention the nun in the wheelchair. She would sit in the doorway of her beautifully wood-paneled office, at the top of the granite staircase, with an air of authority like a mother superior. Sometimes, she sat near me when I was trapped in the paneled room; whether as jailer or comforter I was never quite sure. I vaguely recall her being there late in the night, sometimes silently talking to me or to someone else nearby; overlooking with a stern compassion.

I never saw the gangsters—they were always hidden in dark shadow—but they were a palpable, threatening presence. Only the gangsters' molls—the glitzy cowgirls—were overtly visible and aware of me in the bar. The gangsters wanted the gold demon mask, and I also had something else that they were after, willing to kill me for it but, for some reason, weren't allowed. I had to voluntarily give up whatever it was they wanted: I just had to put my hand in my pocket, remove the object, and hand it over, but I stubbornly and steadfastly refused. I've thought a lot about this. Was it the ultimate existential test: to willingly give up my life?

I really believed I was in that beautiful Belgian hospital on its wooded hillside, with the cobbled-street medieval tourist town below. As I became more aware of my actual surroundings, I found myself hearing the conversations of those around me, particularly the nurses and staff at the various locations around my bed. I was picking up on accents, and these were shifting my perception of where the hospital was located.

But why Belgium? About ten years previously, I had a couple of short stays and was impressed with the narrow, cobbled streets in the medieval town centers. During one of those holidays, we visited the German town of Aachen and I took a long walk to the three borders where Germany, Belgium, and Holland all meet. Part of the walk was rural, and I could see on a low hillside in the distance, surrounded by trees, Aachen hospital shining white in the sun. Hence, perhaps, all of this fed in to create the hospital in my dreams and a natural place for me to heal and recover.

By far the worst of the entrapment dreams was the Cushioned Room. This manifested in a number of incarnations, but the small furnished room with the ticking clock was much the worst. It was like being entombed. And how odd that an object of comfort, a cushion, should become a thing of malevolent threat!

The dream of "alien" figures drifting past, and the continuous swishing sound, was also a disturbing, seemingly interminable dragging of time, which can also be interpreted in the light of goings-on around my bed. I'm myopic, and the aliens were probably my blurred, drugged perception of nurses and staff passing by. There was a table nearby with a very large folder containing tabulated sheets for documenting my progress. As the large pages were turned, they made a swishing sound, hence: swish, swish, swish.

The dream of my mother beckoning to follow along the road was very poignant, as she had passed away less than a year before. I was convinced I had, or someone had, a photograph or card of her posing in her nurse uniform with the "lollipop" sign. This was an example of my being unable to distinguish between dream and actual, for this photograph never existed.

The ice rink and the great gray building I recall clearly and are part of what I call the solace dream for the comfort it gave me; it often occurred late in the evening, when the ward was deserted and quiet. It gave me hope, peace, succor, following the rigors of entrapment.

Nighttime was the longest, loneliest period of the day. I can recall the feelings of abandonment and isolation when the lights went out and the ward became quiet. I think this is reflected in the dreams.

These dreams are now long in the past, but occasionally a sound, a play of light, a song on the radio, triggers a memory and transports me fleetingly back to the world of the Belgian hospital, sometimes to the Cushioned Room but never, thankfully, as a prisoner there.

I'm filled with gratitude toward all the doctors, nurses, physiotherapists, and staff of the critical care unit at the Royal Liverpool University Hospital for saving me from the brink of death and nursing me back to life. There isn't a day goes by without them in my thoughts, and I thank them from my heart.

Rory (Continued): I'm Not Alone

Rory, who spent seven days in a coma after suffering a horrific home invasion, shares the following about life after his coma.

• • •

My therapy did very, very little to help me with my PTSD or the trauma of my coma experience. I don't honestly think doctors have the first clue about what it's like to be in a coma. The only people who really know are the ones who've suffered through it themselves.

The coma has absolutely changed my views on life and death. Sometimes, I'm in a total state of panic, believing I'm still in the coma and this life isn't real. This is happening less over the years, but it's total panic, a full-on anxiety attack when it does happen. I never thought about death or dying before, I just enjoyed my life. Now I am absolutely terrified of dying and think about it all the time.

The coma changed me as a person. I'm very withdrawn now and don't really like much company. I have a huge dislike of crowds and loud noises. I've become reclusive. I regularly have flashback dreams about the events. They usually result in my waking, shaking and sweating. I have to take powerful sleeping pills when this gets bad. I have random daily things that trigger memories, and I'll start shaking and have to have a moment to try and be calm. I suffer with my mental health as a result. The coma fucked my head and my life up.

For the most part of my coma, I had absolutely no idea I was even in hospital and definitely didn't know I was in a coma. It's funny because I don't even remember being told that I had been in a coma after the event. My mum told me recently that I shouldn't have been in one for as long as I was and that I took a lot longer to come out of it than the doctors thought. She said she was by my side every day, talking to me, but I only have one memory of her being by my bedside—and that was a nightmare.

I found that the nurses and doctors played significant roles in my experiences. My surgeon and a number of nurses took on terrifying forms in my coma. I can only conclude that I must have opened my eyes at times and seen them. All these evil characters in my dreams trying to hurt or abuse me actually turned out to be hospital staff. Doctors, nurses, even cleaners.

Needless to say, I was terrified when I actually did come out of my coma and began to see all these same people. I was very slowly woken up from my coma and I was on a lot of heavy morphine, so, even though I was half awake, I was still hallucinating very badly. The scary Asian man who was always there, doing or trying to do me harm, was in fact my surgeon, and he was actually a very, very nice man. The scary canteen women were all nurses who were on the ICU unit and, again, all very lovely people. The big Black lady? I have absolutely no idea who she was to this day. I know it sounds awful, but whenever I see a large Black lady it triggers my PTSD badly.

I had a counselor come to talk to me twice while I was in hospital, but I really didn't want to speak to anyone at the time and made this very clear to her. I sought help the following year and saw a psychologist. He was the one who thought my coma experience was so traumatic and scary because the last thing that happened was my attack. While I was laying bleeding to death, I thought I was going to die and was in complete panic and terror. The thing is, so many different things happened in that time that I'm not sure if I will ever really remember it all. To this day, I will see or hear something, and it will come crashing back into my brain like lightning.

The only people I've ever managed to find who understand are those on the Facebook Coma Survivors Group. It's just comforting to know I'm not alone, that others understand what kind of mindset this puts you in.

Nikki (Continued): A Life Changer

Nikki, who gave birth to the baby with the ice-blue eyes, spent more than eight months in the hospital after developing double pneumonia that led to complete organ failure and thirty-four days in a medically induced coma.

. . .

Personally, it was only by looking online that I saw other people experience coma dreams, that it's an actual thing! I genuinely thought I was losing my mind!

I was on a different planet with drugs. I was so confused and in pain. It took everything out of me. Talking about it was extremely painful. I didn't understand the whole life-changing experience I'd been through, and, to be honest, the consequences of the whole thing took months to sink in.

I was offered no counseling for the mental health issues it caused. It wasn't until a year or so that it became clear I wasn't coping day to day, dealing with the new physical me. The relationships with my son and husband were becoming more and more damaged. I lost eighteen months' memory when my eldest little boy was only three. It took years for me to repair my relationship with him. My relationships with my husband and son had to restart and develop into something very different. Thankfully, my husband is very understanding and supportive.

I went to the doctor, told him about the flashbacks, and he said I had PTSD. Luckily, I was able to go private for counseling and to see a psychologist. She diagnosed depression and anxiety. I was told I needed to grieve. I have a few coma memories. All but one were recurring nightmares. Generally, they don't affect me unless something gives me a flashback, like seeing a basement in films or seeing burn victims.

It may sound selfish given the whole COVID pandemic, but long COVID is now a medical diagnosis and yet it's very similar to what I've been suffering for years, but I've been ignored, or told that I'm lucky, given everything. Get over it. Deal with it. *It's very hard to explain when you've experienced the brink of life and death, and then the terrible journey back, trying to become a new person with "fog" due to the brain damage.*

It's funny when people say, You're lucky to be alive. *People around you don't realize the hell you're locked into.* And why are you grieving for a child that didn't exist? *I was told by one family member that I couldn't have been in a proper coma because I didn't hear my family talking to me! They thought I'd made it all up, 'cos her father-in-law was in an actual coma and heard everything. Trying to explain levels of sedation was lost on them. But it's something many people don't want to talk about; it's too different from what we're told, especially in the media. It's taken me years to forgive it.*

Now, in COVID time, for so many, life is hell. Those families need help. To know that they're not always sleeping peaceful. It's essential for people to know what they're going through and that they won't just simply get over it. It's a life changer.

Chrissy (Continued): No One Explains

While in a coma, I remember getting an infection in my arm and a mark being drawn where the infection was to see how it was spreading. I also remember the pain, and I heard conversations as they tried to drain the infection. They thought I was deeper under than I really was. When I was on the open ward, I asked the nurse looking after me about the incident and she confirmed everything that happened. She was really surprised.

If only someone had explained to me what was happening! I would have been much calmer. When I woke up, I couldn't move or talk. I had the feeling that someone was sitting on my chest, and I was so scared. I thought one nurse was trying to kill me and was terrified of her. I went through total nightmares of the darkest kind that you can imagine and some you can't. It was terrifying.

My nightmares involved drowning on a ship, rape, euthanasia, and war, together with my former partner trying to kill me. I was fighting my way out of a dark well that I was sinking into and fighting to get out.

They had a TV on for me, so this is where nightmares and reality cross over. When you're sleeping, they stroke your face to wake you up. But in my eyes they looked like claws or oriental dancers with long nails—they terrified me. I saw many dead people in these nightmares and endless mutilation. I still struggle sleeping at night but can sleep like a baby in the daytime when I know people are about.

Isobel (Continued): Just So Barbaric

I went back to the ICU and tried to tell them about my experiences inside coma, and everyone was like, That's weird. Oh, really? And when I saw my surgeons and my anesthetist no one could understand what I was talking about. It was only when I went to rehab and spoke to the trauma counselor and told her that no one knows about this and she said, Well, I do. We get this all the time. *I told her I work at the hospital. We have the best doctors in the country, they really know their stuff. We've been intubating and sedating patients for years; why is this not known? She told me she thought everyone knew about it.*

So I went to Facebook support groups, and there's one called I Survived a Coma. Actually, I started off going to COVID support groups, but that was ridiculous for me because it didn't cover what I'd been through; there were people there who hadn't even been to hospital. But the coma group, you have to have survived a coma, and that's where I found so many people who'd been through the same thing—just the sheer numbers! So I saw all these people having the same experiences, the correlations, and I asked myself, Why don't people know about this?

And then I came across Kali Dayton and I found out that coma doesn't really need to be an option. Obviously, I thought we had no choice in the matter, that there were no other options. I mean, I didn't need to be put under!

At my hospital, last year [2021] I must have seen twenty-five deaths. They were just dropping like flies. So finding Kali has made a huge difference. I actually don't think I'd know about it if it wasn't for her. I showed a lot of doctors the Awake *and* Walking *videos,[7] and they were shocked—physicians, ENT and other surgeons, anesthetists—no one has even heard of it.*

If someone came to me now with propofol to put me in a coma, I'd be like, Get away from me! *I'd sooner die than let that happen to me again. I'm working very hard to live a normal life. I have lots of physio. But there's cognitive damage. When I woke up I couldn't even do the alphabet. And there's definitely still gaps; I'm still learning vocabulary. Before the coma I was very good at English. Now I'm having to relearn words. In order to learn the word "tree," I had to ask what's that thing that grows out of the ground?*

Coma, you know, is so dramatic—just so barbaric that it's happening at all. I think one day, we're gonna look back and be horrified!

10

So, Who's Going to Pay for All This?

(Every One of Us, Unless We Bring about Change)

The argument goes that most hospitals are cash-strapped these days, that there are too few nurses, doctors, and other specialists, and that the last thing anyone needs is to make more work for staff. And while few can doubt this, there is a far more convincing argument that if we get it right in the first place, then patients will have better outcomes and far fewer will need the continuing care elsewhere in the system. It is not the initial costs that need to be focused upon but the ultimate extra expense to both health facilities and those who have to suffer down the line.

"Sure, they say we don't have enough staff," says Kali Dayton. "This is the argument coming from the ICU side because they recognize the extra workload that all of this causes, so they keep them sedated. But what is cost-effective can be contrary with our mission as health care workers and the objective of the ICU. For example, early death is often more cost-effective but not in line with our societal values. But they don't get to see the delirium and damage that they've caused. They send them to care facilities, and they don't recognize how much more work this is. They have to understand the process and the problems that we've caused in order to understand the harm and expense being incurred."

And while on the face of it caring for patients lying senseless in bed might appear easier than dealing with their continuous needs while awake, the opposite is known to be the case. "When hospital systems force ICU nurses to struggle to care for four patients instead of one or two, they are creating a storm of death, suffering, and incredible expense," underlines Dayton. "When nurses do not have the support, training, and opportunity to avoid sedation, prevent delirium, and mobilize their patients, then they end up doing far more work running to change sedation drips, they break their backs to turn obese, flaccid bodies every two hours, and they bear the emotional trauma of constant poor outcomes."

Much of this should, in fact, be obvious, she maintains. "We know that the more sedation a patient receives, the longer they're going to be in hospital. And the longer you're sedated, the longer you're going to be on the ventilator, and everything to do with the ventilator is expensive. When patients don't move and their diaphragm atrophies, then they can't breathe independently, and then they're going to need even more time on the ventilator and far longer to rehabilitate the diaphragm."

But it does not stop there. The longer the ICU stay, the more frequent are hospital-acquired infections and complications, from bed sores, wasted muscles, and calcified joints, to acute nerve and cognitive damage, all of which require treatment elsewhere in the system. "This bigger picture of ICU care—the rehabilitation, length of stay, return to work, outpatient care, long-term health care costs—are not captured in any cost analysis that I could find," she insists.

Almost all of the financial studies that we could find date back more than a decade, well before the pandemic, and do not reflect current costs or rising inflation. However, given the frequency of these conditions in ICU patients, vast savings are likely to be made by targeting specific issues such as delirium, Dayton maintains, pointing out that around 80 percent of ICU patients develop this condition and that just one episode of delirium adds around 40 percent to both ICU and general hospitalization costs.[1] Patients with delirium were shown in one study[2] to spend nearly five days longer in the ICU than those who avoided the condition. Other studies have shown that delirious patients stay twice as long in the hospital generally, doubling the amount of nursing care required.[3]

The first step in both cutting direct costs and decreasing the instances of delirium is to reduce the amount of sedatives prescribed. For example, just 1 mg of Ativan, used to treat anxiety in the ICU, increases the risk of delirium by 20 percent. "So if you give two milligrams every six hours, that's a one hundred and sixty percent increase in risk in just twenty-four hours," she points out, while benzodiazepines such as midazolam, sold under the brand name Versed, each day add a staggering 840 percent risk of ICU delirium if administered at a "low dose" of 5 mg/hr. Or, to put it another way, it is a total given that lengthy sedation with either of these two drugs will result in acute brain failure while adding considerably to the cost of care.

"So," she says, "rates of delirium depend on the agent, dose, depth, and duration of sedation, which directly impact patient harm or complications and health care costs, and we know that decreasing—and especially avoiding—sedation drastically prevents and decreases delirium."

One study by the SCCM covering over twenty-thousand patients showed that by implementing the A2F bundle, health care costs were significantly reduced by cutting the number of days in coma by up to half. Another study showed that the bundle cut delirium rates by nearly 80 percent.[4]

Another obvious means of reducing delirium and overall costs is to institute early mobility in the ICU by employing physical and occupational therapists to work with the awake patients and by investing in mobility equipment that helps nurses take the strain out of lifting.

"We know that physical therapy in the ICU can decrease time on the ventilator, time in the ICU, and time in the hospital," Dayton points out. "It improves discharge home rates, long-term functional status, and decreases hospital and ICU readmissions. All resulting in decreased health care costs."

A recent study in Brazil showed that having physical therapists in the hospital around the clock resulted in decreased medical and staff costs by drastically reducing the length of stay and time on the ventilator. "Perhaps that's why I'm getting so many incredible pictures and videos from Brazil of COVID patients with high ventilator settings playing volleyball," smiles Dayton. "So when hospital systems refuse to invest in hiring more rehabilitation clinicians, such as occupational and physical therapists, are they really being financially responsible and driving down health care costs?"

Each year, the Johns Hopkins University School of Medicine admits around nine hundred patients. In 2008, they decided to spend $358,000 annually to cover the additional costs of dedicated physical and occupational therapists in their intensive care units. Within just one year, the average length of stay in the ICU dropped by nearly a quarter, down from six and a half days to just five days. Transfers to care facilities fell by 18 percent. This is believed to have resulted in a net cost saving for the hospital of about $818,000 per year.

However, due to the lack of research available, hard figures of potential savings are difficult to assess. Nonetheless, the authors of the 2014 report "Reduction of Intensive Care Unit Length of Stay: The Case of Early Mobilization" concluded that the father of modern medicine, Hippocrates, may have got it wrong when he implied that pain is best relieved by bed rest. "Modern day researchers have found that bed rest is potentially harmful with complications of pulmonary edema, atelectasis, bone demineralization, muscle wasting, vasomotor instability, constipation, back pain, pressure ulcers, contractures and blood clots," they stressed.[5]

"While the cost saving benefit is not fully realized by the research available, early mobilization has the potential to reduce length of stay and medical complications," the authors concluded. "Early mobilization in the ICU would likely benefit patients, hospitals and insurance companies. Because of its benefits, early mobilization in the ICU should become a standard of care due to the potential reduction in medical complications."

The lack of adequate research also hampered the authors of the 2016 report "Higher Hospital Spending on Occupational Therapy Is Associated with Lower Readmission Rates," who said the sparsity of literature makes it much harder for hospital executives to allocate scarce resources. However, by examining Medicare insurance claims and cost report data, they were able to analyze the association between hospital spending for specific services and thirty-day readmission rates for heart failure, pneumonia, and acute myocardial infarction. "We found that occupational therapy is the only spending category where additional spending has a statistically significant association with lower readmission rates for all three medical conditions," they concluded. "One possible explanation is that occupational therapy places a unique and immediate focus on patients' functional and social needs, which can be important drivers of readmission if left unaddressed."[6]

"When you think about it," says occupational therapist Andrew Rich, MS, OTR/L CSPHP, "when, in the ICU, do people ever get hope? When do people realize that they're feeling better? It's when they get out of bed. That's usually the first *ah-ha* moment." He believes that every patient in the ICU, even those on mechanical ventilation, needs to walk at least two hundred steps every day. It is not hard to believe that a short trip out onto the porch or into the hospital grounds, even a quick trip up to the helipad, can bring about remarkable change in patients' outlooks, knowing that there is a world outside, ready and waiting for their return.

Another study by the SCCM found that ICU readmissions were cut in half and discharges to nursing homes reduced by 40 percent when the A2F bundle had been fully implemented in ICUs. The society also found that two-thirds of ICU survivors had failed to return to work within several months of discharge, placing a heavy financial burden on both health care systems and survivors.

One 2008 study in Italy—where residential care homes are rare and home nursing is almost universally the norm—it was discovered that nearly one million caregivers, out of a total population of fifty-nine million, had to be hired annually by families struggling to care for ICU survivors, at an average cost per family of over $1,000 a month.

The financial burden for families is one overlooked aspect after discharge, Dr. Leanne Boehm, PhD, RN, ACNS-BC, FCCM, assistant professor at Vanderbilt University School of Nursing, told us. As part of a rare study, she interviewed around forty ICU survivors to learn how they were faring after discharge. "And sometimes after those interviews, I would feel like I needed some therapy myself," she says.

"They look okay, but they're not okay. And people don't understand that, even the patients and family members don't understand. They're just alone and isolated, and so it's very heartbreaking to hear about all of those things," says Dr. Boehm. "There are serious financial issues that come out of this, related to the hospitalization, related to ongoing care needs, related to permanent disability. They can't work anymore. So that's a loss of income."

Suddenly, she says, they discover an entirely new dynamic in the household. "If they were the breadwinner before, they're no longer that now, and then family members have to pick up that burden, while also potentially still having to take care of the survivor, and not understanding that this was a possible eventuality of the ICU hospitalization."

Amidst all this, the person they knew and loved has changed into something else. "They wake up with nightmares every other night. Life has been turned upside down. And there's also the social isolation. All of a sudden, they're afraid to go out in public and be around people because they're afraid they're gonna get sick again, and that's kind of like PTSD, but nobody understands. You talk to your friends, and they just don't get it."

Dayton, one of the most influential leaders in modern critical care, maintains, "By understanding the reality of our practices—that sedation is so often unnecessary and results in expensive, lethal, and inhumane repercussions—then we can use the evidence to speak the language of the stakeholders, which is money. We can talk about human suffering with all our passion, but the strongest card we can play is money. Poor care is expensive care. The misguided approaches to decreasing health care costs and increasing revenue by staffing hospitals at the bare minimum have backfired."

The quest for financial compensation may one day tip the balance, but only once it becomes widely known that existing practices in the ICU are both lethal and life changing. "It's easy to demonstrate that we are generally practicing against decades of evidence," Dayton points out. "It's simple to trace patient harm, suffering, and costs back to sedation and immobility practices and the failure to practice the A2F bundle. What if we started to think, *Wow, how would I defend myself in court for a RASS of –3? How would I explain allowing that dose of midazolam? How could we justify the failure to have this patient out of bed for three weeks?* What if hospital systems and even clinicians felt the pressure of those liabilities?" she asks.

But to bring change via crippling lawsuits that bankrupt hospitals and target individual doctors and nurses would be a terrible way to go, because no medical professional sets out to harm patients and those who staff ICU units are some of the finest in the profession. They do not deserve to have to defend their ingrained practices in a court of law.

Yet no matter how hard people like Kali Dayton and Dr. Ely and Polly Bailey and others push for change within the medical system, change—if it ever does come about—will take decades, and in that time who can say just how many more people will die and how many more lives will be ruined?

THE THREE STAGES OF TRUTH

Anybody wishing to see for themselves the damage done to those who survive ICU only need to visit the HealthUnlocked forum, where survivors daily post the most heartrending questions in their desperate search for answers. Most want to know if they are suffering alone. Have they gone insane? And, more optimistically, when might they ever get better? Does one ever get better? They ask questions like:

I have no idea how I'll get my brain back to normal. I'm constantly tired and have big problems communicating.

My girlfriend was in a medically induced coma for ten days. Since waking up, she doesn't remember anything and refers back to people from fifteen or twenty years ago. Will her memory ever come back?

My husband came out of a fifteen-day coma almost a week ago. Now he just won't respond. Is he ever going to wake up?

This makes for painful reading when, every day, we receive updates from the forum in our mailbox. It is also unsettling to see just how many survivors share among themselves the simplified explanations for events within coma, seeing them in terms of conscious happenings such as hallucinations or delirium, even when they were most likely deep in coma with their brains offline. Whatever they do remember are just coma dreams or false memories, often conjured up in the very instant of wakefulness as the mind's way of filling in blanks. None of it was real. And none of this could be further from the truth.

When it comes to cognitive and physical harm after coma, the depth of their illness—not the sedatives or lack of mobility—is most often seen as the likely cause and, given that they were so critically ill, such complications appear a foregone conclusion. Now that we know differently—that these distressing events are invariably the result of the critical care they received—each post becomes even more heartbreaking, and our desire to open eyes becomes more imperative by the day.

When we first approached Dr. Murphy, he laughed at us when we explained the purpose of this book. "I'm going to tell you this," he said. "The world is going to view you as some kind of weirdo. Actually, to any reasonable doctor or nurse, what you're saying will just sound crazy." He knows from long experience that most of those within his field readily accept that deep sedation is an essential tool for the critical ill. To go against the grain will just invite scorn. He even likens those who reject sedation avoidance to Brazilian loggers who fail to see the connection with climate change.

Conversely, many things that sound crazy today—to both the medical world and to people generally—were once readily accepted as perfectly normal. Few doctors today would ever think of draining blood from those at death's door in order to balance their humors, yet this was standard practice for over two thousand years, from the fifth century BCE to the late nineteenth century. And, hopefully, there are few mental institutions in the world today that still charge a small admission fee to allow the public to torment the inmates, but this was standard practice for centuries. Such a thought today is horrifying.

But these changes did not happen overnight, and today they may still not be universally accepted. All medicine is a learning curve, a process of trial and error, research, study, and experimentation. Dr. Charles Sydney Burwell (1893–1967), an earlier professor of medicine at Vanderbilt University (1928–1935) and a director of Harvard Medical School, famously told his students, "Half of what you are taught as medical students will in ten years have been shown to be wrong. And the trouble is, none of your teachers know which half!"

Even so, doctors and nurses can be some of the most conservative of professionals, sticking to what they know best, reticent to introduce change and embrace concepts that appear counter to intuition. There was a time when doctors laughed at the notion that they should wash their hands before touching patients. When Dr. Ignaz Semmelweis (1818–1865) first suggested the idea, he was ridiculed and cast from society, he suffered verbal and physical abuse, and he was eventually consigned to the madhouse by doctors who knew better. There he was beaten and tormented daily until he died prematurely at age forty-seven. Today, we would be appalled by any doctor who failed to scrub up before delivering a baby or delving into a patient's chest.

This is a prime example of what the nineteenth-century German philosopher Arthur Schopenhauer (1788–1860) termed "The Three Stages of Truth," by which he said all truth passes through three stages: First, it is ridiculed. Second, it is violently opposed. Third, it is accepted as self-evident.

To take a more recent example, today we accept as fact that people who undergo extremes of stress—during combat or from physical or sexual assault—are suffering what we now term post-traumatic stress disorder (PTSD). But not so long ago, any soldier in combat exhibiting the classic PTSD symptoms would have been brutally dealt with as either a malingerer or coward.

Theoretically, the United States Uniform Code of Military Justice still proscribes cowardice in combat as a crime punishable by death. And it is only in very recent years that the Pentagon finally recognized PTSD as an actual "thing," to be treated with compassion and understanding. Now the fight is on to convince the U.S. military that NDEs are also a "thing," given that so many serving in combat have experienced the effect when confronted by seemingly imminent death. As a group, those in combat are far more likely to experience an NDE than the public at large.

"The military does not take NDEs seriously," laments Roberta Moore, the former vice president of IANDS, "despite the similarities between an NDE, PTSD, and traumatic brain injuries. It's the third part of the triangle, and it's totally omitted and misdiagnosed," she says. "The military and the medical profession often consciously choose to omit NDEs because it's not something that fits into their worldview. It's not something to be concerned with. They shy away from it."

But, she says, views toward NDEs are now changing, given the frequency of their reported happenings. "Many people have been helped by doctors who actually do understand. It's divided between those who are completely materialistic in their outlook, with closed minds, and those who are not. But to have the experience ignored or dismissed is very harmful because these are deeply impactful, emotional experiences and to have them dismissed is shocking."

And if, one day, NDEs are as generally accepted as PTSD is today, how will doctors explain their occurrence deep within coma? Are they to remain as false memories or hallucinations? And if they are to be recognized, what then of the other events from within coma, from the nightmarish episodes through to the past or alternate lives? Will these one day cease to be treated as creations of disturbed, drugged-up minds?

Given the proliferation of medical and scientific papers advocating the A2F bundle and the complete lack of papers calling for deep sedation, one might wonder why the bundle is not an accepted part of the curriculum of all medical schools? Part of the blame, according to Dr. Murphy, is the lack of any leadership. "For reasons that I cannot fathom, our thought leaders and societies and the government have put no pressure on the medical field to evaluate these issues and come up with a satisfactory response. It just doesn't make sense."

He is most scathing of the SCCM—a U.S.-based but international organization that advocates improvements in critical care—for the lack of any leadership role, despite their seeming "ownership" of the A2F bundle. "As a result of this, I think we're going to unnecessarily harm and cause horrific damage to thousands of patients, maybe hundreds of thousands, if not millions, every year. And I see no evidence that it's going to change," he tells us.

We are, he says, trapped "in the middle of an accidental conspiracy of ignorance and inertia. The people that I work with every day—excellent physicians, nurses, and administrators—have almost zero insight into this issue. The whole ICU experience needs a thorough independent evaluation by medical and nonmedical providers. There is a relative code of silence where clinicians are reluctant to criticize one another because I think we all perform less than ideally on any given day. I think it's a survival instinct, but one that comes with considerable cost."

When we put these points to the society, they failed to respond. Over a period of many months, the SCCM were invited to contribute to this book, but they say they were not able to provide anyone to discuss their work, pointing us instead to the information on their website. And while individuals and a small but growing number of ICUs will bring about change eventually through the early adopter bell curve, such change will likely take many decades and may never be universally accepted.

Dr. Fuchita, the anesthesiologist from Denver, would also like to see outside intervention. "It takes lots of courage to be able to do something different, and people will point fingers telling you that you're doing something wrong," he stresses. So, in order for change to come about, he believes a large, respected body, or even government, needs to intervene to bring about swifter change. He also believes that money will play a part but that, currently, few see the financial incentives necessary to drive change.

"But the public, if they believe in what you write, then there might be outrage. But that may not be met with immediate change, because it's something that's ingrained in the ICU culture around the world. It might take five to ten years for the culture to transform across the globe. I think having public awareness will push toward [a change in] health care structures, but there's going to be a gap between what the public wants and what medicine can provide," he says.

"But once they know what's best for the patients, different people will seek it out, and so that's what makes me feel optimistic; that once we—as in the patients, the families, and the medical community in general—know that this is the way to go, I think change is possible."

Deborah (Continued): I Am a Ghost

I do think the experience of the patient is so different but no less traumatic than the experience of the family. My husband, Adam, has been really supportive. He'll bring me breakfast in bed. He does everything around the house, and I feel quite useless.

I tell him, I'm a bit of an asshole. I'm not a nice person. I'm not the person you married. So if you want to leave, feel free. I won't hold it against you. And what a horrible thing to say! But I have a numbness about it all. Is he better off without me? Am I just existing and he's just existing and we're just coexisting together? The amount of relationships that break down after people have been in comas is quite astronomical.

It's like Invasion of the Body Snatchers. *To him, I look exactly the same, my mannerisms are quite similar. My intrinsic morals and ethics are broadly the same. But part of me takes much bigger risks than I ever used to. I have to remember that the world doesn't revolve around me. I'm not the center of everything.*

It might be easier if he realized that the person he was in love with is not real anymore; they've become a ghost. It's exhausting trying to be a carbon copy of the person I was before because I'm not that person. And that's real. That's hard. You almost have to grieve with your family.

Darren: Fight for Your Life

Darren, who had earlier been screaming for his dad, fearing he would never wake up from the coma doctors were about to induce, says he does not remember much, if anything, of the first five days of his coma.

. . .

One of the nurses said, You looked so sad and frightened. We would handwash you and you wouldn't react. You just lay there helpless. *He said my eyes always made him want to cry. He said my eyes would weep tears now and then.*

He said if your wife or parents or siblings rang, we would sit and hold your hand and say things like Your wife called and asked how you are. They want you to get better, to come home. So you must keep fighting for your life. *Apparently, I would grip his hand when he said this. He said it would always give them hope and comfort, knowing that I could hear them.* In a coma, you were part-aware of what was being said, and in particular when we said fight for your life.

I think the message fight for your life *resonated and stayed with me, and it clearly showed them that I was fighting. So that's one thing that shows where my head was at.*

When I came home, I was still so worried that my breathing would stop when I slept, that I'd not wake up. I wouldn't want to close my eyes, and when I did I would see the other patients in the ICU in their comas and on ventilators. Those thoughts and images still stay with me today, along with the constant bleeping of machines.

I've gone on to donate convalescent plasma twenty-four times. This has helped my emotional recovery and given me a sense of "giving back." For the past few months, I've built up my fitness, and today I ran ten kilometers. I have no long COVID issues and my health and fitness are back to pre-COVID levels. I'm the most prolific convalescent plasma donor in the UK! I'm one of the lucky ones to survive.

When a nurse sits next to you, as you wake from a coma after having the ventilator removed, and she's holding my hand, stroking my arm, saying Darren, you're alive, you're back with us *and she FaceTimes my wife from her personal phone to show her I'm alive, and she's crying with emotion, these acts of kindness break my heart. They show our National Health Service at its best.*

Ted's Dad (Continued): Nothing to Fear

Ted's Dad—the composer Stephen Watkins—technically died twice before they could complete his aneurysm operation. Within his medically induced coma, he had rather a nice time, traveling the world and listening to his music being performed in an ancient German church. His recovery went well, but he was left with one major problem—he had lost the ability to compose music.

. . .

I am a musician, a conductor, and performer. There are certain skills which have not been affected. I can still play. I can write down what anyone else plays. I can even improvise still, but the ability to create extended pieces at will has gone; so has any desire for promotion of my work.

The barrier to the place where my imagination used to work is real. I can't get there. It's not the sort of thing that I expect anyone medical to be able to put right. No one understands how this works anyway. Maybe my hallucinations have used up my imagination for now. I refused all painkillers, and I wonder whether this helped with being relatively unscathed from bad delusions, although they were real enough at the time.

I really don't remember anything about being dead, although I have lots of memories of the coma experience. I am left with the thought that maybe the visitor to the other side experiences what they expect. As an atheist, I wouldn't expect there to be anything other than nothing.

In fact, my biggest emotion was, Well, that's not really anything to be afraid of, is it? But at the same time, I'm grateful to have spared those who love me. To have spared them all of the hassle and unhappiness by having come back to life. Although I take no credit for being a fighter or anything like that; I was just lucky. But strange how the ultimate spiritual experience should be a damp squib.

Andrew: No One Talks about It

Andrew Elkan, who formed the Facebook Coma Survivors Group after spending twenty-eight days in a coma, says his perspective on everything—his understanding or lack of—changed as a result of his coma.

• • •

I'm learning daily. My body and brain are physically damaged and I do the best I possibly can. Others have suffered far worse and have no complaints, only an appreciation for life. Others have suffered far less and complain daily.

Judgment, I'm learning, is not my job. I focus on healing and sharing knowledge. Enjoying the moment. That's all we have. I started the Facebook group shortly after Facebook got popular. I knew there was a need for such a community because I couldn't find anything after surviving my coma.

Once you are stable and gaining strength, they discharge you. I wasted away to around ninety pounds in my coma. I continued occupational and physical therapy for a couple months afterward but then was left on my own. At the time, there was no understanding of my limitations or how to seek support. I ended up not being able to return to my previous job fully as a vet technician because of memory issues. I found it difficult to do much of any work. My short-term memory was severely damaged from the coma.

I don't think mentally I had the strength to recognize what I went through. Once I was back, once I was away from the coma, I was left with the pain and the physical exhaustion. I had to learn to walk and read and write and all that kind of stuff again. It was just an overwhelming experience being back.

When I was released, I'd say it was probably a good month or more before I was able to reflect on everything and start speaking to people. For the most part—other than speaking with my parents—most people don't talk to me about it ever. So it's really not discussed ever.

Most have medical issues and struggle to explain their experiences to family or friends. Most struggle with long-term relationships because outside of our community most expect the injuries or trauma to pass. So it's a lack of understanding or empathy long term.

Corey (Continued): My Faith Reignited

Corey Agricola, the Alabama hospital chaplain, finally got to pop the question to his intended. They got married soon after he left hospital.

. . .

I remember having such peace, that if I'd died in that moment it would have been okay. And, you know, I heard hymns from my church back when I was a kid, It is well with my soul. *Just hearing the choir sing, I was right there in that moment. I interpreted this as God telling me it's going to be okay, trust me.*

I didn't see an image of God. I didn't see a vision of Jesus or anything like that. I just saw a mountain of light. And I saw scripture verses that were real. Versus that I didn't know. And to me, the experience proved my faith was real.

I don't have a fear of dying. I don't have the fear of it or the worry of it. And I learned that just as God gives us grace throughout life, so he does as we're nearing the end of life. He gives exceedingly more grace.

I had a gentleman one time whose daughter was on my unit, and she was in the exact same room that I was in, and she was in a medically induced coma. He was scared. So I encouraged him to talk to her because there's a good chance she can hear what you're saying. It was so encouraging to him—that someone understood that from the patient perspective—that there was something he could do. I told him what it was like being trapped inside your body.

I've spoken with other coma survivors. They describe very similar things to what I described. They didn't have really a lot of fear. I know some do, but mine was not that way. Everything about mine was entirely peaceful. You can't discount an experience like that. But if someone has doubts or questions the experience, that's okay with me because they can't change what I know. I know what I experienced and what happened to me. That doesn't discount my experience.

It changed my life and my ministry, you know. Prior to this happening, I was getting burned out. I've probably visited fifteen thousand patients in this hospital. We've got about twelve hundred beds here in this hospital. UAB is a city within itself, and I was getting burned out dealing with people's grief and people's pain and suffering. Walking families through loss. I was getting tired, and the burdens felt like they were pressing me down.

But this experience just reignited my faith. There's a purpose to what I do. I'd been lost in the doing of the ministry and I forgot about being Corey the person, not Corey the chaplain. It just reaffirmed my calling, of why I do what I do. I'm put here to love people and to let them know they're not alone. If there's somebody that loves them, if there's nobody else, there'll be a chaplain that comes by to love them while they're here in this hospital. That's my mission.

This experience just reaffirmed what I've always believed. It brought a realness to it that I'd never have experienced without it.

Nick (Continued): So Intense, So Pure

Have you ever seen the movie Hard to Kill *with Steven Seagal? The guy's in a coma and after two years is able to jump right up, drink coffee, start fighting, and looks amazing. Yeah, that's not true. Recovering from this was very, very hard, and I wish no one to experience it. Learning to walk again, talk again, eat again, basically doing everything again at thirty-five years old is humbling, to say the least.*

That's just the physical side of it. The mental side is way more taxing and long-lasting. PTSD and ADHD are here now. I'm struggling with that constantly but working to get better. The whole experience changed me, and I'm not sure if it's ever going to go back the way it was.

But there's no crazy emotional swings or confusion now. I did discuss my experiences with a lot of different nurses and it pretty much blew their minds. Same with my parents and fiancée, but they were mostly glad I was alive. My fiancée told me, Honestly, I don't think you had ICU delirium at all. It's something I read about and looked for, and the doctors looked for it but it never came up. You weren't especially confused or psychotic after what happened. I mean, you needed to have explained what happened and, of course, you were a bit like "Holy shit!," but your comprehension was pretty on point as the medicine wore off.

PTSD is real and can be paralyzing. I think that's mostly where my issues are from. But I'm not sure what really happened. But it stays with you, that void, it ripples like a butterfly effect rippling through two different realities at the same time. That's what made me start to think about the question of dreams and what exactly is the dream world? How some people can use astral projection and live on the line of both realities knowingly. It also begs the question, when you're having a coma dream, is that really a dream or is the coma dream reality?

I could go on with other stuff, but I'll just say this: I am very grateful for what that experience gave me but I'm still traumatized from it at the same time. It made me one hundred percent without a doubt not afraid to die because I know there's something else out there.

I'm not saying heaven or hell, I'm just saying another mission similar to this one. I'm not religious, but I'm very spiritual. I feel more connected to nature and to the stars and space. I don't know how to explain. When I came back here, I looked in the sky and remember having conversations with the moon and stars because I was an extended part of the universe. At one point, I felt like I was intense colors that I've never seen before, so vivid and beautiful.

The downside is I feel further from that human connection. I am constantly reminded by flashbacks or thoughts of the experience, and it's difficult. Coming back online and being thrown back into life has been difficult. To wrap it up, like I said, I'm definitely very aware of death and dying, aware but not afraid. I don't want to die because I'm also very aware of life and all its beautiful, majestic peculiarities.

Hands down, the most unbelievable, metaphysical situation of my life happened to me. It was so intense, it was so pure, it was so worry-free, it was so thoughtless, it was so meaningful, it was so powerful. It was an incredible feeling that I've been searching for ever since and don't think I'll ever find it again—not until death.

<><><><><><><><><><>

A REQUEST

If you have been helped by this book—either personally or professionally—please recommended it to others whom you think it will also help. Only when the knowledge contained in this book becomes general knowledge will there ever be any hope of putting an end to the practice of deep sedation in critical care.

THANK YOU,
ALAN AND BEVERLEY PEARCE

A Call to Arms

Kali Dayton, DNP, AGACNP-BC, Nurse Practitioner and ICU Consultant

"I work in the ICU so I don't have to talk to people," my precepting ICU nurse told me. "So don't even dream of this being social hour." My nineteen-year-old nursing student heart shattered. I had felt called to work in critical care medicine and arrived at my first student rotation with naive enthusiasm and eagerness to fulfill my destiny. The unit was dark and silent save for occasional beeps from the monitors. I felt coldness beyond what the thermostat could reveal. This was not what I had gone to nursing school for. My innocent and joyful heart yearned for human connection and felt intensely deprived during that week of rotations. I was no longer sure that I belonged in the ICU.

Despite my morgue-like introduction to the ICU, I couldn't shake the spiritual promptings pushing me to apply to intensive care units. My flame was not completely extinguished as I entered my first interview with Nancy Bardugon, my future nurse manager at LDS Hospital's medical surgical intensive care unit. Even her bright countenance sparked a sense of hope for critical care medicine within me. In the interview she casually asked, "Would you be willing to walk intubated patients on mechanical ventilation?" In my ignorance and nervousness, I responded, "Yes! Teach me everything!" Only ten years later do I fully appreciate the weight of that question.

Everything was new to me. I was overwhelmed but filled with a sense of security being surrounded by seasoned, competent, kind, and compassionate colleagues who were willing to train and help me. They were so calm and composed throughout the tasks of ICU nursing care—especially when helping patients walk while intubated and connected to ventilators. No one explained to me why we were doing it, but it seemed natural to everyone involved. I suppose I never questioned it, as I saw my patients as human and it made sense that they would be awake, communicative, autonomous, and mobile during the day and then be allowed to sleep at night. Everyone seemed to treat this process as being as routine as giving an antibiotic.

I had incredible moments of human connection and immense joy during my years as an ICU nurse at LDS Hospital. I came to truly know my patients, as they would answer questions about themselves, tell me jokes, express their feelings of fear, pain, anxiety, and gratitude on paper, whiteboard, or phone. I knew their favorite songs, foods, how many children they had, what they did for a living, their preferences in care, etc. I watched them fight for their own lives and revel in their success as they got off the ventilator and walked out the door by themselves. I made eternal friendships with families and was honored to be a witness to incredible love and connection between families and patients through pivotal and sometimes final moments of their lives.

I learned from my expert colleagues how to give patients choices, autonomy, and accountability in their own care. I watched how they fought to preserve their dignity and independence even during some of their most vulnerable moments. They guided me to develop skills of assessment, communication, and humane care in response to agitation, anxiety, pain, and delirium. It was innate to allow almost all patients to wake up after intubation and mobilize them promptly. In truth, I barely knew how to start or titrate sedation, as my exposure to it had been so rare. For years, their process of care was the only way I knew, and I loved it. It resonated with who I was, a nurse and human being. My first ICU exposure quickly slipped into the back of my mind like a remote nightmare as if it had never happened. Until I became a travel nurse.

Polly Bailey was the only one to warn me with a simple statement of "Things will be different elsewhere." I was young, unattached, and looking for adventure. New and different experiences did not intimidate me until I later realized what she meant. In my first assignment, I immediately noticed the lights were low during the day, every patient was in bed, and the only sign of life in them were flashing vitals from the monitors. I was met with complete disbelief and opposition when I tried to take sedation off my patients, even questioning the reason for it. My inquiries made everyone doubt the reality of my years of ICU experience.

Although I knew *how* to allow patients to wake up after intubation and *how* to mobilize them with all the lines, tubes, drains, machines, etc., I, too, was a victim of the same systemic gap in education. I didn't understand *why* those interventions were so vital. I didn't fully have the understanding and tools to critically think, let alone defend my inclinations to defy the widely accepted treatments in my new ICUs. I didn't know the reality of medically induced comas and immobility and the harm patients suffer during and after. I took the "when in Rome" approach and went with what was "normal" to everyone else I worked with. To this day, it still haunts me. I have dedicated the rest of my career to repenting of the harm and perhaps death I surely caused many patients.

The ABCDEF Bundle is an acronym for "**A**ssess, prevent, and manage pain; **B**oth awakening and breathing trials; **C**hoice of analgesia and sedation; **D**elirium: assess, prevent, and manage; **E**arly mobility and exercise; and **F**amily engagement and empowerment." It is a protocol widely recognized in the critical care community as the guideline to evidence-based sedation and mobility practices. It utilizes delirium screening with CAM scores and agitation scoring with a RASS level. It is mentioned in most critical care conferences and is generally undisputed. Despite the compelling research behind this approach and the astounding impact to patient outcomes, standardization of this approach has been a challenge throughout the years for most ICU teams.

During my travels, the only utilized element of the ABCDEF bundle was "awakening trials" in one unit. Within the ABCDEF bundle, this is supposed to be a step to wean *off* sedation and mobilize most patients. As the awake and walking ICU rarely starts sedation drips, I was unfamiliar with the term and routine of *awakening trials*. A nurse explained to me, "You just turn down the sedation enough to see them start to flail and then you turn it back on since you can see that the patient couldn't tolerate the ventilator. Then you document it as a "failed awakening trial."

I recall being surprised and confused by this method. I didn't know what it was supposed to accomplish. I still was unable to do a neurological exam. I didn't know what was causing the agitation and doubted it was just the endotracheal tube and ventilator making the patient be so uncomfortable, as I had seen most patients be able to acclimate and be very calm and compliant. I now look back and realize how much one questions themselves and fails to use their own critical thinking skills when enveloped in an environment with a unanimous group mentality. I now cringe to think that I did as I was told, despite my previous experiences.

After a few years of being a travel nurse, I returned to the awake and walking ICU at LDS Hospital as a nurse practitioner. I immersed myself into the mentorship of nurse practitioners Polly Bailey and Louise Bezdjian as well as the decades of research. I compared what I was seeing in that ICU and learning in the literature to what I had experienced and done as a travel nurse. They seemed to be worlds, if not centuries, apart. From having jaws drop at the idea of a patient walking on a ventilator to being back to walking through the halls and seeing all intubated patients sitting in their chairs, flipping through the TV channels, and waiting for their walk around the unit, shook my core.

For years as a travel nurse, I had been treated as the "naive and crazy nurse with dangerous ideas." I felt confident and at home in the awake and walking ICU. I relished the opportunity to provide the best care and witness incredible outcomes. After years of watching most patients be dehumanized and essentially decompose before my eyes, only to die or have a tracheostomy and be sent to rehabilitation, I felt I was watching daily miracles. Yet I knew this was not my final destination. My soul wrestled between the ease at LDS Hospital and the knowledge that the rest of the ICU community was unaware of what was possible and best in critical care medicine.

My joining of Facebook groups for critical care clinicians and ICU survivors solidified a conviction and indignation that consumed my entire being. Sitting at my computer, I could see in black and white the dichotomy between the discussions, jokes, and memes from clinicians wanting patients that were intubated and "snowed" with sedation and the survivors discussing the pain and horrors they experienced during and after being in medically induced comas.

The research reaffirmed survivor testimonials, and yet the ICU community seemed blissfully unaware. I kept thinking back to the nine other ICUs I had worked in. I worked with smart, competent, and especially compassionate clinicians who would never intentionally harm patients. So why was the critical care community at large still automatically sedating every patient after intubation despite the proven lethal and inhumane repercussions? I couldn't shake the thought, *If they REALLY knew, they would change.*

I came to realize that the ABCDEF bundle is often misunderstood and inconsistently practiced. For many teams, the ABCDEF bundle is a checklist of CAM, RASS, and awakening and breathing trial documentation, and they have the mentality that it is "just another pointless and burdensome task to fulfill documentation requirements and make clinicians' jobs harder." In truth, I felt this during my contract that required awakening trials.

As a nurse, it was very difficult to turn down sedation after a patient had received sedation for a prolonged period of time. They usually did come out of sedation with agitation and thrashing. They were very difficult to manage. What I did not fully recognize at the time was how severely they were suffering from delirium and that by continuing the unit's cultural habit of running back to sedation, I was likely causing, exacerbating, and prolonging their delirium and consequent damage.

What I wish the ICU community understood is that the ABCDEF bundle is not for perpetuating the habit of turning on sedation and then only taking brief breaks from sedation once ventilator settings are decreased. As Brenda Pun, one of the creators of the ABCDEF bundle stated, the goal of the bundle is "to produce patients that are more awake, cognitively engaged, and physically active, which ultimately serves to facilitate patient autonomy and the ability to express unmet physical, emotional, and spiritual needs."[1] I realized that we were neither teaching teams the truth about their traditional sedation and immobility practices nor providing for them the vision of having patients awake, free of delirium, and spared from ICU-acquired weakness.

It is my observation that implementation of the ABCDEF bundle with persistent, automatic, continuous sedation right after intubation, failure to utilize all the elements—such as early mobility and family engagement—and a lack of understanding of the "why" increases the burden on nurses and sets teams up for failure. It is unsafe and unfeasible to continue a process of care that launches patients into delirium and ICU-acquired weakness and then obligates nurses to unmask delirium and be left to treat it without support, while being expected to mobilize large, flaccid adults who are too weak to move themselves. Starting sedation after intubation is like pulling a pin from a grenade and then passing it down, shift to shift. It is going to explode on some unfortunate nurse who has to do the awakening trial.

It is my witness and shared experience with those who have implemented the Bailey Method that the practice of allowing most patients to be awake, oriented, and even mobile shortly after intubation makes the goal of the ABCDEF bundle much more feasible. Patients are much more likely to be oriented, calm, cooperative, and able to get themselves out of bed and walk. This sets the ICU team and patients up for ease in workload, fewer complications, and greater success.

Without oversimplifying the obstacles faced in transitioning to this process of care, if teams were to habitually ask after each intubation, *"Does this patient have an indication for sedation? Is sedating this patient worth the risk and repercussions of sedation and immobility? Can we afford the extra expense and workload to care for this patient when they develop complications of this sedation later?"* then continuous sedation after intubation would become the exception rather than the norm. Cutting the cord between automatic sedation and mechanical ventilation must be one of our initial steps to becoming awake and walking ICUs, second to providing true education and training.

In December 2019, I felt compelled to start the podcast *Walking Home From the ICU* before I had any awareness of the global pandemic that was on the brink of consuming my field. I interviewed ICU survivors of sedation and immobility as well as survivors of the awake and walking ICU who had walked on maximum ventilator settings and walked out the doors to go home. I interviewed my colleagues from each discipline to share their roles in this process of care and their personal convictions and experiences related to avoiding sedation and mobilizing intubated patients. I was exploring the depths of the research about ICU survivorship and the ABCDEF bundle. I was alive with motivation to bring this perspective and the evidence to the ICU community—and then COVID-19 hit.

I witnessed a stark contrast between the treatments and outcomes described on social media among ICU clinicians and what I was witnessing in the awake and walking COVID ICU. We saw severe ARDS, very sick patients. We lost some, but most were still able to be awake and mobile on the ventilator and later be extubated and discharged home. I was hearing on social media and from podcast listeners of the normalization of automatic deep sedation, benzodiazepines, weeks of paralytics, massive mortality, and the inability to later transfer debilitated patients with tracheostomies due to overwhelmed rehabilitation facilities struggling to care for the masses of COVID-19 ICU "survivors."

COVID-19 brought an unprecedented level of devastation and desperation to the ICU community. The awake and walking ICU at LDS Hospital also had to make adaptations to their process of care but were able to hold true to their well-founded culture and ethics of avoiding sedation and optimizing mobility. Unfortunately, such drastic changes in practices were not feasible for most ICUs, and patients and teams alike have suffered greatly. My connections with clinicians who listen to and are striving to implement the principles within the podcast fuel my inextinguishable determination that ICU clinicians are some of the most resilient and benevolent people in the world.

I have the honor of helping visionaries who, despite their own exhaustion and trauma, are still ready to fight for change within their ICUs. When I started to present in-person at medical conferences, I was filled with trepidation. *After all they have been through the past few years, how will they receive this information? How do I tell them that the practices they have been taught and practiced are harmful and lethal to patients? How quickly will I be kicked off the stage?* I have been humbled by the incredible responses of excitement, motivation, and compassion from audience members. They have approached me with tears in their eyes and shared with me their personal trauma from watching patients suffer and the hope they feel in learning about a better way. They tell me they are on the verge of leaving critical care medicine, but if they could have moments and successes like those in the case studies I shared, then they would stay in the ICU.

I deeply believe that when ICU clinicians truly understand the *why* behind the ABCDEF bundle, then they will find their *how*. Patients are not suffering and dying from sedation and immobility because most clinicians are not *willing* to change. Our ICU teams deserve to have true support in the form of intensive education, training, and safe staffing ratios. It is my pleasure to work with ICU teams as a consultant to support their process of revolution. Most clinicians are open and excited to learn how to give their patients the best opportunity to survive and thrive. It thrills me to hear their reports and success stories and watch the fire spread within their teams. It is my suspicion that humanizing the ICU will save critical care medicine. Until we support our clinicians in providing the best evidence-based medicine, they will suffer burnout and moral injury and will continue to leave.

It is my hope that the damage and desperation of COVID-19 will propel us into a revolution in sedation and mobility practices, if not for compassion then, now, for necessity. Greater awareness and advocacy on all sides of the ICU bed will expedite these changes to save lives and prevent lifelong suffering. By confronting the darkness of the past and present, we can move forward toward a brighter future.

Kali Dayton

Spokane, Washington

Kali Dayton, DNP, AGACNP-BC, is a critical care nurse practitioner, host of the *Walking Home From The ICU* and *Walking You Through The ICU* podcasts, and critical care outcomes consultant. She is dedicated to creating awake and walking ICUs by ensuring ICU sedation and mobility practices are aligned with current research. She works with ICU teams internationally to transform patient outcomes through early mobility and management of delirium in the ICU.

Acknowledgments

The authors of this book hold deep gratitude to **Kali Dayton**, DNP, AGACNP-BC, for all the help and encouragement she has given us and for the changes in ICU care she is helping to bring about.

We are also deeply indebted to both **E. Wesley Ely**, MD, Professor of Medicine, and **Matthew F. Mart**, MD, Instructor in Medicine, Vanderbilt University Medical Center.

Special thanks to **Andrew Elkan**, coma survivor and founder of the Facebook Coma Survivors Group.

And total gratitude to Professor **Jeffrey J. Kripal**, Associate Dean of the Humanities, J. Newton Rayzor Professor of Philosophy and Religious Thought, Rice University, Houston, Texas.

Our sincere thanks as well to Richard Grossinger, who championed publication, and to all of the helpful and kind folks at Inner Traditions who made it happen, and for the care, attention, and skill shown by our editor, Kayla Toher.

. . .

Thank you to the coma survivors who helped us with this book and shared their experiences in the hope of helping others:

Chrissy Statham

Rev. Corey Agricola, MDiv, BCC-APC

Darren Buttrick

"Debbie"

Deborah Mayo

Chiara from Piedmont

James Morrall

Isobel Wells

Jo Nelson

Kathryn Drown

Megan Johnson

Nick MacDonald

Nicky Marcos

Nikki Milne

Rory Atherton

Simon Newton-Smith

Stephen Taylor

Stephen Watkins (Ted's Dad)

Zara Slattery

We are also indebted to the following people and organizations who helped guide us or contributed directly to this book:

Dr. Peter J. Murphy, Assistant Dean, Professor, and Chief of Medicine at California Northstate University College of Medicine

Adison Pusateri, BSN, RN

Susan Cockerton

The Lancet

Arnold Mindell, PhD—aamindell.net

Bernardo Kastrup—(@BernardoKastrup)

Christina Jones, Reader in Clinical Health Psychology, PhD, CPsychol, AFBPsS, FHEA

Professor Charles M. Stang, Director of the Center for the Study of World Religions, Harvard Divinity School

Professor Edward Francis Kelly, PhD, Division of Perceptual Studies, University of Virginia

Gregory Shushan, PhD, Honorary Research Fellow, Religious Experience Research Centre, University of Wales Trinity Saint David

Professor Elizabeth Loftus, UCI School of Social Ecology

Professor Gianluca Tosini, PhD, FARVO

Dr. James L. Bernat, Professor of Neurology, Active Emeritus, Geisel School of Medicine, Dartmouth

Janice Miner Holden, EdD, LPC-S, ACMHP, President, International Association for Near-Death Studies—iands.org

Martin W. Ball, PhD, Nondual Entheogenic Educator and Author

Dr. Pim van Lommel—pimvanlommel.nl/en

Professor Paul Fletcher, Bernard Wolfe Professor of Health Neuroscience at University of Cambridge

The Society of Critical Care Medicine—sccm.org

Near-Death Experience Research Foundation—nderf.org

Andrew Gallimore, Neurobiologist, Chemist, and Pharmacologist

Anthony Peake—anthonypeake.com

Chad Charles—chadcharles.net

Robert Mentzer

Larry Shroyer

Katerina Sokolova

Andrea of the Samyama Meditation Center—samyama.com

Emma Carruthers of the Hermitage Retreat—thehermitageretreats.com

Helen Cox

Lindsay Cox

Norman Cox

Stephen Nicklen

Jan Simonsz-Coe

Jimo Borjigin, PhD, Associate Professor, Molecular and Integrative Physiology, University of Michigan Medical School

John Chavez—dmtquest.org

Kalianey—kalianey.com

Andy Rich, MS, OTR/L, CSPHP

Professor Michele Balas, PhD, RN, CCRN-K, FCCM, FAAN

Dr. Thomas Strøm, University of Southern Denmark

Jill Larkin Storer, BSN, RN, CCRN

Louise Bezdjian, ACNP

Nora Raher, BSN, RN, CCRN

Leanne Boehm, PhD, RN, ACNS-BC, FCCM, Assistant Professor, Vanderbilt University School of Nursing

Dr. Mikita Fuchita

Roberta Moore, MA, MBA—youtube.com/c/NDEvideo

Useful Links

FACEBOOK GROUPS

Names are styled exactly how they are displayed at the time of printing.

Coma Survivors Group

Coma Survivors (Survivors of Life Support)

Coma survivors

Coma Survivors around the United States

I Survived A Coma

Covid Long Haulers, Coma Survivors, and Caregivers

ICU Survivor Support Group

Facebook Near Death Experiences

OTHER RESOURCES

HealthUnlocked—healthunlocked.com

ICUsteps—icusteps.org

Critical Care Support Network—cc-sn.org

International Association for Near-Death Studies—iands.org

Critical Illness, Brain Dysfunction, and Survivorship Center—icudelirium.org

PODCAST

If you would like to share your story—either as a survivor, family member, or clinician—please visit the homepage of our podcast to contact us: comapodcast.com

Notes

CONTRIBUTOR'S PREFACE.
COMA AND CONSCIOUSNESS

1. The full conversation is available here: Jeffrey Kripal, "Alternative Realities," interviewed by Shahidha Bari, *Arts and Ideas*, BBC, April 21, 2020.
2. The American edition is Jeffrey J. Kripal, *The Flip: Epiphanies of Mind and the Future of Knowledge* (New York: Bellevue Literary Press, 2019). The British edition was published as *The Flip: Who You Really Are and Why It Matters* (London: Penguin, 2020).

INTRODUCTION.
A WHOLE OTHER LIFE

1. Ely, "The ABCDEF Bundle."

CHAPTER I.
YOU'RE NOT JUST SLEEPING YOUR TIME AWAY

1. Slattery, *Coma*.
2. Read more about Arnold Mindell's work on the Amy and Arnold Mindell website: aamindell.net.
3. Jung, *Memories, Dreams, Reflections*.
4. Jung, *The Interpretation of Nature of the Psyche*, 507.
5. Van Lommel, *Consciousness Beyond Life*.
6. Fenwick, "Science and Spirituality."

7. Liverpool University's Intensive Care Research Group, "Intensive Care: Easing the Trauma," 641.

CHAPTER 2.
FANTASIES, DREAMS, AND LUCKY GUESSES

1. Van Lommel, *Consciousness Beyond Life*.
2. Moody, *Life after Life*.
3. Cassol et al., "Near-Death Experience Memories Include More Episodic Components Than Flashbulb Memories."
4. Martial et al., "Near-Death Experience as a Probe to Explore (Disconnected) Consciousness."
5. Much of Kenneth Ring's work, including full essays, links to interviews, and more, can be explored on his website. See also Raymond Moody's work on the Life after Life website.
6. To listen to Dr. Alexander describe the experience in his own words, watch "Eben Alexander—The Nature of Consciousness," Westminster Town Hall Forum, or visit his website to review the body of his written work.
7. Van Lommel, Wees, Meyers, and Elfferich, "Near-Death Experience in Survivors of Cardiac Arrest: A Prospective Study in the Netherlands."
8. Christopher French, "Commentary."
9. Shears, Elison, Garralda, and Nadel, "Near-Death Experiences with Meningococcal Disease."
10. Laugrand, "The Beauty of the Afterlife Among the Inuit of Nunavut."
11. Shushan, "The Sun Told Me I Would Be Restored to Life."
12. Fernandez, *Bwiti: An Ethnography of the Religious Imagination in Africa*.
13. Fenwick, published as "Perceptions of Beyond the Near Death Experience and at the End of Life."
14. Bush and Greyson, "Distressing Near-Death Experiences."

CHAPTER 3.
BLINDED BY SCIENCE

1. Sharp, *After the Light*.
2. Sheldrake, *Science Set Free*.
3. Tononi, "Integrated Information Theory of Consciousness: An Updated Account."

4. Kelly, *Consciousness Unbound*.

5. Fenwick, "Science and Spirituality."

6. Jenkins, "A Catch-22."

7. Kardec, *Spiritist Codification*.

8. The story of Shanti Devi and the following story of Giriraj Soni are shared in Swami, *New Doctrine on Mental Diseases based on Evidence on Reincarnation and Survival of Soul*.

9. Kripal, *The Flip*.

10. Alexander, "Eben Alexander—The Nature of Consciousness." Westminster Town Hall Forum.

11. Backster's research can be read about in Wilcox, *The Use of the Polygraph in Assessing, Treating, and Supervising Sex Offenders*.

12. Valandrey, *De cœur inconnu* (Of Heart Unknown).

13. Amy's story was shared in *Women First Magazine*, September 19, 2011, p. 48.

CHAPTER 4.
THE CHATTERING MONKEY

1. Spinney, "Anarchy Discovered in the Honeybee Hive."

2. Van Lommel, *Consciousness Beyond Life*.

3. Jaynes, *The Origin of Consciousness in the Breakdown of the Bicameral Mind*.

4. Kelly, *Consciousness Unbound*.

5. Van Lommel, "About the Continuity of Consciousness."

6. This story has been adapted from Moorjani, "Dying to Be Me."

7. Harari, *Sapiens*.

8. Queensland Brain Institute, "Where Are Memories Stored?"

9. Pribram, "The Neurophysiology of Remembering." See also karlpribram .com.

10. Berkovich, "A Note on Science and NDE."

11. Van Lommel, "About the Continuity of Consciousness."

12. Van Lommel, *Consciousness Beyond Life*.

13. Lewin, "Is Your Brain Really Necessary?"

14. Harvard University Department of Psychology, "Karl Lashley."

15. Boyle, Benderev, Klahr, Vedantam, and Penman, "How Derek Amato Became a Musical Savant."

16. Treffert, "Genetic Memory."

17. No author, "As Dementia Sets In, Artistic Genius Emerges."

18. Mizzou News, "Selflessness—The Core of All Major World Religions—Has Neuropsychological Connection, MU Study Finds."

19. Cristofori et al., "Neural Correlates of Mystical Experience."

20. Kastrup, "Transcending the Brain."

21. Newberg, *Principles of Neurotheology*.

22. Kastrup, "Transcending the Brain."

23. Timmermann et al., "DMT Models the Near-Death Experience."

24. No author, *German Neuroscientists*.

25. Raichle et al., "A Default Mode of Brain Function"; Raichle, "The Brain's Dark Energy"; Raichle, "The Brain's Default Mode Network."

26. Raab, *The Empowerment Diary* blog.

27. The *thought torrent* and *motor minding* are described in Maciuika, *Conscious Calm*.

28. Raab, *The Empowerment Diary* blog.

29. Tolle, *The Power of Now*.

30. Killingsworth and Gilbert, "A Wandering Mind Is an Unhappy Mind."

31. Norton et al., "Disruptions of Functional Connectivity in the Default Mode Network of Comatose Patients."

32. Heine et al., "Resting State Networks and Consciousness."

33. Taylor, "My Stroke of Insight."

CHAPTER 5.
DELIRIUM, HALLUCINATIONS, AND SOMETHING ELSE

1. Gunk, "Magic Carpets, Sensory Deprivation and Entheogenic Ceremonial Magick."

2. Seth, "Your Brain Hallucinates Your Conscious Reality."

3. Ely, *Every Deep-Drawn Breath*.

4. Adamis et al., "A Brief Review of the History of Delirium as a Mental Disorder."

5. American Psychiatric Association, *Diagnostic and Statistical Manual of Mental Disorders*.

6. Liester, "Toward a New Definition of Hallucination."

7. Ian Stevenson quoted in Liester, "Toward a New Definition of Hallucination."

8. Barrett and Griffiths, "Classic Hallucinogens and Mystical Experiences."

9. Ruscio et al., "Social Fears and Social Phobia in the USA."

10. Roberta Moore, NDE Video website and YouTube channel.

11. Daniel and Mason, "Predicting Psychotic-Like Experiences during Sensory Deprivation."

12. Jan and del Castillo, "Visual Hallucinations."

13. Kornfeld, Zimberg, and Malm, "Psychiatric Complications of Open-Heart Surgery."

14. Slocum, *Sailing Alone Around the World.*

15. Adams, *Chasing Liquid Mountains.*

16. Ritter, *A Woman in the Polar Night.*

17. Alotaibi, "A Neuroimaging Investigation into Hallucination Proneness in a Healthy Population."

18. Daniel and Mason, "Predicting Psychotic-Like Experiences during Sensory Deprivation."

19. Grassian, "Psychiatric Effects of Solitary Confinement."

20. Heron, "The Pathology of Boredom."

CHAPTER 6.
APACHES AND POETS

1. All quotes from Morris E. Opler or his informant Antonio are from his article "The Use of Peyote by the Carrizo and Lipan Apache Tribes."

2. Wilson, *Cosmic Trigger.*

3. Slotkin, *The Peyote Religion,* 34, 28.

4. Mitchell, "Remarks on the Effects of *Anhalonium lewinii* (the Mescal Button)."

5. Ellis, "Mescal: A New Artificial Paradise."

6. All Huxley quotes, except those later specified, are from *The Doors of Perception* and *Heaven and Hell.*

7. Pontvianne, "Psychedelics and Buddhism."

8. The four characteristics and the quotes below come from Watts, "Psychedelics and Religious Experience."

9. Pontvianne, "Psychedelics and Buddhism."

10. James, *The Varieties of Religious Experience.*

11. The story shared later in this chapter is by Ariel Levy, "The Drug of Choice for the Age of Kale."

12. Spruce, *Notes of a Botanist on the Amazon and Andes.*

13. Reinberg, "Contribution à l'étude des boissons toxiques des indiens du Nord-ouest de l'Amazon, l'ayahuasca, le yagé, le huanto."
14. Huxley, *Heaven and Hell.*
15. Shanon, *The Antipodes of the Mind.*
16. Palhano-Fontes et al., "The Psychedelic State Induced by Ayahuasca Modulates the Activity and Connectivity of the Default Mode Network."
17. Horák and Verter, *Ayahuasca in the Czech Republic.*
18. Two good examples are Schenberg, "Ayahuasca and Cancer Treatment," and Pollan, *How to Change Your Mind.*
19. Heuser, "Ayahuasca Entity Visitations."
20. Barker, "LC/MS/MS Analysis of the Endogenous Dimethyltryptamine Hallucinogens, Their Precursors, and Major Metabolites in Rat Pineal Gland Microdialysate."
21. Dean et al., "Biosynthesis and Extracellular Concentration of N, N-dimethyltryptamine in Mammalian Brain."
22. All of Rick Strassman's quotes are from his book *DMT: The Spirit Molecule.*
23. Quoted in Szára, "Dimethyltryptamin."
24. Bilton, "Divine Molecule Talks at Tyringham—Part II, Exploring Entheogenic Entity Encounters."

CHAPTER 7.
DARK BRINGS LIGHT

1. Kalianey's remarks come from a mix of interviews and the post "40 Days Dark Retreat" on her website blog.
2. Chia, *Darkness Technology.*
3. See the website of Chad Charles.
4. Strassman, *DMT: The Spirit Module,* and Strassman, *The Psychedelic Handbook.*
5. Timmermann et al., "DMT Models the Near-Death Experience."
6. Greyson, "The Near-Death Experience Scale."
7. Liester, "Ayahuasca 'Vine of the Soul' and NDEs."
8. Jon Dean and John Chavez, "Groundbreaking DMT Research That Could Change Everything w/ Dr. Jon Dean and John Chavez."
9. Chavez, *Questions for the Lion Tamer.*
10. Norton et al., "Disruptions of Functional Connectivity in the Default Mode Network of Comatose Patients"; Jombík et al., "Some Quantitative

EEG Features in Default Mode Resting State Network under General Anaesthesia"; Garrison, "Meditation Leads to Reduced Default Mode Network Activity beyond an Active Task."

CHAPTER 8.
THE ICU DEATH TRAP

1. Pun et al., "Prevalence and Risk Factors for Delirium in Critically Ill Patients with COVID-19 (COVID-D): A Multicentre Cohort Study," notes C8, 11.

2. Shehabi et al., "Early Intensive Care Sedation Predicts Long-term Mortality in Ventilated Critically Ill Patients"; Tanaka et al., "Early Sedation and Clinical Outcomes of Mechanically Ventilated Patients."

3. Visit the Dayton ICU Consulting website.

4. *Walking Home from the ICU* podcast can be found on the Dayton ICU Consulting website.

5. Balas, "ABCDEF ICU Bundle of Care."

6. Guttormson et al., "Nurses' Attitudes and Practices Related to Sedation."

7. Grap et al., "Sedation in Adults Receiving Mechanical Ventilation."

8. Parshley, "You Can't Use Ventilators without Sedatives. Now the US Is Running out of Those, Too."

9. Romero-García and la Calle "Moral Distress, Emotional Impact and Coping in Intensive Care Units Staff during the Outbreak of COVID-19."

10. Desai, "France Sees 1,300 Nursing Students Resign amid COVID Pandemic."

11. "COVID-19 Takes Toll as 20,000 Nurses Quit, Rapid Test Shortages." Private video posted by 9 News on YouTube.

12. Saunders and Duggan, "Record Numbers of NHS Staff Quit as Frontline Medics Battle Covid Pandemic Trauma."

13. Schubert et al., "A Hospital-Wide Evaluation of Delirium Prevalence and Outcomes in Acute Care Patients."

14. Tanaka et al., "Early Sedation and Clinical Outcomes of Mechanically Ventilated Patients."

15. Dziegielewski, "Delirium and Associated Length of Stay and Costs in Critically Ill Patients."

16. Gehlbach et al., "Temporal Disorganization of Circadian Rhythmicity and Sleep-Wake Regulation in Mechanically Ventilated Patients Receiving Continuous Intravenous Sedation."

17. Mistraletti et al., "Sleep and Delirium in the Intensive Care Unit."

18. Pun et al., "Prevalence and Risk Factors for Delirium in Critically Ill Patients with COVID-19 (COVID-D)."

19. Griffiths and Jones, "Seven Lessons from 20 Years of Follow-up of Intensive Care Unit Survivors."

20. Pandharipandh et al., "Lorazepam Is an Independent Risk Factor for Transitioning to Delirium in Intensive Care Unit Patients"; Yang et al., "Risk Factors of Delirium in Sequential Sedation Patients in Intensive Care Units"; Davydow et al., "Posttraumatic Stress Disorder in General Intensive Care Unit Survivors."

21. Lin et al., "Risk Factors for the Development of Early-Onset Delirium and the Subsequent Clinical Outcome in Mechanically Ventilated Patients"; Rello et al., "Risk Factors for Developing Pneumonia within 48 Hours of Intubation."

22. Cox et al., "Pressure Injury Risk Factors in Critical Care Patients."

23. Minet et al., "Venous Thromboembolism in the ICU."

24. Vanhorebeek et al., "ICU-Acquired Weakness."

25. Shehabi et al., "Early Intensive Care Sedation Predicts Long-Term Mortality in Ventilated Critically Ill Patients"; Tanaka et al., "Early Sedation and Clinical Outcomes of Mechanically Ventilated Patients."

26. Pereira et al., "Dexmedetomidine versus Propofol Sedation in Reducing Delirium among Older Adults in the ICU."

27. Carenzo et al., "Return to Work After Coronavirus Disease 2019 Acute Respiratory Distress Syndrome and Intensive Care Admission."

28. Strøm et al., "Sedation and Renal Impairment in Critically Ill Patients: A Post Hoc Analysis of a Randomized Trial."

29. Lipshutz and Gropper. "Acquired Neuromuscular Weakness and Early Mobilization in the Intensive Care Unit."

30. De Jonghe et al., "Paresis Acquired in the Intensive Care Unit."

31. Parry and Puthucheary, "The Impact of Extended Bed Rest on the Musculoskeletal System in the Critical Care Environment."

32. Lipshutz and Gropper, "Acquired Neuromuscular Weakness and Early Mobilization in the Intensive Care Unit."

33. American Hospital Association, "Fast Facts on U.S. Hospitals, 2022."

34. Viglianti and Iwashyna, "Toward the Ideal Ratio of Patients to Intensivists."

35. Ely, *Every Deep-Drawn Breath*.

36. Morandi et al., "The Association between Brain Volumes, Delirium Duration, and Cognitive Outcomes in Intensive Care Unit Survivors."

CHAPTER 9.
THE AWAKE AND WALKING ICU

1. Bailey et al., "Early Activity Is Feasible and Safe in Respiratory Failure Patients."
2. Visit the Perme ICU Rehab Seminars website.
3. Perme and Chandrashekar, "Early Mobility and Walking Program for Patients in Intensive Care Units."
4. Society of Critical Care Medicine, "ICU Liberation Bundle A–F."
5. Dattilio and Castaldo, "Differentiating Cognitive Impairment from Symptoms of Anxiety in Postcoronary Artery Bypass Grafting Encephalopathy."
6. ICUsteps, "Intensive Care: A Guide for Patients and Relatives."
7. Visit the Dayton ICU Consulting website page "Case Studies."

CHAPTER 10.
SO, WHO'S GOING TO PAY FOR ALL THIS?

1. Kyeremanteng et al., "ICU Delirium, Clinical Outcome and Cost."
2. Dziegielewski, "Delirium and Associated Length of Stay and Costs in Critically Ill Patients."
3. Schubert et al., "A Hospital-Wide Evaluation of Delirium Prevalence and Outcomes in Acute Care Patients."
4. Smith and Grami, "Feasibility and Effectiveness of a Delirium Prevention Bundle in Critically Ill Patients."
5. Hunter, Johnson, and Coustasse, "Reduction of Intensive Care Unit Length of Stay."
6. Rogers et al., "Higher Hospital Spending on Occupational Therapy Is Associated with Lower Readmission Rates."

LAST WORDS.
A CALL TO ARMS

1. Pun et al., "Caring for Critically Ill Patients with the ABCDEF Bundle."

Bibliography

Adamis, Dimitrios, Adrian Treloar, Finbarr C. Martin, and Alastair J. D. Macdonald. "A Brief Review of the History of Delirium as a Mental Disorder." *History of Psychiatry* 18 (72 Pt 4) (December 2007): 459–69.

Adams, David. *Chasing Liquid Mountains: Adventures of a Solo Yachtsman.* London: Pan Macmillan, 1997.

Alexander, Eben. "Eben Alexander—The Nature of Consciousness." Westminster Town Hall Forum, November 21, 2013. Posted to YouTube by MySPNN, November 27, 2013.

Alotaibi, Abdullah. "A Neuroimaging Investigation into Hallucination Proneness in a Healthy Population." PhD diss., University of Liverpool, 2020. ProQuest Dissertations Publishing, 2020. 28403746.

American Hospital Association. "Fast Facts on U.S. Hospitals, 2022." American Hospital Association website.

American Psychiatric Association. *Diagnostic and Statistical Manual of Mental Disorders.* Washington, D.C.: Generic Tyzek, 2015.

Bailey, Polly, George E. Thomsen, Vicki J. Spuhler, Robert Blair, James Jewkes, Louise Bezdjian, Kristy Veale, Larissa Rodriquez, and Ramona O Hopkins. "Early Activity Is Feasible and Safe in Respiratory Failure Patients." *Critical Care Medicine* 35, no. 1 (January 2007): 139–45.

Balas, Michelle. "ABCDEF ICU Bundle of Care." Interview from the Orlando Convention Center Posted to YouTube by allnurses on August 8, 2019.

Barker, Steven A., Jimo Borjigin, Izabela Lomnicka, and Rick Strassman. "LC/MS/MS Analysis of the Endogenous Dimethyltryptamine Hallucinogens, Their Precursors, and Major Metabolites in Rat Pineal Gland Microdialysate." *Biomedical Chromatography* (July 23, 2013).

Barrett, Frederick S., and Roland R. Griffiths. "Classic Hallucinogens and Mystical Experiences: Phenomenology and Neural Correlates." *Current Topics in Behavioral Neuroscience* 36 (2018): 393–430.

Berkovich, Simon. "A Note on Science and NDE." Near-Death Experience Research Foundation website. Accessed June 26, 2023.

Bilton, Anton. "Divine Molecule Talks at Tyringham—Part II, Exploring Entheogenic Entity Encounters." Private research symposium hosted by Anton J. G. Bilton at Tyringham Hall, May 29–June 1, 2017. Symposium overview available on Academia website.

Boyle, Tara, Chris Benderev, Renee Klahr, Shankar Vedantam, and Maggie Penman. "How Derek Amato Became a Musical Savant." NPR's *Hidden Brain,* February 23, 2016.

Bush, Nancy Evans, and Bruce Greyson. "Distressing Near-Death Experiences: The Basics." *Missouri Medicine* 111, no. 6 (November–December 2014): 486–91.

Carenzo, Luca, Francesca Dalla Corte, Ryan W. Haines, Chiara Palandri, Angelo Milani, Alessio Aghemo, Daniela Pini, Alessandro Protti, and Maurizio Cecconi. "Return to Work After Coronavirus Disease 2019 Acute Respiratory Distress Syndrome and Intensive Care Admission." *Critical Care Medicine* (May 2021 online).

Cassol, Héléna, Estelle A. C. Bonin, Christine Bastin, Ninon Puttaert, Vanessa Charland-Verville, Steven Laureys, and Charlotte Martial. "Near-Death Experience Memories Include More Episodic Components than Flashbulb Memories." *Frontiers in Psychology* 11 (May 13, 2020): 888.

Charron, Chaitanya. "The Mysterious Phenomenon of Consciousness: Exploratory Studies in Reincarnation." Center for Indic Studies website. Accessed September 1, 2021.

Chavez, John. *Questions for the Lion Tamer: Delving into the Mystery That Is DMT.* n.p.: CreateSpace, 2017.

Chia, Mantak. *Darkness Technology: Darkness Techniques for Enlightenment.* Available at the Universal Healing Tao e-products store.

Cox, J., S. Roche, and V. Murphy. "Pressure Injury Risk Factors in Critical Care Patients: A Descriptive Analysis." *Advances in Skin and Wound Care* 31, no. 7 (2018): 328–34.

Cristofori, Irene, Joseph Bulbulia, John H. Shaver, Marc Wilson, Frank Krueger, and Jordan Grafman. "Neural Correlates of Mystical Experience." *Neuropsychologia* 80 (January 8, 2016): 212–20.

Daniel, Christina, and Oliver J. Mason. "Predicting Psychotic-Like Experiences during Sensory Deprivation." *BioMed Research International* (2015): 439379.

Dattilio, Frank M, and John E Castaldo. "Differentiating Cognitive Impairment from Symptoms of Anxiety in Postcoronary Artery Bypass Grafting Encephalopathy." *Neuropsychiatric Disease and Treatment* 2, no. 1 (March 2006): 111–16.

Davydow, D. S., J. M. Gifford, S. V. Desai, D. M. Needham, and O. J. Bienvenu. "Posttraumatic Stress Disorder in General Intensive Care Unit Survivors: A Systematic Review." *General Hospital Psychiatry* 30, no. 5 (2008): 421–34.

Dayton, Kali. "Case Studies," "Home," and "Walking Home from the ICU Podcast." Dayton ICU Consulting website. Accessed May 8, 2023.

Dean, Jon, and John Chavez, "Groundbreaking DMT Research That Could Change Everything w/ Dr. Jon Dean and John Chavez." Interview and posted to YouTube by Aubrey Marcus, June 9, 2021.

Dean, Jon G., Tiecheng Liu, Sean Huff, Ben Sheler, Steven A Barker, Rick J. Strassman, Michael M. Wang, and Jimo Borjigin. "Biosynthesis and Extracellular Concentration of N,N-dimethyltryptamine in Mammalian Brain." *Scientific Reports* 9, no. 1 (June 27, 2019): 9333.

De Jonghe, Bernard, Tarek Sharshar, Jean-Pascal Lefaucheur, François-Jérome Authier, Isabelle Durand-Zaleski, Mohamed Boussarsar, Charles Cerf et al. "Paresis Acquired in the Intensive Care Unit: A Prospective Multicenter Study." *Journal of the American Medical Association* 288, no. 22 (2002): 2859–67.

Desai, Shweta. "France Sees 1,300 Nursing Students Resign amid COVID Pandemic." Anadolu Agency website (October 30, 2021).

Dziegielewski, Claudia. "Delirium and Associated Length of Stay and Costs in Critically Ill Patients." *Critical Care Research and Practice* 2021, no. 3 (April 2021).

Ellis, Havelock. "Mescal: A New Artificial Paradise." *Contemporary Review* 73 (1898).

Ely, E. Wesley. "The ABCDEF Bundle: Science and Philosophy of How ICU Liberation Serves Patients and Families." *Critical Care Medicine* 45, no. 2 (February 2017): 321–30.

Ely, E. Wesley. *Every Deep-Drawn Breath: A Critical Care Doctor on Healing, Recovery, and Transforming Medicine in the ICU.* New York: Scribner, 2021.

Fenwick, Peter. Published as "Perceptions of Beyond the Near Death Experience and at the End of Life." Presented at the International Association for Near-Death Studies 2004 Annual Conference.

———. "Science and Spirituality: A Challenge for the 21st Century." The Bruce Greyson Lecture presented at the International Association for Near-Death Studies 2004 Annual Conference. Available on the IANDS website.

Fernandez, J. W. *Bwiti: An Ethnography of the Religious Imagination in Africa.* Princeton, N.J.: Princeton University Press, 1982.

French, Christopher. "Commentary." *The Lancet* 358 (2001): 2010–11.

Garrison, Kathleen A. "Meditation Leads to Reduced Default Mode Network Activity beyond an Active Task." *Cognitive, Affective, and Behavioral Neuroscience* 15, no. 3 (September 2015): 712–20.

Gehlbach, Brian K., Florian Chapotot, Rachel Leproult, Harry Whitmore, Jason Poston, Mark Pohlman, Annette Miller et al. "Temporal Disorganization of Circadian Rhythmicity and Sleep-Wake Regulation in Mechanically Ventilated Patients Receiving Continuous Intravenous Sedation." *Sleep* 35, no. 8 (August 1, 2012): 1105–14.

Grap, Mary Jo, Cindy L. Munro, Paul A. Wetzel, Al M. Best, Jessica M. Ketchum, V. Anne Hamilton, Nyimas Y. Arief, et al. "Sedation in Adults Receiving Mechanical Ventilation: Physiological and Comfort Outcomes." *American Journal of Critical Care* 21, no. 3 (May 2012) 21: e53–e64.

Grassian, Stuart. "Psychiatric Effects of Solitary Confinement." *Washington Journal of Law & Policy* 22 (January 2006).

Greyson, Bruce. "The Near-Death Experience Scale: Construction, Reliability, and Validity." *Journal of Nervous and Mental Disease* 171, no. 6 (June 1983): 369–75.

Griffiths, Richard D., and Christina Jones. "Seven Lessons from 20 Years of Follow-up of Intensive Care Unit Survivors." *Current Opinion in Critical Care* 13, no. 5 (October 2007): 508–13.

Gunk, Wretch. "Magic Carpets, Sensory Deprivation and Entheogenic Ceremonial Magick." Available on the Academia website.

Guttormson, Jill L., Linda Chlan, Mary Fran Tracy, Breanna Hetland, and Jay Mandrekar. "Nurses' Attitudes and Practices Related to Sedation: A National Survey." *American Journal of Critical Care* 28, no. 4 (July 2019): 255–63.

Harari, Yuval Noah. *Sapiens: A Brief History of Humankind.* New York: Harper, 2015.

Heine, Lizette, Andrea Soddu, Francisco Gómez, Audrey Vanhaudenhuyse, Luaba Tshibanda, Marie Thonnard, Vanessa Charland-Verville, et al. "Resting State Networks and Consciousness: Alterations of Multiple Resting State Network Connectivity in Physiological, Pharmacological, and Pathological Consciousness States." *Frontiers in Psychology* 3 (August 27, 2012): 295.

Heron, Woodburn. "The Pathology of Boredom." *Scientific American* (January 1, 1957).

Heuser, J. "Ayahuasca Entity Visitations." PhD diss., California Institute of Integral Studies, 2006. UMI Microform 3218522.

Horák, Miroslav, and Nahanga Verter. *Ayahuasca in the Czech Republic.* Brno, Czechia: Mendel University in Brno, 2019.

Hunter, Alex, Leslie Johnson, and Alberto Coustasse. "Reduction of Intensive Care Unit Length of Stay: The Case of Early Mobilization." *Health Care Management* 33, no. 2 (April–June 2014): 128–35.

Huxley, Aldous. *Heaven and Hell.* New York: Harper Brothers, 1956.

Huxley, Aldous. *The Doors of Perception* and *Heaven and Hell.* New York: Harper Perennial Modern Classics (1954 and 1956, respectively), 2009.

ICUsteps. "Intensive Care: A Guide for Patients and Relatives." Accessed May 8, 2023.

James, William. *The Varieties of Religious Experience: A Study of Human Nature.* New York: Longmans, Green, and Co., 1902.

Jan, Tiffany, and Jorge del Castillo. "Visual Hallucinations: Charles Bonnet Syndrome." *Western Journal of Emergency Medicine* 13, no. 6 (December 2012): 544–47.

Jaynes, Julian. *The Origin of Consciousness in the Breakdown of the Bicameral Mind.* Boston: Mariner Books, 2000.

Jenkins, Hannah. "A Catch-22: PSI and Explanation." Paper presented at the Parapsychological Association 51st Annual Convention, West Downs Centre, the University of Winchester, Winchester, England, August 13–17, 2008.

Jombík, Peter, Michal Drobny, Beata Saniova, Martin Fischer, Petra Kaderjaková, Marianna Lajčiaková, Erika Bakosova, et al. "Some Quantitative EEG Features in Default Mode Resting State Network under General Anaesthesia." *Neuroendocrinology Letters* 38, no. 4 (August 2017): 261–68.

Jung, Carl. *The Interpretation of Nature of the Psyche.* Oakland, Calif.: Ishi Press, 2012.

Jung, Carl. *Memories, Dreams, Reflections,* rev. ed. New York: Vintage, 1989.

Kalianey. "40 Days Dark Retreat." *Kalianey* blog, January 17, 2016.

Kardec, Allan. *Spiritist Codification,* 2nd ed. Miami: United States Spiritist Council, 2016.

Kastrup, Bernardo. "Transcending the Brain." *Scientific American* (March 29, 2017).

Kelly, Edward F. *Consciousness Unbound: Liberating Mind from the Tyranny of Materialism.* Lanham, Md.: Rowman & Littlefield, 2021.

Killingsworth, Matthew A., and Daniel T. Gilbert. "A Wandering Mind Is an Unhappy Mind." *Science* 330, no. 6006 (November 12, 2010): 932.

Kornfeld, Donald, Sheldon Zimberg, and James R. Malm. "Psychiatric Complications of Open-Heart Surgery." *New England Journal of Medicine* 273 (1965): 287–92.

Kripal, Jeffrey J. *The Flip: Epiphanies of Mind and the Future of Knowledge.* New York: Bellevue Literary Press, 2019.

———. "Alternative Realities." Interview by Shahidha Bari. Arts and Ideas, BBC, April 21, 2020.

Kyeremanteng, Kwadwo, Kalpana Bhardwaj, Dipayan Chaudhuri, Brent Herritt, Madison Foster, Peter Lawlor, Shirley Bush, et al. "ICU Delirium, Clinical Outcome and Cost: Systematic Review & Meta-Analysis." *Critical Care Medicine* 46, no. 1 (January 2018).

Laplana, Joan Pons. *Destiny and Hope: My Life as a Nurse in Great Britain— Brexit, Covid-19 and Vaccines.* Editorial Letra Minúscula, 2021.

Laugrand, Frédéric. "The Beauty of the Afterlife Among the Inuit of Nunavut." In *Death Across Cultures: Death and Dying in Non-Western Cultures,* edited by H. Selin and R. M. Rakoff. Parts of the book series *Science Across Cultures: The History of Non-Western Science,* edited by H. Selin, vol. 9. New York: Springer, 2019.

Levy, Ariel. "The Drug of Choice for the Age of Kale." *New Yorker,* September 5, 2016, September 12, 2016 issue.

Lewin, Roger. "Is Your Brain Really Necessary?" *Science* 210, no. 4475 (December 12, 1980): 1232–34.

Liester, Mitch. "Ayahuasca 'Vine of the Soul' and NDEs." Talk presented at the International Association for Near-Death Studies (IANDS) Conference, Newport Beach, California, August 29, 2014.

Liester, M. B. "Toward a New Definition of Hallucination." *American Journal of Orthopsychiatry* 68, no. 2 (April 1998): 305–12.

Lin, Shu-Min, Chien-Da Huang, Chien-Ying Liu, Horng-Chyuan Lin, Chun-

Hua Wang, Pei-Yao Huang, Yueh-Fu Fang, et al. "Risk Factors for the Development of Early-Onset Delirium and the Subsequent Clinical Outcome in Mechanically Ventilated Patients. *Journal of Critical Care* 23 no. 3 (2008): 372–79.

Lipshutz, Angela K. M., and Michael A. Gropper. "Acquired Neuromuscular Weakness and Early Mobilization in the Intensive Care Unit." *Anesthesiology* 118, no. 1 (2013): 202–15.

Liverpool University's Intensive Care Research Group. "Intensive Care: Easing the Trauma." *The Psychologist* 14, no. 12: 640–642.

Maciuika, Laura. *Conscious Calm: Keys to Freedom from Stress and Worry.* Oakland, Calif.: Tap Into Freedom Publishing, 2013.

Martial, Charlotte, Héléna Cassol, Steven Laureys, and Olivia Gosseries. "Near-Death Experience as a Probe to Explore (Disconnected) Consciousness." *Trends in Cognitive Sciences* 24, no. 3 (March 2020): 173–83.

Minet, C., L. Potton, A. Bonadona, R. Hamidfar-Roy, C. A. Somohano, M. Lugosi, J. C. Cartier, G. Ferretti, C. Schwebel, and J. F. Timsit. "Venous Thromboembolism in the ICU: Main Characteristics, Diagnosis and Thromboprophylaxis." *Critical Care* 19 no. 1 (2015): 287.

Mistraletti, G., E. Carloni, M. Cigada, and E. Zambrelli. "Sleep and Delirium in the Intensive Care Unit." *Minerva Anestesiologica* 74, no. 6 (June 2008): 329–33.

Mitchell, Silas Weir. "Remarks on the Effects of *Anhalonium lewinii* (the Mescal Button)." *British Medical Journal* 2 (1896): 1625–29.

Mizzou News. "Selflessness—The Core of All Major World Religions—Has Neuropsychological Connection, MU Study Finds." University of Missouri News Bureau, December 17, 2008.

Monnet, Vincent, dir. *L'Amour Dans Le Sang* (Love in the Blood). Mon Voisin Productions, 2008.

Moody, Raymond. *Life after Life,* anniversary edition. New York: HarperOne, 2015.

Moorjani, Anita. "Dying to Be Me." TEDxBayArea talk, November 30, 2013. YouTube video.

Morandi, Alessandro, Baxter P. Rogers, Max L. Gunther, Kristen Merkle, Pratik Pandharipande, Timothy D. Girard, James C. Jackson, et al. "The Association between Brain Volumes, Delirium Duration, and Cognitive Outcomes in Intensive Care Unit Survivors." *Critical Care Medicine* 40 no. 7 (July 2012): 2182–89.

Newberg, Andrew B. *Principles of Neurotheology*. Routledge Science and Religion Series Indianapolis: Routledge, 2016.

No author. "As Dementia Sets In, Artistic Genius Emerges." *Neurology Today* (June 2003).

No author. *German Neuroscientists: Emil Kraepelin, Alois Alzheimer, Hans Gerhard Creutzfeldt, Alfons Maria Jakob, Emil Du Bois-Reymond, Hans Berger*. Memphis, Tenn.: Books LLC, 2010.

No author. *Women First* magazine, September 19, 2011.

Norton, Loretta, R. Matthew Hutchison, G. B. Young, and Donald H. Lee. "Disruptions of Functional Connectivity in the Default Mode Network of Comatose Patients." *Neurology* 78, no. 3 (January 17, 2012): 175–81.

Opler, Morris E. "The Use of Peyote by the Carrizo and Lipan Apache Tribes." *American Anthropologist* 40 (1938): 271–85.

Palhano-Fontes, Fernanda, Katia C. Andrade, Luis F. Tofoli, Antonio C. Santos, Jose Alexandre S. Crippa, Jaime E. C. Hallak, et al. "The Psychedelic State Induced by Ayahuasca Modulates the Activity and Connectivity of the Default Mode Network." *PLoS ONE* 10, no. 2 (February 2015): e0118143.

Pandharipandh, P., A. Shintani, J. Peterson, B. Truman, G. Wilkinson, R. Dittus, G. Bernard, and W. Ely (2006). "Lorazepam Is an Independent Risk Factor for Transitioning to Delirium in Intensive Care Unit Patients." *Anesthesiology* 104.

Parry, Selina M., and Zudin A. Puthucheary. "The Impact of Extended Bed Rest on the Musculoskeletal System in the Critical Care Environment." *Extreme Physiology and Medicine* 4, no. 16 (2015).

Parshley, Lois. "You Can't Use Ventilators without Sedatives. Now the US Is Running out of Those, Too." Vox website (April 6, 2020).

Pereira, J. V., R. M. Sanjanwala, M. K. Mohammed, M. L. Le, and R. C. Arora. "Dexmedetomidine versus Propofol Sedation in Reducing Delirium among Older Adults in the ICU: A Systematic Review and Meta-analysis." *European Journal of Anaesthesiology* 37, no. 2 (2020): 121–31.

Perme, Christiane, and Rohini Chandrashekar. "Early Mobility and Walking Program for Patients in Intensive Care Units: Creating a Standard of Care." *American Journal of Critical Care* 18, no. 3 (May 2009): 212–21.

Perme ICU Rehab Seminars website. Accessed May 8, 2023.

Peterson, Dan. "Anatomically and Functionally Impossible?" *Patheos* blog, September 3, 2018.

Pollan, Michael. *How to Change Your Mind,* reprint ed. New York: Penguin Books, 2019.

Pontvianne, François. "Psychedelics and Buddhism: Inter-Relationship and Ethical Considerations." *MACS Research Essay* (May 2014). Available on the Academia website.

Pribram, Karl H. "The Neurophysiology of Remembering." *Scientific American* 220 (1969).

Pun, Brenda T., Michele C. Balas, Mary Ann Barnes-Daly, Jennifer L. Thompson, J. Matthew Aldrich, Juliana Barr, Diane Byrum, et al. "Caring for Critically Ill Patients with the ABCDEF Bundle: Results of the ICU Liberation Collaborative in over 15,000 Adults." *Critical Care Medicine* 47, no. 1 (2019): 3–14.

Pun, Brenda T., Rafael Badenes, Gabriel Heras la Calle, Onur M. Orun, Wencong Chen, Rameela Raman, Beata-Gabriela K. Simpson, et al. "Prevalence and Risk Factors for Delirium in Critically Ill Patients with COVID-19 (COVID-D): A Multicentre Cohort Study." *The Lancet Respiratory Medicine* (March 2021) 9(3): 239–50.

Queensland Brain Institute. "Where Are Memories Stored?" University of Queensland, Australia website. Accessed May 9, 2023.

Raab, Diana. *The Empowerment Diary.* (*Psychology Today* blog).

Raichle, Marcus E. "A Default Mode of Brain Function." *PNAS* 98, no. 2 (January 16, 2001): 676–82.

Raichle, Marcus E, Ann Mary MacLeod, Abraham Z. Snyder, William J. Powers, Debra A. Gusnard, and Gordon L. Shulman. "The Brain's Dark Energy." *Scientific American* (March 1, 2010).

Raichle, Marcus E. "The Brain's Default Mode Network." *Annual Review of Neuroscience* 38 (July 8, 2015): 433–47.

Reinberg, P. "Contribution à l'étude des boissons toxiques des indiens du Nord-ouest de l'Amazon, l'ayahuasca, le yagé, le huanto." *Journal de la Societé des Américanistes* 13, no. 1 (1921): 25–54.

Rello, J., E. Diaz, M. Roque, and J. Vallés. "Risk Factors for Developing Pneumonia within 48 Hours of Intubation." *American Journal of Respiratory and Critical Care Medicine* 159 no. 6 (1999), 1742–46.

Ring, Kenneth. *Life and Death.* New York: William Morrow and Company, 1980.

Ritter, Christiane. *A Woman in the Polar Night.* London: Pushkin Press, 2019.

Rogers, Andrew T., Ge Bai, Robert A. Lavin, and Gerard F. Anderson. "Higher Hospital Spending on Occupational Therapy Is Associated with Lower Readmission Rates." *Medical Care Research and Review* 74, no. 6 (December 2017): 668–86.

Romero-García, Marta, and Gabriel Heras la Calle. "Moral Distress, Emotional Impact and Coping in Intensive Care Units Staff during the Outbreak of COVID-19." *Intensive and Critical Care Nursing* 70 (June 2022): 103206.

Ruscio, A. M., T. A. Brown, W. T. Chiu, J. Sareen, M. B. Stein, and R. C. Kessler. "Social Fears and Social Phobia in the USA: Results from the National Comorbidity Survey Replication." *Psychological Medicine* 38, no. 1 (January 2008): 15–28.

Saunders, Tom, and Joe Duggan, "Record Numbers of NHS Staff Quit as Frontline Medics Battle Covid Pandemic Trauma." iNews website (January 7, 2022).

Schenberg, Eduardo E. "Ayahuasca and Cancer Treatment." *SAGE Open Medicine* (October 18, 2013).

Schubert, Maria, Roger Schürch, Soenke Boettger, David Garcia Nuñez, Urs Schwarz, Dominique Bettex, Josef Jenewein, et al. "A Hospital-Wide Evaluation of Delirium Prevalence and Outcomes in Acute Care Patients: A Cohort Study." *BMC Health Services Research* 18, no. 1 (July 13, 2018): 550.

Seth, Anil, "Your Brain Hallucinates Your Conscious Reality." TED talk, posted July 18, 2017. YouTube video.

Shanon, Benny. *The Antipodes of the Mind: Charting the Phenomenology of the Ayahuasca Experience*. Oxford: Oxford University Press, 2010.

Sharp, Kimberly Clark. *After the Light: What I Discovered on the Other Side of Life That Can Change Your World*. Bloomington, Ind.: iUniverse, 2003.

Shears, Daniel, Sarah Elison, M. Elena Garralda, and Simon Nadel. "Near-Death Experiences with Meningococcal Disease." *Journal of the American Academy of Child and Adolescent Psychiatry* 44, no. 7 (July 2005): 630–31.

Shehabi, Yahya, Rinaldo Bellomo, Michael C. Reade, Michael Bailey, Frances Bass, Belinda Howe, Colin McArthur, et al. "Early Intensive Care Sedation Predicts Long-term Mortality in Ventilated Critically Ill Patients." *American Journal of Respiratory and Critical Care Medicine* 186, no. 8 (2012): 724–31.

Sheldrake, Rupert. *Science Set Free*, ill. ed. La Jolla, Calif.: Deepak Chopra [publishing], 2013.

Shushan, Gregory. "The Sun Told Me I Would Be Restored to Life: Native American Near-Death Experiences, Shamanism, and Religious Revitalization Movements." *Journal of Near-Death Studies* (Spring 2016): 127–50.

Slattery, Zara. *Coma*. Brighton: Myriad Editions, 2021.

Slocum, Joshua. *Sailing Alone Around the World*. n. p.: Create Space Independent Publishing Platform, 2014.

Slotkin, J. S. *The Peyote Religion*. Glencos, Ill.: The Free Press, 1956.

Smith, Claudia DiSabatino, and Petra Grami. "Feasibility and Effectiveness of a Delirium Prevention Bundle in Critically Ill Patients." *American Journal of Critical Care* 26, no. 1 (December 2016): 19–27.

Society of Critical Care Medicine. "ICU Liberation Bundle A–F." Society of Critical Care Medicinewebsite. Accessed May 8, 2023.

Spinney, Laura. "Anarchy Discovered in the Honeybee Hive." *New Scientist* (January 12, 2005).

Spruce, Richard. *Notes of a Botanist on the Amazon and Andes: Being Records of Travel on the Amazon and its Tributaries, the Trombetas, Rio Negro, Uaupés, Casiquiari, Pacimoni, Huallaga and Pastasa*. Cambridge: Cambridge University Press, 2014.

Strassman, Rick. *DMT: The Spirit Molecule*. Rochester, Vt.: Park Street Press, 2000.

Strassman, Rick. *The Psychedelic Handbook: A Practical Guide to Psilocybin, LSD, Ketamine, MDMA, and Ayahuasca (Guides to Psychedelics & More)*. Berkeley, Calif.: Ulysses Press, 2022.

Strøm, Thomas, Rasmus R. Johansen, Jens O. Prahl, and Palle Toft. "Sedation and Renal Impairment in Critically Ill Patients: A Post Hoc Analysis of a Randomized Trial." *Critical Care* 15 no. 3 (2011): R119.

Swami, Rama C. *New Doctrine on Mental Diseases based on Evidence on Reincarnation and Survival of Soul*. Bangalore Reincarnation Research Centre, 1982.

Szára, S. "Dimethyltryptamin: Its Metabolism in Man; The Relation of Its Psychotic Effect to the Serotonin Metabolism." *Experientia* 12 (1956), 441–42.

Tanaka, Lilian Maria, Luciano Cesar Azevedo, Marcelo Park, Guilherme Schettino, Antonio Nassar Junior, Alvaro Rea-Neto, Luana Tannous, et al. "Early Sedation and Clinical Outcomes of Mechanically Ventilated Patients: A Prospective Multicenter Cohort Study." *Critical Care Research and Practice* 18, no. 4 (July 21, 2014).

Taylor, Jill Bolte. "My Stroke of Insight." TED talk, posted March 13, 2008. YouTube video.

Timmermann, Christopher, Leor Roseman, Luke Williams, David Erritzoe, Charlotte Martial, Héléna Cassol, Steven Laureys, et al. "DMT Models the Near-Death Experience." *Frontiers in Psychology* 9 (August 15, 2018).

Tolle, Eckhart. *The Power of Now—A Guide to Spiritual Enlightenment*. Novato, Calif.: New World Library, 2004.

Tononi, G. "Integrated Information Theory of Consciousness: An Updated Account." *Archives Italiennes de Biologie* 150, no. 2–3 (June–September 2012): 56–90.

Treffert, Darold. "Genetic Memory: How We Know Things We Never Learned." *Scientific American* (January 28, 2015).

Valandrey, Charlotte. *De cœur inconnu* (Of Heart Unknown). Paris: J'ai Lu, 2013.

Vanhorebeek, I., N. Latronico, and G. Van den Berghe. "ICU-Acquired Weakness." *Intensive Care Medicine* 46, no. 4 (2020): 637–53.

Van Lommel, Pim. "About the Continuity of Consciousness: A Concept Based on Scientific Studies of Near-Death Experiences." Article for the Galileo Commission website, 2018.

———. "About the Continuity of Our Consciousness." In *Brain Death and Disorders of Consciousness: Advances in Experimental Medicine and Biology*, vol. 550, edited by Calixto Machado and D. Alan Shewmon, 115–32. Boston: Springer, 2004.

———. *Consciousness Beyond Life*. New York: HarperOne, 2011.

Van Lommel, Pim, Ruud van Wees, Vincent Meyers, and Ingrid Elfferich. "Near-Death Experience in Survivors of Cardiac Arrest: A Prospective Study in the Netherlands." *The Lancet* 358, no. 9298 (2001): 2039–45.

Viglianti, Elizabeth M., and Theodore J. Iwashyna. "Toward the Ideal Ratio of Patients to Intensivists: Finding a Reasonable Balance." *JAMA Internal Medicine* 177, no. 3 (March 2017): 396–98.

Watts, Alan. "Psychedelics and Religious Experience." *California Law Review* 56, no. 1 (January 1968): 74–85.

Wilcox, Daniel, ed. *The Use of the Polygraph in Assessing, Treating, and Supervising Sex Offenders: A Practitioner's Guide*. Malden, Mass.: Wiley Blackwell Publishing, 2009. Also available on the VDoc website.

Wilson, Robert Anton. *Cosmic Trigger*. Grand Junction, Colo.: Hilaritas Press, 2016.

Yang, J., Y. Zhou, Y. Kang, B. Xu, P. Wang, Y. Lv, and Z. Wang. "Risk Factors of Delirium in Sequential Sedation Patients in Intensive Care Units." *BioMed Research International* (2017).

Index